States, Parties, and Social Movements

Studies of social movements and of political parties have usually treated them as separate and distinct. In fact, they are deeply intertwined. Social movements often shape electoral competition and party policies; they can even give rise to new parties. At the same time, political parties and campaigns shape the opportunities, personnel, and outcomes of social movements. In many countries, electoral democracy itself is the outcome of social movement actions. This book examines the interaction of social movements and party politics since the 1950s, both in the United States and around the world. In studies of the U.S. civil rights movement, the New Left, the Czechoslovak dissident movements, the Mexican struggle for democracy, and other episodes, this volume shows how party politics and social movements cannot be understood without appreciating their intimate relationship.

Jack A. Goldstone is Professor of Sociology and International Relations at the University of California, Davis. He received the American Sociological Association Award for Distinguished Scholarly Publication for his book *Revolution and Rebellion in the Early Modern World* (1991).

Cambridge Studies in Contentious Politics

Editors

Doug McAdam *Stanford University and Center for Advanced Study in the Behavioral Sciences*
Sidney Tarrow *Cornell University*
Charles Tilly *Columbia University*

Ronald Aminzade et al., *Silence and Voice in the Study of Contentious Politics*
Doug McAdam, Sidney Tarrow, and Charles Tilly, *Dynamics of Contention*
Jack A. Goldstone, ed., *States, Parties, and Social Movements*

States, Parties, and
Social Movements

Edited by

JACK A. GOLDSTONE
University of California, Davis

CAMBRIDGE
UNIVERSITY PRESS

PUBLISHED BY THE PRESS SYNDICATE OF THE UNIVERSITY OF CAMBRIDGE
The Pitt Building, Trumpington Street, Cambridge, United Kingdom

CAMBRIDGE UNIVERSITY PRESS
The Edinburgh Building, Cambridge CB2 2RU, UK
40 West 20th Street, New York, NY 10011-4211, USA
477 Williamstown Road, Port Melbourne, VIC 3207, Australia
Ruiz de Alarcón 13, 28014 Madrid, Spain
Dock House, The Waterfront, Cape Town 8001, South Africa

http://www.cambridge.org

First published 2003

Printed in the United States of America

Typeface Janson Text 10/13 pt.   *System* LaTeX 2_ε [TB]

A catalog record for this book is available from the British Library.

Library of Congress Cataloging in Publication Data
States, parties, and social movements / edited by Jack A. Goldstone.
p.   cm. – (Cambridge studies in contentious politics)
Includes bibliographical references and index.
ISBN 0-521-81679-3 – ISBN 0-521-01699-1 (pb.)
1. Political parties.   2. Social movements.   I. Goldstone, Jack A.   II. Series.
JF2011 .S73   2003
303.48′4–dc21   2002067649

ISBN 0 521 81679 3 hardback
ISBN 0 521 01699 1 paperback

*To my family, whose support makes all things possible,
and to the Mellon Group of contentious politics scholars,
whose efforts made this volume possible*

Contents

List of Figures and Tables

Figures

Tables

Foreword

Doug McAdam

This volume arose from a unique collaborative project that began in the early 1990s and stretched into the new millennium. Ultimately, the project involved twenty-one core participants and a host of others who attended one or more of the nine mini-conferences that structured the project. In form and function, the project resembled nothing so much as an extended collaborative conversation concerning the nature and dynamics of "contentious politics."

Motivated by a shared concern that the study of social movements, revolutions, democratization, ethnic conflict, and other forms of nonroutine, or contentious, politics had grown fragmented, spawning a number of insular scholarly communities only dimly aware of one another, the project was committed above all else to exploring possible lines of synthesis – empirical and theoretical – that might transcend some of the scholarly conventions that still largely divide the field. Among these conventions are persistent theoretical divisions between rationalists, culturalists, and structuralists; putative differences between various forms of contention (e.g., social movements, revolutions, peasant rebellions, industrial conflict); and the long-standing assumption of area specialists that any general phenomenon – such as contentious politics – can only be understood in light of the idiosyncratic history and cultural conventions of the locale in which it takes place. While respectful of these conventional distinctions, the project has been committed to exploring their limits and embracing promising new approaches and topics in the study of political contention.

A bit of history: The project began in 1993 with a casual conversation between Sid Tarrow and me, in which we found that we shared a deep ambivalence regarding the proliferation of work on social movements. On the one hand, we were delighted that a topic long regarded as peripheral by political scientists and sociologists alike had come to be seen as a legitimate subject of so much academic work. On the other hand, we were concerned about the increasing narrowness of the field and its disconnect from other proximate fields of study. Wouldn't it be great, we mused, if scholars from these separate fields could together explore the possibilities for synthesis across these nominally distinct subfields? In turn, the conversation led to a concrete suggestion: Why not submit a proposal to the Center for Advanced Study in the Behavioral Sciences to convene a one-year Special Project to be devoted to the kind of exploration and synthesis we had in mind? Why not, indeed! After we enlisted Chuck Tilly as a third coconspirator, a proposal was drafted, ably vetted by Phil Converse and Bob Scott (then director and associate director, respectively, of the Center), and in 1994 approved by both the Center's Advisory Committee on Special Projects and its board of trustees.

Once the Special Project was secured, the enterprise took a fateful and felicitous turn. Knowing how ambitious – yet amorphous – our aims were, Bob Scott encouraged us to seek the additional monetary support that would allow us to stretch the project over a longer time frame. At his suggestion, we applied in 1995 to the Mellon Foundation's Sawyer Seminar Series seeking support for a three-year seminar series organized around the broad topic of "contentious politics." To our delight and surprise, Mellon granted our request.

The challenge now centered on finding the right core faculty around whom to build the ongoing conversation. Eventually, we were lucky enough to attract four other colleagues for the project: Ron Aminzade, Jack Goldstone, Liz Perry, and Bill Sewell. We could not have asked for a more qualified and generous group of conversationalists. (Speaking personally, the opportunity to interact with all six of these colleagues over the life of the project has been one of the most rewarding experiences of my career. None of them can possibly know just how much I have learned and continue to learn from them.)

Though neither our Center nor the Mellon sponsors required us to do so, the seven of us agreed immediately that we wanted to involve graduate students in the project. Who better to offer fresh perspectives on important topics than promising young scholars not wedded to disciplinary boundaries and subfield conventions? The model we hit on for facilitating student involvement in the project was a yearly competition to select five graduate Fellows drawn from applicants solicited nationally from across a range of social science disciplines. The results of our first competition confirmed the approach. The voices of the five members of that first graduate cohort – Lissa Bell, Pamela Burke, Robyn Eckhardt, John Glenn, and Joseph Luders – blended so seamlessly into the conversation that, in the end, they forced us to revise our plan to limit the fellowships to one year and to approach Mellon for funding to enable us to retain all graduate Fellows for the life of the project. Mellon came through for us a second time. Nine more talented students – Jorge Cadena-Roa, David Cunningham, Manali Desai, Debbie Gould, Hyojoung Kim, Heidi Swarts, Nella Van Dyke, Heather Williams, and Kim Williams – joined us over the next two years, bringing the total number of graduate Fellows on the project to fourteen. It is a number of these younger scholars whose path-breaking efforts have produced this volume.

These younger scholars have more than fulfilled our hopes for fresh approaches to the study of contentious politics. Their many interventions, provocative queries, and fresh takes on familiar topics enlivened our discussion and taught us new ways of seeing social movements and social change. The essays in this volume crash through any barriers that once separated the study of institutional politics, social movements, political parties, and revolutionary change. Embracing topics as widely divergent as the collapse of communism in Eastern Europe, the foundation of communist parties in India, the development of democracy in Mexico, the New Left and civil rights movements in the United States, and local politics in U.S. cities, these essays nonetheless share a common focus on demonstrating how political change emerges from the complex interplay of states, parties, and social movements. Far from being separate spheres of activity, the essays in this volume repeatedly demonstrate that social protest and institutional politics have been deeply intertwined, both in advanced democracies and in developing countries.

In addition, these brave scholars have taken on the standard shibboleths of social movement theory. Drawing on their rich empirical research, they show that our conventional view of social protest as rooted in political opportunities, sympathetic framing, and mobilization networks is far too simple to embrace the dynamics of protest and institutional change. Again and again, these essays show that political opportunities interact with specific issues, elite alignments, and the choices of movement and political party leaders to generate diverse outcomes. Framing is not an autonomous process of conceptualization, but is mediated by the path-dependent experiences of activists and movement organizations. And while mobilization networks are crucial to protest activity, these scholars repeatedly demonstrate that the results of protest are not simply related to the scale or intensity of mobilization and protest activity. Interactions with political leaders and agendas, as well as shifting state, public, and elite responses, can either produce dramatic changes from relatively modest mobilization or frustrate even widespread popular protest activities.

In short, we have much to learn from a new generation of research on the dynamics of social movements and political institutions. We are proud and delighted that the scholars who have given us so much during the Mellon project have allowed us to present the first fruits of their research in this volume.

Menlo Park, CA
April 20, 2000

Acknowledgments

A highly diverse set of individuals and institutions provided the support to make this volume possible. To understand why so many gracious scholars played a role, it will help to know something about the way the broad project was structured. In each of the three years of the Mellon project (1995–6, 1996–7, and 1997–8), the core faculty organized three two-day mini-conferences, each focused on a specific topic relevant to a general understanding of contention. Among the topics explored in these sessions were religion and contention, emotion and contention, the globalization of contention, identity and networks in contention, and the like. Besides featuring graduate Fellows and core faculty, each of these conferences included participation by two or three invited experts on the specific topic of the gathering. We owe these colleagues a vote of thanks as well. Many of the ideas pursued in the essays benefited from insights gleaned from this or that conversational guest. A complete list of these distinguished colleagues follows: Mark Beissinger, Craig Calhoun, Bill Gamson, Jeff Goodwin, Roger Gould, Susan Harding, Michael Hechter, Lynn Hunt, Jane Jenson, Arthur Kleinman, Hanspeter Kriesi, Marc Lichbach, John Meyer, Ann Mische, Aldon Morris, Maryjane Osa, Gay Seidman, Kathryn Sikkink, Verta Taylor, Mark Traugott, Paul Wapner, and Timothy Wickham-Crowley.

The contributors to this volume also wish to acknowledge the help and advice offered on individual essays by Guy Baldwin, Peter Bearman, Irenee Beattie, Paul Burstein, Margarita Favela Casanova, Elisabeth Clemens, Michael Dauderstadt, Steven Epstein, Pablo Gonzalez, Ronald Herring, Greta Krippner, Charles Kurzman, Petr Lom, Sarah Mendelson, Pam Oliver, Rachel Rosenfeld, Philippe Schmitter, Christian Smith, David Snow, Jack Snyder, Sarah Soule, Brad Usher, Maurice Zeitlin, Jan Zielonka, and the members of the University of North Carolina's Seminar on

Structure in Process. Thanks also to Magdalena Hernandez and Rene Francisco Poitevin for their valuable research assistance.

The research presented in this volume was supported by the following granting agencies: The Andrew Mellon Foundation; The Aspen Institute Nonprofit Sector Research Fund for Doctoral Dissertation Grant 99–NSRF–24; the Carnegie Corporation; a Mellon Graduate Fellowship from Cornell University; The National Science Foundation: No. SBE–9521536, SBR–9701585; the Social and Behavioral Sciences Research Institute at the University of Arizona; the Institute on Global Conflict and Cooperation of the University of California; and the International Studies Overseas Program at UCLA. We also thank the editors of *Social Forces* for permission to reprint portions of Essay 6, which first appeared in "Party Formation, Political Power, and the Capacity for Reform: Comparing Left Parties in Kerala and West Bengal, India," *Social Forces* (2001), vol. 80, pp. 37–60. We also thank Lew Bateman, our editor at Cambridge University Press, who has supported publication of the Contentious Politics series, and Louise Calabro, our skilled production editor, who oversaw preparation of this volume. J. Zach Schiller provided valuable research assistance and compiled the index.

We have reserved two very special institutional acknowledgments. We refer, of course, to our two institutional sponsors, who responded creatively and generously to our requests for support. To the Mellon Foundation, and Harriet Zuckerman in particular, we offer a sincere vote of thanks for their creative stewardship of the project. Without Mellon's funds, we would never have been able to undertake such a unique and ambitious project.

And then there is the enormous debt of gratitude we owe the Center for Advanced Study in the Behavioral Sciences. It was the prospect of a Center Special Project that set us in motion in the first place. It was Bob Scott's vision of a longer-term project that led the faculty to approach Mellon for support. It was the consistent support of two Center directors – Phil Converse and later Neil Smelser – that sustained the project over the long term. And, we are convinced, it was the special quality of the Center experience that allowed the larger Mellon group to become so close and so successful over the life of the project. We therefore salute the entire Center staff for their critical role in the success of the enterprise. More prosaically, much of the work on the volume was carried out at the Center, either as part of the Special Project or in connection with the various mini-conferences held there in 1995–8.

Acknowledgments

Finally, all of the Mellon junior Fellows would like to offer their collective and heartfelt thanks to the senior Fellows in the Mellon seminar – Doug McAdam, Sidney Tarrow, Charles Tilly, Elizabeth Perry, Ron Aminzade, Bill Sewell, and especially Jack A. Goldstone, who so generously agreed to edit this volume. For us, the seminar, which covered a period of three years from 1995 to 1998, with meetings every three to four months, was one of the most rewarding experiences of our graduate training. The senior Fellows generously shared their ideas and knowledge and took a considerable amount of time to discuss our dissertation projects with each of us. For many of us, the drawing together of disparate areas and subfields of the study of social movements was a rich source of ideas. For others, the attention to "silences" in the research in social movements, such as emotions or religion, was invaluable. We made new connections, both in our work and interpersonally, that will stay with us for the rest of our careers. For this we must thank the warmth and collegiality (and humor!) of the senior Fellows. They ensured that the seminar would be an experience to remember and treasure.

Contributors

Jorge Cadena-Roa received his Ph.D. in sociology from the University of Wisconsin-Madison. He is currently at the Centro de Investigaciones Interdisciplinarias en Ciencias y Humanidades at the Universidad Nacional Autónoma de México (UNAM). He recently published "Symbolic Politics and Emotions in the Creation and Performance of a Masked Crusader in Mexican Urban Movements" in *Mobilization*.

David Cunningham earned his Ph.D. in sociology at the University of North Carolina at Chapel Hill. He is currently an Assistant Professor in the Department of Sociology at Brandeis University. His research interests include the organization of state repression against a wide range of left- and right-wing challengers, as well as the emergence of collective identities within youth subcultures in suburbia.

Manali Desai received her Ph.D. from the Department of Sociology, UCLA. She is currently Assistant Professor of Sociology at the University of California, Riverside. Her interests include globalization, social inequality, gender, and social theory.

John K. Glenn (Ph.D., Harvard University, 1997) is the Executive Director of the Council for European Studies, hosted at Columbia University, and a Visiting Scholar at New York University. He has been a Junior Visiting Fellow at the Institute for Human Sciences, Vienna; Jean Monnet Fellow at the European University Institute, Florence; and EU Center Postdoctoral Fellow at New York University. His publications include *Framing Democracy: Civil Society and Civic Movements in Eastern Europe* (Stanford University Press, 2001) and *The Power and Limits of NGOs: A Critical Look* *at Building Democracy in Eastern Europe and Eurasia*, coedited with Sarah Mendelson (Columbia University Press, 2002).

Jack A. Goldstone is Professor of Sociology and International Relations at the University of California, Davis. He is the author of the prize-winning *Revolution and Rebellion in the Early Modern World* (University of California Press, 1991) and editor of *The Encyclopedia of Political Revolutions* (Congressional Quarterly, 1998) and *Revolutions of the Late Twentieth Century* (Westview, 1991). He has been a Fellow of the Center for Advanced Study in the Behavioral Sciences at Stanford University and has held fellowships from the American Council of Learned Societies, the Research School of Social Sciences at the Australian National University, and the Canadian Institute for Advanced Research.

Joseph Luders received his Ph.D. in political science from the New School for Social Research. He is currently Assistant Professor of Political Science at Yeshiva University in New York City. He has written on economic explanations of social movement success, racial conflict, the impact of the Mississippi Sovereignty Commission on the civil rights movement, and the politics of American social policy. His general research interests include American political development, racial politics, and political economic approaches to the study of social movements.

Doug McAdam is Professor of Sociology and Director of the Center for Advanced Study in the Behavioral Sciences at Stanford University. He is the author of *Freedom Summer* (Oxford University Press, 1988), winner of the C. Wright Mills Award; of *Political Process and the Development of Black Insurgency: 1930–1970* (Chicago University Press, 1970); and coauthor of *Dynamics of Contention* (Cambridge University Press, 2001), with Sidney Tarrow and Charles Tilly.

Heidi J. Swarts received her Ph.D. in government from Cornell University. She is Assistant Professor of Political Science at the Maxwell School of Citizenship and Public Affairs, Syracuse University. She recently completed a dissertation comparing the resources, ideologies, tactics, and results of different strategies of organizing poor and working-class Americans to develop civic skills, influence policymaking, and gain political power.

Charles Tilly is the Joseph L. Buttenwieser Professor of Social Science at Columbia University. He received the Distinguished Scholarly Publication

Award of the American Sociological Association for *Durable Inequality* (California University Press, 1998) and for *The Contentious French* (Belknap Press, 1986). His most recent book is *Dynamics of Contention* (Cambridge University Press, 2001), coauthored with Doug McAdam and Sidney Tarrow.

Nella Van Dyke gained her Ph.D. in sociology from the University of Arizona. She is now Assistant Professor of Sociology at Ohio State University. Recent publications include "Gendered Outcomes: Gender Differences in the Biographical Consequences of Activism," with Doug McAdam and Brenda Wilhelm; *Mobilization* (2000); and "Hotbeds of Activism: Locations of Student Protest," *Social Problems* (1998). Her current research focuses on social movement coalitions, cultural outcomes of social movements, and the mobilizing effect of structural social change.

Kim M. Williams received her Ph.D. from Cornell University. She completed her dissertation, *"Boxed In: The U.S. Multiracial Movement,"* in 2001. She is now Assistant Professor of Public Policy at the Kennedy School of Government, Harvard University, and specializes in racial-ethnic politics and social movements. She has received fellowships and awards from the Ford Foundation, Dartmouth College, the Horowitz Foundation for Social Policy, the Center for Advanced Study in the Behavioral Sciences at Stanford University, Mathematica Policy Research Inc., and the American Political Science Association. She is contributing to two forthcoming edited volumes: *Multiracial Identity Politics* and *The Politics of Multiracialism*.

Introduction

BRIDGING INSTITUTIONALIZED AND NONINSTITUTIONALIZED POLITICS

Jack A. Goldstone

Some years ago, Craig Jenkins and Bert Klandermans (1995, p. 3) stated that "Surprisingly little attention has been paid to the interaction between social movements and the state." If that statement was at all valid then, it certainly is no longer valid now. The last half-decade has seen an enormous outpouring of work on the mutual influences between social movements and the state, ranging over such topics as framing protest issues (Gamson and Meyer 1996), repression (Kurzman 1996; Rasler 1996), movement outcomes (Dalton 1995; Misztal and Jenkins 1995), and, most commonly, political opportunity structures (Kriesi 1995; McAdam, McCarthy, and Zald 1996; Tarrow 1996).

Nonetheless, there has been a persistent tendency to see this interaction as distinct from normal institutionalized politics occurring through voting, lobbying, political parties, legislatures, courts, and elected leaders. As Jenkins and Klandermans state this distinction: "[S]ocial movements... constitute a potential rival to the political representation system" (1995, p. 5). This separation of movement politics from institutionalized politics was concretized in Charles Tilly's (1978) enormously influential schema presenting social movements as "challengers" seeking to enter the institutionalized world of "polity members" who have routinized access to the levers of power. It was strongly reinforced by William Gamson's (1990) depiction of social movements as "outsider" groups whose challenges succeed, in one sense, as such groups become recognized actors in institutional politics. As Mary Fainsod Katzenstein (1998, p. 195) expressed this view: "Students of social movements commonly associate institutionalization with demobilization.... Social movements... are necessarily extrainstitutional."

One obvious conclusion of this view is that as social movement actors gain institutionalized access to the political system, we expect that protest action

1

by such actors would (and indeed, normatively *should*) fade away. Pereira et al. (1993, p. 4) argue that "if reforms are to proceed under democratic conditions, distributional conflicts must be institutionalized. All groups must channel their demands through the democratic institutions and abjure other tactics." In other words, protest is for outsiders and opponents of the system; normal citizens seeking policy changes or social reforms should stick to supporting political parties and candidates and should use the legal system, petitions, and lobbying to pursue their goals.

The essays in this book advance a different claim, namely, that social movements constitute an essential element of normal politics in modern societies, and that there is only a fuzzy and permeable boundary between institutionalized and noninstitutionalized politics. To be sure, there are distinctly different behaviors at the extreme ends of the spectrum of institutional and noninstitutional politics. Elections, legislative votes, and court decisions are quite different in their conduct and content from protest marches, demonstrations, or boycotts. Yet just as analysts of social movements have come to realize that they cannot study movements independently of their political context, including the operations of normal political institutions, we maintain that the reverse is also true. To restate a claim first advanced by Rudolph Heberle (1951) a half-century ago and increasingly voiced by social movement scholars today (Burstein 1998b, 1999; Clemens 1997; Tarrow 1998b), we believe that one cannot understand the normal, institutionalized workings of courts, legislatures, executives, or parties without understanding their intimate and ongoing shaping by social movements. Indeed, as the essays in this volume demonstrate, state institutions and parties are interpenetrated by social movements, often developing out of movements, in response to movements, or in close association with movements.

Meyer and Tarrow (1998a) have made the claim that Western democracies are moving toward becoming "movement societies," in which social movements have become so routine, so institutionalized (through permits for demonstrations and referendums by petition), that they are now part of normal politics. We would agree with this but go further. Social movements are not merely another forum for or method of political expression, routinized alongside courts, parties, legislatures, and elections. Rather, social movements have become part of the environment and social structures that shape and give rise to parties, courts, legislatures, and elections. Moreover, this is true not only in established Western democracies but also, as the essays by Jorge Cadena-Roa, John K. Glenn, and Manali Desai in this volume demonstrate, it is even true in emerging democracies, such as those of Mexico and Eastern Europe, and in non-Western societies such as India.

Indeed, to the extent that democratic institutions are spreading in the world today, this is not merely an adaptation or appropriation of institutions by political elites; it is instead a response to mass social movements seeking democratization as a goal (Markoff 1996; Valenzuela 1989). The normal story of the development of social movements is that they became part of normal politics in response to greater citizenship rights and the development of political party systems in Western democracies (Koopmans 1995; Tilly 1984). Today, the reverse seems to be true: In Eastern Europe, Africa, Latin America, and Southeast Asia, citizenship rights and political party systems are developing out of social movements.

Inside or Outside? Social Movements and Institutionalized Politics

Prior to the 1980s, prevailing images of social movement actors were that they were outsiders. In the words of Jenkins (1995, p. 15), they were "actors who are excluded or marginalized in the political order." Recognition of the role played by the middle class, by intellectual and professional elites, and by students in the so-called "new" social movements – which focused on health, the environment, and peace, among other issues – somewhat changed this view of participants in social movements, but scholars still saw movements as acting mainly outside of institutionalized politics, emerging only for intermittent rounds of conflict with established institutions and authorities (Melucci 1989). Yet empirical research has repeatedly shown that the actors, the fates, and the structures of political parties and social movements are closely intertwined.

Since the Republican movement in nineteenth-century France (Aminzade 1995), the same individuals have often been both social movement activists and political candidates. In the United States, presidential candidate Ralph Nader used a third-party challenge in 2000 to extend his consumerist/environmentalist movement, while in Europe, former environmentalist activists have become members of the German parliament and even ministers as politicians of the Green Party. Gay political activists have run for local offices, and leaders of the movement for research on acquired immunodeficiency syndrome (AIDS) have taken seats on government regulatory bodies (Epstein 1996). The same individuals often give their time and money to both social movements and conventional party campaigns (Dalton 1995; Rucht 1991). As Meyer and Tarrow (1998a, p. 7) explain, "participation in protest activity has not come at the expense of other forms of participation.... People who protest are more, not less, likely to vote and engage in the whole range of conventional citizen politics."

Not only persons but also organizations frequently engage in both protest and conventional political actions. Kriesi et al. (1995, pp. 152ff) point out that social movement organizations sometimes act like protest groups, organizing protest actions, while at other times they act like normal lobbies, seeking to provide information and advice to officials, and at still other times they act like parties or party auxiliaries, helping to get out the vote for particular candidates.

Indeed, in the United States and Western Europe, political parties and social movements have become overlapping, mutually dependent actors in shaping politics, to the point where even long-established political parties welcome social movement support and often rely specifically on their association with social movements in order to win elections, as with the U.S. Republican Party and the religious right (Green, Guth, and Wilcox 1998). Conversely, many social movements can barely exist and certainly not succeed without sponsorship from institutionalized political parties (Jenkins 1985). For example, Maguire (1995) shows how both the British Campaign for Nuclear Disarmament (CND) and the Italian peace movement depended on support from established parties. CND initially grew and seemed likely to gain success when the Labour Party supported it; yet as soon as Labour decided that CND was not in its interest and turned against the movement, its chances for success dropped to zero and its support dried up. In Italy, the peace movement "could emerge only with PCI [Italian Communist Party] support, and it was organizationally and financially dependent on the party" (Maguire 1995, p. 225).

The stance taken by institutionalized parties toward social movement issues often determines the approach and fate of social movements (della Porta and Rucht 1995; Kriesi 1995); in return, the support or lack of support given by social movements to political parties can determine the latters' electoral success (Dalton and Kuechler 1990; Koopmans 1995; Lo 1990). Even at the local level, as the essay in this volume by Heidi J. Swarts shows, elected city councils and mayors rely on guidance from social movements to set their agenda and provide information for decision making, while at the national level, as shown by Nella van Dyke's essay, cycles of protest and cycles of electoral change seem to be remarkably synchronized.

This overlap and interpenetration of social movement actors and actions with conventional political participation and political parties is not something new, nor is it limited to established Western democracies. In Europe, all of the major labor movements of the nineteenth century worked simultaneously to build unions for organizing protest and to build labor parties for organizing voting and electing representatives. In the United States in the 1930s, the Roosevelt welfare program was advanced by the Democratic Party in conjunction with labor-based and reformist social movements, which meshed protest and conventional political mobilization (Amenta 1998; Cloward and Piven 1999; Piven and Cloward 1979), leaving a long-term legacy of active participation of the labor movement in Democratic Party politics. On the right, Nazism began as a social movement but triumphed as a political party (Brustein 1996).

Going further back in time, in the United States all of the major nineteenth- and early-twentieth-century social movements that spawned social movement organizations – the American Anti-Slavery Society, the Farmers' Alliance, and the Anti-Saloon League – also spun off political parties that ran candidates in local and national elections: the Free Soil, Populist, and Prohibition parties, respectively. The fate of the movements was intimately tied to the fates of those parties and vice versa: The Free Soil Party later developed into the Republican Party of Abraham Lincoln, who eventually brought success to the abolitionist cause. The Populist Party polled twenty-two electoral votes in 1892, elected several governors and members of Congress, and later fused with the Democratic Party; the Democrats' defeat in William Jennings Bryan's 1896 campaign then brought the collapse of one of the most widespread and challenging protest movements in the United States since the Civil War. Although the Prohibition Party never was a significant player in national elections, the Anti-Saloon League and the Women's Christian Temperance Union eventually succeeded by embracing normal politics at the state level, namely, by leading referendum campaigns for dry laws in numerous states, which provided the foundation for national prohibition. The fates of major political parties were thus closely tied to the social movements that integrated with them. Of the major pre–World War I social movements, only the women's suffrage movement remained largely uninvolved in institutionalized political campaigns and party organizations.[1]

---

[1] Women's suffrage movements did, in fact, engage in initiative drives in a few states, but these were the exceptions in what were primarily campaigns of lobbying and protest (Banaszak 1998; Costain 1998).

Outside the United States, we find that social movement activists and political party organization again overlap, even in the earliest emergence of democratic party institutions. Jan Kubik (1998) found that among four Eastern European nations that recently developed democratic institutions, namely, Poland, the former East Germany, Hungary, and Slovakia, democratic participation and protest activity were not alternatives, but rather complements, that rose and fell together. Those states that had the most active political party participation – Poland and East Germany – also had the most protest. In Russia, the activists of the Democratic Russia Party, which successfully backed Boris Yeltsin in his challenge to the Communist Party, were recruited from among dissident leaders of the human rights movement and from among environmental activists who had been among the first organizers of social movements in the former Soviet Union (Brovkin 1990). And in South Africa, the politics of the now democratically elected ruling African National Congress bear the indelible marks of that party's origins in the violent struggle of protest against apartheid (Seidman 2001).

Why have many scholars come to treat protest not merely as one aspect of social movement activity, but as the normal or primary mode of action for social movements and quite separate from institutionalized political actions? I think it may be because social movement theory as it emerged in the 1950s and 1960s lost sight of the essential complementarity of both social protest and electoral politics by focusing on somewhat peculiar movements, namely, movements in democratic societies that mainly involved people who were legally debarred from voting. Black civil rights and New Left student movements (before the voting age was lowered to eighteen) could draw a fairly clean line between normal political activity (voting, running for office) and protest activity (association, demonstration, protest) because *for those groups* only the latter was viable.

In addition, New Left and Black Power groups also often self-identified with more revolutionary movements (with such anticapitalist heroes as Che Guevarra and Fidel Castro) that were clearly outside of and opposed to the establishment. It is certainly true that for many protest movements, the question of self-identification sometimes involves a decided stance as "outside of" and "opposing" established parties and political systems precisely to avoid the taint of cooptation or excessive compromise. However, social scientists should not treat these strategic or tactical positionings by movement actors as if they represented *inherent* characteristics of movement activity. In fact, as this volume makes clear, social movements' stance of alliance with, or opposition to, conventional political parties and officials is a pivot of multiple possibilities and shows frequent shifts.

The complementarity of protest and conventional political action (lobbying, participation in election campaigns, voting) suggests that studies of the effectiveness of *protest* (Gamson 1990) in terms of the characteristics of protest groups may have been wrongly conceived. Rather, it may be the ability of groups to combine *both* protest *and* conventional tactics for influencing government actors that best conduces to movement success (Andrews 2001; Cress and Snow 2000).[2]

Moreover, the temporal contrast that most researchers drew was between the protest cycle of the 1960s and 1970s and the relatively quiescent trough of protest activity in the immediate post–World War II period of the late 1940s and 1950s (Kriesi et al. 1995; Rucht 1998). The earlier period was seen as representing conventional politics, while the 1960s cycle was viewed as "normal" protest. The somewhat different character of earlier protest cycles, such as the labor protests of the 1930s (Piven and Cloward 1979) or the middle-class movements of the nineteenth century referred to earlier, such as abolitionism and prohibition (Calhoun 1995), were overlooked. The implicit assumption was that once those groups leading the 1960s protest cycle succeeded and were incorporated into the polity – for example, given the right to full political participation – they would use that standing to influence policy by conventional politics, and social movements would fade or continue to be drawn from the excluded.

Yet it has not turned out that way at all. The women's movement, the student left (which focused on international peace, antiapartheid efforts, cultural diversity on campus, and other issues), and the civil rights movement continued to use protest tactics in conjunction with normal political processes to seek their agendas, now expanded beyond mere access to voting to include a variety of issues of fairness (economic as well as political) and welfare (Koopmans 1995; Rucht 1998). Their repertoire of contentious action did not shift from protest to politics; rather, it expanded to include both. "New" social movements such as the environmental movement and the antiabortion movement, which never had formally disenfranchised actors, from their inception pursued and to this day pursue a variety of protest,

---

[2] Andrews (2001) points out that even for the civil rights movement in Mississippi, "Local movements used a variety of conventional tactics, but they did not abandon the politics of protest. . . . Rather, movements were most influential when they built local organizations that allowed for an oscillation between mass-based tactics and routine negotiation with agency officials" (p. 89).

associational, and political party actions all aimed at making state policies conform to their goals (Costain and Lester 1998).

The reasons for this close ongoing relationship between protest and institutionalized politics have become more clear from Charles Tilly's pathbreaking explorations of the emergence of social movement activity in the late eighteenth and early nineteenth centuries (Tilly 1995; Tilly and Wood in press). Social protest repertoires emerged in England at roughly the same time as repertoires for influencing elections to Parliament, and with the same purpose – to influence the outcomes of Parliament's deliberations. This was not a coincidence but represented a fundamental evolution in the nature of politics: *Both* democratization *and* social movements built on the same basic principle, that ordinary people are politically worthy of consultation. Both protests and normal electioneering seek to influence the decisions of representative bodies by presenting to the public and to those bodies the degree of popular support behind particular goals (Burstein 1999). Social movement activity and conventional political activity are different but parallel approaches to influencing political outcomes, often drawing on the same actors, targeting the same bodies, and seeking the same goals.

Social protest and routine political participation are complementary in several ways. First, institutional politics, for most ordinary people, is a highly intermittent process, focusing on electoral cycles. Protest and associational actions can go on throughout the seasons and throughout the years. Second, most conventional political participation only allows a fairly crude expression of choices – one votes for or against a candidate or party that may have a wide variety of positions. Protest and associational actions can focus on particular issues, giving greater specificity to actions; indeed, protests can shape party behavior in this respect, as Elisabeth Clemens (1997) has shown for the role of protest in making parties more responsive to specific social groups and their claims. This is not always the case; anticommunist or prodemocratic movements have very broad goals, while conventional referendum campaigns or lawsuits are often very issue-specific. However, in general, protest actions allow a degree of focus that is often difficult for ordinary citizens to attain in routine voting and political party participation.

Third, protest and associational actions offer an ongoing method to refine and reinforce the results of conventional elections (Imig 1998). Left movements may protest more when a rightist government is in power (and vice versa) to keep their agenda in view or to moderate the actions of the new government; in other cases, left movements may protest more when a leftist movement is in power (and vice versa) to push that government to make good on campaign promises and honor its commitments. The essay by Nella Van Dyke in this volume gives evidence of both processes operating in the United States, interestingly in different ways at the national and state levels of governance.

Fourth, social movements, not just parties, can affect the *outcome* of institutionalized electoral contests. Movements can affect elections not only by mobilizing their supporters to vote and support a particular party, but also by increasing the salience of issues that are identified with particular parties or politicians (Burstein 1999, p. 15). Thus, the U.S. civil rights movement not only mobilized blacks to vote Democratic in northern states where Democrats had a thin margin in state elections; by dramatizing the injustices of segregation and raising the salience of civil rights issues, the movement also shifted the support given to antisegregation parties and politicians across the nation.

To sum up, there is no reason to expect that protest and conventional political action should be substitutes, with groups abandoning the former as they become able to use the latter. While some groups may, at different times, be more "in," in the sense of being more aligned and integrated with the institutional authorities, while other groups are more "out," there is neither a simple qualitative split nor a "once and for all" crossing of some distinct line separating challengers from insiders. It is more accurate to think of a continuum of alignment and influence, with some groups having very little access and influence through conventional politics, others having somewhat more, and still others quite a lot; but groups may move up and down this continuum fairly quickly, depending on shifts in state and party alignments. Protest may sometimes be a means of moving upward along the continuum, or a response to movement downward, or even an option that becomes easier and more available as institutionalized access increases (Meyer and Tarrow 1998a). The dynamics of protest thus have a complex and contingent relationship to a group's integration into institutionalized politics. The notion that there are in-groups and out-groups, and that the latter engage in protests while the former engage in politics, is a caricature with little relation to reality.

Protest actions have certain advantages over and complementarities with conventional political action that make protest both an alternative and a valuable supplement to the latter. Indeed, one would expect, and we generally find, that as societies gain and extend their institutionalized political participation through parties and voting, they *also* extend their institutionalized repertoires of, and participation in, social movements and political protests. Both voting and social protest are avenues of political action that open up to ordinary people with the advance of democratization.

This still leaves the puzzle of why democratic social movements have, in recent years, been a major factor in nondemocratic countries (Markoff 1996), at least since the Gandhi-led independence movement in India in the 1940s. I believe this is rightly characterized as one of the impacts of globalization (Meyer et al. 1997). When expectations that democratic rights are a natural entitlement of adults spread (as they are now spreading to the developing world, just as they spread from England to France and thence to Europe and Asia in the eighteenth, nineteenth, and early twentieth centuries), that encourages people both to protest and to seek democracy; both efforts are rooted in the belief that the actions and desires of ordinary people should count and will be seen by the world (if not by their current regime) as worthy of support.

Moreover, if the spread of national democracies is the natural setting for the development of new repertoires of social protest and movement organizations, it should not be surprising that the international spread of democratic beliefs and norms alongside the growth of international organizations and multinational associations and agreements should be fertile ground for the development of new international organizations seeking to influence those organizations and associations, such as the international advocacy organizations studied by Margaret Keck and Kathryn Sikkink (1998). Such advocacy organizations, focusing on issues such as human rights, environmental protection, and promoting democracy, typically draw on experts and focus on lobbying, party building, and other conventional political activity (Wapner 1995). Yet such groups have developed alongside the more contentious protest actions organized at such sites as the World Bank and International Monetary Fund meetings. Again, even as political activity extends to new globalized arenas and issues, we find the same close interweaving of institutional and social protest actions as complementary approaches to influencing the outcomes of deliberative and policymaking bodies.

Appreciation of the complex dynamics of protest and institutional politics also calls for new reflections on the role of violence. The simple dichotomy of in-groups and out-groups provided a simple theory of the role of violence in protest: Out-groups would be both the target and the source of the most violence; as groups gained more access to institutionalized politics, the level of violence they needed to employ to gain attention, or that would be deployed against them, should decrease. Yet this has been only partially true. Studies of protest and repression have long recognized that groups with virtually no resources and no access to institutionalized politics have little means for effective disruption or violence and no defenses against repression. Groups with no access are thus as unlikely to engage in sustained protest actions as groups with very high access. The relationship between political access and political violence is therefore generally considered to be curvilinear, with more violent protests in states with intermediate levels of repression and political access (Muller 1985; Weede 1987).

However, even this simple curvilinear scheme does not cover temporal patterns that are also important. When does a state decide that a protest group is a threat requiring repression? Does it depend on the size of the group, its intensity of protest, its level of violence? The essay in this volume by David Cunningham suggests that none of these is a solid guide to government repression (see also Davenport 2000). Studies of revolution and rebellion have shown that it is often not groups that were most distant from institutionalized political access, but those groups that had made considerable gains in institutional power and then were suddenly excluded, or that had acquired considerable economic power and felt entitled to a greater political role, that produced the most violent or revolutionary mobilization (Goldstone 1991; Goodwin 2001; Walton 1984). In the U.S. civil rights movement, popular violence by blacks increased most rapidly *after* initial gains in civil rights legislation were made, as it became clear that even those victories in gaining institutionalized recognition and participation rights were not going to yield much immediate economic benefit or relief from residential, work, and other forms of discrimination (McAdam 1982). The U.S. labor movement suffered exceptional violence from employers in the late nineteenth century precisely as it began to gain unusual success in broad-based mobilization (Voss 1993). Indeed, as the essay in this volume by Joseph Luders demonstrates, in a lesson clear from Voss's work on U.S. labor conflicts, violence is sometimes a deliberate product of governments pitting different groups against each other, or simply failing to intervene to impose order amid group conflicts, rather than a matter of out-groups facing overt state repression or choosing violent methods of protest.

The wall that once separated studies of social movements from the study of institutionalized politics is now crumbling under a barrage of new findings and criticism. Leading social movement scholars now take it for granted that we must challenge the boundary between institutionalized and noninstitutionalized politics (Costain and McFarland 1998; McAdam,

Tarrow, and Tilly 2001; Tarrow in press). We can no longer treat institutionalized politics in the realm of elections and parties as somehow primary and the noninstitutionalized actions of social movements acting from outside the polity as merely an effort to influence the former's decisions. The very existence, actions, and structure of institutionalized political actors are permeated by social movement activity on an ongoing basis. Understanding how social movements give rise to parties, shape political alignments, and interact with normal political institutions has become essential to comprehending political dynamics.

However, this means that a whole new range of questions regarding social movements requires attention. If we are not merely going to batter down the wall between institutionalized and noninstitutionalized politics, but to scale it and move beyond it, we need to ask precisely *how* social movements influence states and parties, and how states and parties shape and influence social movements. We need to understand the impact on party structures of shifts in social movements. We need to go well beyond the most visible recent cases of social movements that have been the grist for social movement theory in recent decades and explore the interactions of states, parties, and social movements in a wide variety of regional and political settings. This is precisely what the essays in this volume set out to do.

Political Dynamics of State-Party-Movement Interaction

The essays in this book focus on the dynamics interweaving state actions, the emergence and strategies of political parties, and social movements. They present new findings regarding these dynamics in local and national settings ranging from the United States to Mexico, India, and Eastern Europe, and covering such issues as civil rights, democracy, urban politics, and the New Left.

States and Social Movements

We usually think of social movements as seeking to influence states, but the reverse is also true – states often act to influence the reception of social movements. Moreover, we typically think of states as responding to movements by repression or efforts to maintain state authority. Yet in his study of variations in the intensity of civil rights protest in the American South in the 1960s, Joseph Luders illuminates more subtle relationships. Luders shows how southern states' decisions on whether to encourage or suppress countermovements was a major element of their strategy in responding to civil rights protests. In fact, certain state governments deliberately chose to abdicate their authority in order to allow greater scope for countermovement violence against civil rights protestors. Luders shows that variations in the degree of anti-rights violence across southern states was not simply due to differing levels of black protest or white racism. Rather, the intensity of the conflict was deliberately modulated by the actions of states.

State governments varied greatly in their willingness to punish anti-rights violence by private groups and to prevent violent anti-rights action by local authorities. While certain state governments, such as those of Mississippi and Louisiana, tolerated a great deal of anti-rights violence by private actors and even local authorities, sometimes even encouraging actions by the Ku Klux Klan, other states adopted a strict law-and-order policy that repressed anti-rights agitators as much as or more than civil rights protestors. This was not out of any sympathy with the cause of civil rights, for the latter states, such as North and South Carolina, remained as strongly segregationist as federal laws would allow. Rather, this was a decision not to allow violence and disorder to take over their states; to this end, they even assigned state law officers to infiltrate the Klan and took authority away from local sheriffs and police when the latter threatened to let racial contention get out of hand.

We generally think of states as simply either repressing or accepting movements, with countermovements acting independently to compete for public and state support. The images of Birmingham's public safety commissioner, Bull Connor, setting the dogs on protestors in Alabama, or of courageous Freedom Summer volunteers facing murder at the hands of Klansmen in Mississippi, are etched on our consciousness of social movement history. Yet Luders shows that these confrontations were less a result of fierce movement action than of deliberate *inaction* on the part of state governments. Where state governors resolved to avoid violence – whether by or against civil rights protestors, and whether by private countermovements or their own local authorities – fierce racial contention, despite the existence of equally strong passions, simply did not occur. State actions, as much as or more than the movements themselves, determined the intensity of contention between the movements seeking civil rights and the countermovements of white supremacy. Luders's essay offers a profound lesson for those who see the ethnic conflicts among different groups around the world as an inevitable product of racial passions and movement mobilization.

David Cunningham also revisits the 1960s and sheds additional light on the complexities of repressive state actions against movements. Cunningham points out that most of the social movements literature dealing with the effects of repression assumes that repression is open and visible to all, so that its dissuasive effects will be clear to movement sympathizers, bystanders, and opponents alike. In fact, much state action against social movements is not overt and is not merely a punitive response to movement actions. In the 1960s, the Federal Bureau of Investigation (FBI) developed a proactive department – a domestic counterintelligence program (COINTELPRO) – designed to quietly undermine and dissolve New Left, white hate, and black hate movements from within. Using campaigns of misinformation and infiltration, the FBI acted – often with fair success – to sow discord and confusion among movements, preventing actions rather than using force to suppress them. Luders noted that some southern U.S. governors did the same to weaken white supremacy groups that threatened violence, and we would have reason to expect that ever since the development of secret police, overt violence and punishment against protest movements may be only the tip of the iceberg of state efforts against opposition movements. Beyond the scale of these covert repressive efforts, Cunningham finds that contrary to what we might expect, it was not the most active, the largest, or the most violent protest groups that drew the greatest preemptive efforts at covert repression. Rather, it was those groups whose ideology and behavior seemed most threatening to the values that the FBI, and in particular its director, Edgar J. Hoover, held to be critical to preserving American society. Despite the claims that new social movements rooted in lifestyle changes are apolitical (Melucci 1989), it was precisely the counterculture aspects of the New Left that seemed to draw disproportionate interest from the repressive forces of the American state as embodied in the FBI. Cunningham makes a compelling argument that there is usually far more to state–movement interactions than meets the eye through the overt repression aimed at protestors.

While Cunningham illuminates the phenomenon of covert repression, Heidi J. Swarts demonstrates that much protest over government policy is also invisible. Swarts examines the campaigns of two local church-based social movement organizations that sought changes in the agenda and decisions of local governments in San Jose, California, and St. Louis, Missouri. Though they indeed engaged in sustained confrontations with authorities, these social movement organizations' actions were rarely clearly visible because they took place almost entirely behind closed doors. Instead of the marches and public protests that we traditionally identify with social movements, these organizations staged public assemblies of hundreds or even thousands of people in "prayer services," "accountability sessions," "learning summits," and "town hall meetings." These are clearly not merely lobbies or interest groups that submit expert advice or pay lobbyists to influence local government. The chief tactic of these groups was to quietly confront elected officials with mass demonstrations of interest and commitment to their issues.

Moreover, Swarts's findings about the conditions of success of these movements also reveal much that is usually unseen and is counter to prevailing wisdom regarding political opportunity and social movements. First, aside from such factors as popular support, organization, and elite support, it crucially mattered to movement success how the specific issues being contested interacted with the government structure faced by the movement. In San Jose, the church-based protest groups faced a fairly centralized city government, and sought an incremental diversion of resources to projects to address crime and support education in poor neighborhoods. The combination of a strong centralized city government and the choice of an incremental issue that would not strain the resources controlled by that government was conducive to success. In contrast, in St. Louis the church-based groups faced an extremely fragmented set of urban and suburban governments over an issue – urban sprawl – that none of the governments truly controlled. Success would have required coordinating significant changes in direction among a variety of separate government actors dominated by different elites. Not surprisingly, they failed to make much headway.

In addition, the interaction of elites, states, and social movements is not reducible to the typical formula that divided elites conduce to protest success. In St. Louis, political and business elites were divided, with the mayor of St. Louis and many urban planners supporting the movement's demand to halt or reduce the sprawl that was sucking much economic growth out of the city, while suburban and state politicians, and business elites throughout the area, were in favor of continued expansion. The problem was not merely that the protestors found themselves on the wrong side of the elite divide, as the coalition of suburban and statewide officials and business leaders was able to counter any plans to halt sprawl; rather, the divisions among elites coincided with such fractured authority that even winning over powerful local elites gave the movement little leverage. By contrast, in San Jose, although the initial victory of incremental funding increases for crime and education programs relied on an elite split, with the mayor siding with the protestors against the conservative City Redevelopment Agency, once the programs were in place, their demonstrable efficacy in improving youth behavior in the city won over supporters, so that united elite support for sustaining and expanding the programs developed and led to further movement success. In short, if a movement can win over a united state and business elite, that is often better than facing a state or an elite split so badly that even winning over significant actors provides no leverage for change. Swarts shows, once again, that the interactions of states and social movements offer far more than usually meets the eye, and that simple formulas do not capture the realities of those interactions or the paths to movement success.

Jorge Cadena-Roa also demonstrates how social movement actions interweave with institutional politics in his study of the recent emergence of electoral democracy in Mexico. Cadena-Roa convincingly repudiates the view that elite "pacts" can suffice as the analytical focus for explaining transitions from authoritarian to democratic regimes. He demonstrates that the emergence of democracy in Mexico, recently capped with the election of the first non–Institutional Revolutionary Party (PRI) president in seventy-one years in the person of Vicente Fox, was the result of a complex struggle among elite factions and popular movements that gradually undermined the PRI's exclusive control of the symbols of legitimacy and the levers of political power. This was not simply a matter of elites being influenced in their actions by popular pressures, or of political parties being assisted or reinforced by outside agitation by opposition groups. Rather, the interplay of political parties, of economic, political, religious, and intellectual elites, and of opposition movements and leaders was one of fluid intermingling and shifting coalitions. Students, clerics, intellectuals, and popular leaders alternately founded parties and engaged in electoral politics, or joined social movement oppositions or even guerrilla groups, depending on the openings and allies available to them. The PRI alternately gave concessions to social movements to outflank opposition political parties while engaging in repression and arbitrary actions that drove even mainstream political and economic elites to join those opposition parties. Social movements demanded and monitored elections that were not manipulated by the PRI, thus providing the essential conditions for other political parties to achieve electoral victories. In what looks very much like a "slow-motion revolution," unrolling from 1970 to 2000, the shifting orientations and relationships among the PRI, opposition electoral parties, moderate social movements, and radical guerrilla movements all combined to create a competitive democratic framework for politics in the space that had formerly been wholly dominated by the PRI. This transition is simply not comprehensible without detailing the intimate relationship between Mexico's political parties and the social movements that cleared and reshaped that political space.

Parties and Social Movements

John K. Glenn, like Cadena-Roa, also examines a democratic transition, this time in Eastern Europe. In Czechoslovakia, social movements did not merely influence and assist in the creation of democratic governance; they became the government. Yet this created a new tension: How should movements transition into ruling entities? Should they become conventional political parties, unconventional parties-cum-movements, or simply fade away? International actors, particularly prodemocracy nongovernment organizations from the United States, promoted a conventional party model. But this option was resisted by the intellectual dissidents who had founded and led the anticommunist movement. The result was an opportunity for political entrepreneurs to use transnational assistance to build their own party machines and seize power from the civic movements that had first assumed leadership after the fall of the communist regime. These new parties were political instruments rooted neither in existing societal cleavages nor in the prior social movements. Rather, they were the product of transnational assistance and models subsequently adapted to win local support. One outcome of this development was something that no one – not the original anticommunist movements, nor the transnational actors, nor the population of Czechoslovakia – had foreseen: the fission of Czechoslovakia into two separate nations under two separate political parties, each the instrument of its leader: Vaclav Klaus in the Czech Republic and Vladimir Mečiar in Slovakia.

Manali Desai also examines a case of social movements that became governing parties, and as in Czechoslovakia, with different results in different parts of the country. Her study of the Communist parties in the states of Kerala and West Bengal in India further emphasizes Glenn's argument that one cannot simply read off the policies and future of a political party from the social movement from which it sprang. The encounter of movement leaders with the realities of political competition often transforms them, and the choices they make shape their parties. Desai thus speaks of the "autonomy of parties" to make it clear that parties – even those rooted in social movements – are not merely the instruments of those movements. On the other hand, the details of the history of how parties emerge from movements does matter, as does the impact of that history on the relationships between party leaders and their followers. Desai first forcefully demonstrates that the structural conditions facing Indian peasants in these two states did not determine the emergence, goals, or strategies of leftist movements in those regions; areas with similar tenant–landlord relations developed very different leftist movements, while areas with quite different land relations followed the same parties. Second, she shows how the leftist movement in Kerala was distinct from that in Bengal in two ways: (1) the Kerala Communist leaders joined tenant–landlord issues to attacks on the caste system, stressing egalitarian policies, and (2) the Kerala Communist leaders initially cooperated with the anti-British nationalist Congress Party, winning supporters among a wide range of groups who sought Indian self-determination. In contrast, the Bengali Communists campaigned against economic landlord domination while maintaining their elite-caste status, embarking on a tactical course of elite-conducted terrorist attacks rather than grassroots organizing. The result was that when these two movements came to power in their states, their political situation and hence their policy approaches were quite different. With broad support and a commitment to their grassroots base, the Communists in Kerala adopted wide-ranging welfare state reforms, devoting exceptionally large resources to distributing land, increasing access to education, and improving public health. As a result, Kerala has been celebrated for its success in raising quality-of-life indicators such as literacy and life expectancy far above Indian norms. Yet the Communist Party in Bengal, with a much narrower social base among workers and small cultivators, was forced to compromise its radicalism to achieve political success; moreover, its elite orientation and its distance from the masses left its leaders with no strong personal commitments to enforce egalitarian welfare policies. As a result, although the Communist Party in Bengal has implemented some land reforms, its achievements in social welfare are no greater than those of many other Indian states.

Kim Williams offers further new insights into the subtlety of movement–party relations in her study of state-level voting on legislation to add a "multiracial" category to official demographic records. In the mainstream pluralist model of U.S. politics, movements try to influence parties to achieve certain outcomes. Strength of commitment, number of supporters, and mobilization efforts are all supposed to matter to success. But in this case, the voting to adopt multiracial categories was generally unanimous, rather than a matter of one party or the other achieving a victory. In fact, there was only a tenuous relationship at best between the strength and activity of the multiracial category movement in a particular state and the outcomes in that state. Thus, the relationship between movements and parties is clearly incomplete; what matters is the triangle of movements, parties, and constituencies. Party-based legislators clearly have considerable autonomy to determine whether responding to a social movement will result in actions that help them with their broader constituencies. Even in the absence of countermovements, the degree of mobilization and the number of active supporters may be poor guides to movement success (cf. Goldstone 1980). Rather, the role of the movements seems to be to raise issues that are potentially valuable to legislators in gaining the support of constituencies, even if the majority of the constituents are not active in the movement. Then the response to those issues depends on how legislators assess the value of that action – not the value to the movement and its known supporters, but rather to their overall (in this case suburban and upper-class) constituencies. This research suggests a relationship between movements and parties that is less direct, but perhaps no less pervasive, than the typical pluralist or interest-group model. If some movements work mainly by framing issues as potentially valuable to legislators with their broader constituencies, even if those constituencies are not mobilized for the issue, then the influence of movements on legislatures may be far more extensive than studies of mobilization or social movements that focus on the movements themselves presume. Instead, movements may be an ongoing factor in the shaping of party deliberations and actions out of all proportion to the magnitude of the movement mobilization. Thus, understanding legislative politics may often require us to see even limited social movements as mediating broadly between whole constituencies and party politicians.

Legislative politics is also a theme of Nella Van Dyke's study of political party alignments and student protest in the United States from the 1930s through the 1980s. Contrary to simple political opportunity models, Van Dyke finds that the frequency of student protest decreased when the Democratic Party, presumably more sympathetic to left movements, controlled the presidency or state governorships. Evidently, a Republican, and presumably more hostile, chief executive was more likely to precipitate protests. Threat thus mattered as much as opportunity. Nonetheless, Democratic control of the legislature did produce more protest; thus, allies at the legislative level apparently promoted movement efforts.

To complicate matters still further, Van Dyke also found that it mattered whether or not the state and national governments were divided, with different parties controlling the executive and the legislature – but the results varied by level of government. At the federal level, a divided government was associated with less frequent student protests, but at the state level, a divided government was associated with more frequent protests. Again, the relationship between state, party, and movements is surprisingly complex. Parties can offer allies or impose threats to left movements; both conditions can spur protest. Thus, no simple explanation of protest activity based on party alignments is possible; it apparently matters at what level of government allies and antagonists appear, and in what branch of the state government as well. Chief executives appear to provoke the most protest by threatening students' interests, but legislatures appear to promote the most protest when they offer support.

Patterns of Influence: Social Movements, Parties, and States

The conventional wisdom in studies of social movements has often presumed a separation of institutional and noninstitutional politics; that protest dynamics consisted mainly of movements initiating protest actions and states' responses; and that movement success depended mainly on favorable political opportunities and the extent of movement mobilization. The essays in this volume make it clear that none of these presumptions is wholly valid. Rather, we shall have to broaden our view of state–party–movement interactions to embrace a far wider range of possibilities.

Views of social movements as mainly adversarial often saw movements as having only two possible relationships to the state. Either the state would repress the movement or it would be reluctantly influenced by it. Outcomes were similarly binary: The movement would fail or it would become institutionalized (and cease to exist as a movement), either because its policy goals were achieved or because it had become a "member of the polity" and now functioned as a normal interest group (Gamson 1990).

In fact, the range of relationships is far more varied (Burstein, Einwohner, and Hollander 1995), as the essays in this volume clearly demonstrate. The choices of repression or reluctant influence are only two steps on a much wider scale, especially once one recognizes the internal heterogeneity of "the state" as involving multiple players and parties. States may respond to social movements in any of the following ways:

Introduction

Repression with Institutional Change

If a social movement or movements are perceived as a large enough threat or novel in their methods of protest, the state may evolve new coercive institutions to deal with them, as shown in Cunningham's essay on the FBI. The repressive capacities and operations of the state may thus change markedly as a result of engagement with movements. As Luders demonstrates, states may even orchestrate repression by third parties, such as vigilante groups or countermovements, thus changing the institutions of local power and authority. In either case, state repression may be largely invisible, at least in the sense that violent clashes between protestors and state agents may be absent. Thus, we need to expand our usual notion of "repression" to include a wider repertoire of state sanctions against movements (Barkan 1984).

Repression with no Institutional Change

This is the conventional response to small-scale but radical protests, but as Van Dyke's essay shows, various patterns of state hostility can increase as well as decrease movement activity. Opposition to a movement's goals by conventional party politicians can in fact invigorate movement activity by raising fears of loss of past gains or of new threats to their interests (Goldstone and Tilly 2001; Kurzman 1996; Lindenberg 1989). Whether repression discourages or encourages protest movements depends in complex ways on the constellation of conventional party alignments, the level (local, regional, or national) at which party allies or opponents dominate, and the support or opposition of the public and organized counter or allied movements.

Moreover, as Cadena-Roa shows in the case of Mexico, states may even turn repression against political parties to keep them from gaining adherents. Or as Desai demonstrates for the case of the Communist Party of India, movements may "take refuge" within the covering shell of broader political party organizations in order to mobilize while avoiding repression.

Toleration or Encouragement

Social movements may continue for a long time with little or no effect on or response from the state, particularly if balanced by countermovements or if not part of a major protest wave or cycle. However, and more significantly, states may actually embrace movements and seek their support or their integration into party politics. Luders's essay shows how various states' toleration or even active support of countermovements shaped the civil rights contention in the American South. In recent history, state leaders have orchestrated social movements to achieve their political goals – for example, Mao Zedong in China (in the Cultural Revolution) and Robert Mugabe in Zimbabwe (supporting organized land seizures). As Cadena-Roa shows, the Mexican PRI alternated among repressive, tolerant, and encouraging responses to movement actions, depending on how the party judged its tactical situation versus various political challenges. At times, the PRI embraced and coopted social movements precisely to outflank challenges by conventionally operating political parties.

Influence with no Institutional Change

This is the conventional view of social movement success; a state reluctantly enacts policies derived from, or accepts the legitimacy and institutionalization of, a protest group's point of view. However, no major institutional changes are involved. Yet as Swarts shows, even such success does not generally end a movement's activity; protest groups may develop ongoing relationships with institutional actors and continue to use protest mobilization to shape the latter's agenda. Movements need not "enter the polity" and cease to be "challengers" to have influence, to use Gamson's (1990) terms. Many movements, such as the church-based movements that Swarts studies, aim to have long-term influence precisely by maintaining long-term popular mobilization and pressure on conventional parties and politicians.

Influence with Institutional Change

In many cases, a social movement's influence is so extensive that responding to its policy desires or legitimizing its viewpoint changes basic elements of the institutional structure of parties and government. Nonetheless, those social movements that have gained routine access and even institutions of government to enforce their policies – such as the Environmental Protection Agency for the U.S. environmental movement and the Civil Rights division of the Justice Department for the U.S. civil rights and womens' rights movements – do not thereby cease to engage in periodic protest and movement mobilization (Costain and Lester 1998). Instead, periodic mobilization and protest continue to remain part of their repertoire for influencing politics, whether to raise the salience of their concerns with politicians and the public or to pursue particular policies or new agendas.

Very clearly, for the democracy movements in nondemocratic societies, such as those examined by Glenn and Cadena-Roa, movement success meant substantial institutional change, whether occurring suddenly, as in Eastern Europe, or incrementally over several decades, as in Mexico. Yet especially in those cases, movement success and institutional change did not simply end popular protest in those societies. Rather, space opened for new political parties, which some movement actors joined, while other movement actors (such as the Zapatistas in Mexico) chose to remain mobilized against the new regime. It was very clear that even extreme movement success did not produce a simple transformation of successful movements into conventional parties or political actors.

Influence through Ongoing Alliance

In some cases, a social movement gains influence not by imposing its demands on reluctant polity members, but through the enthusiastic embrace of the state or state actors, who seek an ongoing alliance with the movement. In the United States, Democrats aligned themselves with prominority, labor, and left movements from the 1930s to the 1970s, while Republicans aligned themselves with moral and religious conservative groups, both parties routinely involving the social movements in their political fund-raising and mobilization for elections. This does not end the life of these social movements, but rather creates an ongoing symbiosis between the movement and institutionalized political parties, with sharing of information and strategies, and each gaining from the others' success in mobilization and swaying public opinion. As Williams's essay shows, the embrace of a movement by legislators may occur even with only modest mobilization and action by the movement. Fairly small movements may gain considerable influence by suggesting policies that can benefit legislators with their nonmovement constituents.

Influence through Movement Spin-off of Political Parties

Social movements have always had a tendency to "spin off" conventional political parties that contend for power (Garner and Zald 1987). These parties may remain allied with the movement or become independent and merely somewhat influenced by it. For example, the Labor and Socialist parties in nineteenth-century Europe grew out of the labor movement, just as the Green parties in Europe grew out of ecology movements. In Eastern Europe, nationalist and human rights movements produced new regimes and political parties. These developments did not mean that the labor movement, or the ecology movement, or the human rights movements had ended; rather, they simply marked a new degree to which those movements influenced conventional political institutions. As Desai and Glenn show, the relationship between such parties and the movements that spawned them is complex. Such parties are not merely extensions or instruments of the movement, but rather autonomous actors. As such, they can shape both states and movements in unexpected ways.

The essays in this volume greatly enrich our understanding of the intricate relationships among states, parties, and movements. They show that, far from being separate domains, institutional politics and movement actions are deeply intertwined. Moreover, their relationships are not reducible simply to action and response, opportunity and repression. Movements shape parties, sometimes produce parties, often cooperate with parties, and sometimes suggest potential avenues for party action; in all of these roles, the influence of movements is never a simple product of the size of the movement, or of its level of activity or open support. Rather, it is the role of the movement in the multisided strategic action of state leaders, parties, countermovements, and the public at large, each seeking to use or hinder the others to seek its own ends, that produces the final results.

Movements and states also influence each other, often in subtle ways. While open protest and overt repression are most visible and are the preoccupation of most literature, these essays show that those actions are only part of the spectrum of movement and state activity. Movements influence state actors by agenda-setting and suggesting new political strategies; states, in turn, influence movements by proactive covert repression, and by setting the rules for countermovement as well as movement activities. Perhaps most important, contrary to the view that social movements emerge only in democratic societies, these essays show that movements can help create democratic societies out of colonial, autocratic, and racial supremacist regimes.

These empirically rich and theoretically sophisticated accounts of the complexity of state, party, and movement interactions take us well beyond the conventional demarcation of institutional versus noninstitutional politics. In many ways, they uncover heretofore largely unappreciated patterns in the dynamics of contention.

PART I

States and Social Movements

1

Countermovements, the State, and the Intensity of Racial Contention in the American South

Joseph Luders

In direct and palpable ways, states shape movements. In the case of the civil rights movement, law enforcement officers harassed, arrested, and assaulted demonstrators. States prosecuted civil rights organizations; state sovereignty commissions and legislative investigative committees organized covert surveillance of activists and orchestrated various legalistic and economic reprisals against the proponents of racial equality. Most of these state activities are clear and directly related to movement behavior. Equally important yet far less studied are the many ways in which state and local authorities indirectly affect movements by modulating *counter* movement mobilization. During civil rights protests or desegregation events, public officials were obliged to respond to hostile white crowds and to the activities of countermovement organizations such as the Ku Klux Klan and the White Citizens' Council.[1] Though relatively ignored in the expansive literature on social movements, I argue that studies of the impact of states on social movements must address the manner in which states respond to

---

[1] In this study, I do not distinguish sharply between Klan and Council activity, though these organizations were clearly different. The Council, often described as the "uptown Klan," derived support mainly from elite backers in plantation counties. More devoted to economic reprisals, propaganda, and softer forms of intimidation, this organization formally eschewed violence. Indeed, few incidents of racial violence trace back to this organization. The diverse Klan organizations, by contrast, drew support primarily from working-class and lower-middle-class whites. While likewise formally opposed to violence, Klansmen were often found to be involved in acts of white supremacist violence. Incidents of violence, then, are assumed to have been carried out by Klansmen or racists with no known organizational affiliation. On the Council, see McMillen (1971); and on the Klan, see Chalmers (1965) and U.S. House (1967). On events and the use of events as units of analysis, see Olzak (1989).

countermovement mobilization.[2] Simply put, states shape countermovements and countermovements affect the movement to which they are opposed. By opting to suppress, tolerate, or encourage countermovement mobilization, states can decisively affect the intensity of countermovement activity directed against the initial movement. In the case of the civil rights movement, I assert that a combination of state repression of Klan-type organizations and condemnation of lawlessness substantially reduced the intensity of private anti-rights violence. Conversely, greater violence accompanied civil rights activity to the extent that public officials refused to contain the hostile opponents of the civil rights movement and failed to assume a law-and-order posture.

By examining the civil rights movement and countermovement, I make five specific points and suggest some broader implications of this research for social movement theory and the analysis of ethnic conflict. First, southern states responded to countermovement activity in differing ways. Second, these differences in the regulation of countermovement activity should be viewed as the consequence of an explicit or de facto state policy. Third, these differences fundamentally affected the general intensity of anti-rights contention. Fourth, differences in state response to countermovement activity resulted from political calculations by public officials. To understand the variation in the intensity of movement–countermovement contention and therefore how states indirectly shape movements, it is necessary to pay close attention to political actors and institutions. Fifth, by considering the political calculations of elected officials, I offer a partial explanation for the changing intensity of anti-rights contention over time. Finally, after sketching how political concerns caused the posture of southern officials toward countermovement violence to change from tolerance to active suppression, I conclude with an argument in favor of bringing politics more fully into studies of the contention that accompanies movement–countermovement interactions and, more generally, to research on ethnic conflict.

---

[2] For an excellent survey of the available literature and a set of insightful propositions, see Meyer and Staggenborg (1996); see also Lo (1982), Mottl (1980), Zald and Useem (1987), and della Porta and Reiter (1998). McAdam (1982) addresses state mediation of movement-countermovement interaction, as does Marx (1982). On state-sponsored repression carried out under private auspices, see Rosenbaum and Sederberg (1974); on state-sanctioned terrorism among southern states during the lynching era from 1880 to 1930, see Tolnay and Beck (1992).

Anti-Rights Events

The incidence of anti-rights violence clearly varied across the South. An event count of southern anti-rights actions drawn from the annual *New York Times Index* offers a general depiction of the contours of southern anti-rights contention. Between 1954 and 1965, the *Times* reported over 1,500 anti-rights events initiated by private citizens. Broken down into smaller categories, these events included some 312 incidents of private harassment and intimidation, 43 riots and lesser racial clashes, 174 bombings and arsons, and 345 other incidents involving violence.[3] Together, these actions resulted in about 1,000 reported injuries and at least 29 murders.[4] What this catalog of reported incidents does not capture is the marked unevenness of anti-rights contention across the South (see Figure 1.1). Looking at the total number of unconventional protest events (e.g., demonstrations, sit-ins) next to violent anti-rights events conducted by private citizens, it is clear the citizens of certain states were far more violence-prone than others. Alabama and Mississippi far surpass all other states with respect to the prevalence of private violence, whereas this was a relative rarity in the Carolinas. In between, in Florida, Georgia, Louisiana, and Tennessee, considerable violence accompanied civil rights events. Moreover, the differences across the states cannot be reduced simply to the intensity of pro-rights activity. Florida and North Carolina shared approximately the same number of unconventional pro-rights events, but Florida had over three times the reported number of violent anti-rights incidents. Even though many more civil rights protests took place in Georgia than in Louisiana, private anti-rights violence was more common in the Pelican State. In brief, this statistical sketch of anti-rights violence clearly depicts substantial differences across the South. Instead of regarding the variation in anti-rights violence as manifestations of local racism, I suggest that state and local authorities shaped the variation in anti-rights contention.

Although all of the variation in anti-rights violence cannot be reduced to the posture of public officials, the response of state officials to white countermobilization clearly differed. The event totals for anti-rights violence and state punishment (arrest or conviction) of whites engaged in anti-rights activity serves as a rough indicator of the extent of state suppression

---

[3] Data collected by the author.

[4] These figures do not include incidents of racial violence with no apparent connection to the civil rights movement.

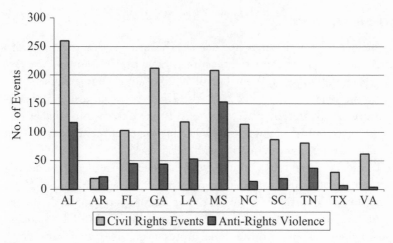

Figure 1.1 Total unconventional pro-rights events and violent anti-rights events initiated by private citizens by state, 1954–65. (*Source: New York Times Index*)

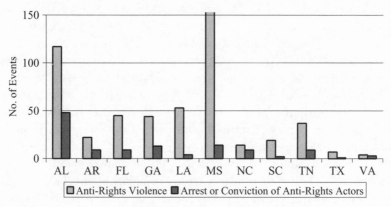

Figure 1.2 Incidents of anti-rights violence and state punishment of counter-movement actors by state, 1954–65. (*Source: New York Times Index*)

of white countermobilization (see Figure 1.2).[5] North Carolina emerges as a bastion of law and order in which almost as many punishment events took place as incidents involving anti-rights violence. By contrast, Louisiana, with somewhat more violent events than Georgia, arrested anti-rights activists much less frequently. Similarly, in Mississippi, violence flourished as law enforcement seldom punished the perpetrators of anti-rights actions.

---

[5] "State suppression" is meant generally to include acts of both state and local law enforcement officials.

While too crude for sweeping generalizations, these figures suggest that southern states differed in their treatment of countermovement activity and that these differences affected the overall intensity of violence directed at the civil rights movement. To further substantiate these assertions, I sketch the responses of states and local authorities to countermovement activity in North Carolina, South Carolina, Mississippi, and Louisiana.

Case Studies

In North Carolina, active state-led suppression of white supremacist mobilization severely limited the prospects for white countermobilization over the 1954–65 period. On numerous occasions, Governors Luther H. Hodges (1954–61) and Terry Sanford (1961–5) warned the Klan against violence and called for law and order.[6] While Hodges denounced the Klan in 1958, his State Bureau of Investigation (SBI) infiltrated and kept close tabs on the Klan as well as the Citizens' Council.[7] An SBI informer reported that, at a Klan meeting in Greensboro, "many of the Klansmen were afraid that they were going to be raided . . . [and] he heard several of the men say they were getting out of the Klan because it was getting too dangerous."[8] Despite the size of the organization, state infiltration and surveillance weakened the ability of the Klan to engage in unpunished terrorism. For example, in 1958, six Klan members were charged with felonies after undercover agents exposed their plot to bomb a black school (*New York Times*, February 22, 1958, p. 32). Despite the large number of Klaverns affiliated with the United Klans of America, the single largest organization in the state, state repression of anti-rights mobilization likely forced the North Carolina Klan to be "relatively nonviolent" (Wade 1987, p. 315).[9] Absent elite condemnation

---

[6] See, for example, "Statement by Governor Hodges," NCDAH (1958b). In Charlotte, the police chief barred the Klan from rallying on the courthouse lawn (*New York Times*, September 2, 1957, p. 26). In the parlance of social movement theory, the political opportunity structure in North Carolina was especially unfavorable because of this willingness and ability of state authorities to repress Klan-type mobilization. On the importance of firm leadership and public warnings against white violence, see Vander Zanden (1965).

[7] There are numerous reports from the SBI describing Klan activity as well as efforts to cultivate a set of informants. See NCDAH (1958a). In contrast to North Carolina's early attention to Klan activity, state law enforcement in Mississippi did not monitor the Klan until 1964.

[8] NCDAH (1958a).

[9] Wade attributes this fact to the influence of the leader of the North Carolina United Klans of America (UKA), Bob Jones, and to a plan to make political use of the organization's large numbers.

and active state suppression, anti-rights intimidation and violence might have been significantly more widespread.

State suppression of white anti-rights violence also included the punishment of whites with no known connection to the Klan. For instance, police in High Point used tear gas to break up a crowd of whites molesting civil rights demonstrators (*New York Times*, September 12, 1963, p. 30).[10] A Highway Patrol report describes an incident in which a police officer told a white youth, who was about to throw a bottle into a group of civil rights demonstrators, that "it would be the greatest mistake he would ever make."[11] In Elm City, state highway patrolmen guarded an African American church that the Klan had threatened to burn and eventually apprehended two white men attempting to do so (*New York Times*, July 15, 1964, p. 16). Firm opposition to anti-rights violence limited the opportunities for Klan-type mobilization and reduced the amount of racial contention to a level below what might have been expected based on the prevalence of the Klan throughout the state.

In South Carolina, after an initial period of support for "massive resistance" to civil rights in the latter 1950s, South Carolina authorities eventually adopted a similar law-and-order stance. Governor Ernest F. "Fritz" Hollings (1959–63), who had won the 1958 gubernatorial election by "out-segging" his opponent, softened the state's intransigent posture in his inaugural address. In the speech, Hollings affirmed his commitment to segregation and then delineated a position in favor of maintaining public order (Muse 1964, p. 257).[12]

To suppress anti-rights harassment and violence, Hollings took several steps. First, as stated previously, Hollings articulated a clear policy of law and order in his public statements and press releases. In the wake of the sit-ins in several communities across South Carolina in 1960, Hollings offered more than the usual denunciation of civil rights protests; he added that his injunction against disorder applied to whites as well, even bystanders. "The threat [to public order] is the same, whether it be by demonstrator or

[10] See also NCDAH (1963a). The police report indicates that "ten rounds of 12 gauge shotgun tear gas were fired into the white crowd and three rounds of 202 (projectiles). . . . The tear gas was very effective and the crowd scattered immediately."

[11] NCDAH (1963b).

[12] In the campaign to win the runoff election, Hollings placed Donald Russell, the former president of the University of South Carolina, on the defensive by attacking his devotion to segregation (Black 1976, pp. 80–2). Hollings, who hailed from Charleston, polled somewhat better in the counties of the eastern low country.

unruly spectator. Law enforcement officers have been directed to apprehend either or both when they threaten violence" (SCDAH 1960). Unlike the governors of other Deep South states who reacted to demonstrations with incendiary rhetoric, Hollings sought to discourage civil rights activity at the same time as he sent a clear signal that white anti-rights violence had no place in South Carolina.

Second, Hollings sought to centralize control over law enforcement.[13] While crediting J. P. "Pete" Strom of the State Law Enforcement Division (SLED) and the sheriffs, Hollings acknowledged that "our city police officers and all were bad." To circumvent local police abuse and interference from the state Highway Patrol (which was under the indirect control of the state legislature), Hollings designated Chief Strom of SLED – who was directly responsible to the governor – as the commander of all law enforcement forces during crises.

So when we [law enforcement] went to Clemson or any other place there would be the chief [Strom], the ranking man from the highway patrol, the sheriff, and the chief of police, and when we brought the guard in – the National Guard, we'd all be in one place at all times, so decisions could be made. But the ultimate decision came from a directive from the governor [by way of] Chief Strom.[14]

In addition, Hollings directed the reliable officers to the trouble spots to "make sure that they enforced the law properly." For example, at the outset of protests in Rock Hill involving Martin Luther King, Jr., Hollings went to the city to supervise the situation. Upon his arrival, Hollings realized that the city police force "was not good and . . . could cause us trouble." To avert a racial clash, Hollings pulled the city officers off duty and, in their stead, he placed all the available African American officers from SLED and from other state and local police forces.

[W]hen Martin Luther King marched in . . . we had black policeman policing the streets and the incidents, and when one of them stepped out of line there was a black policeman leading him into the paddy wagon and they threw away their cameras. They said this isn't what we want. And they went on down to Montgomery where Bull Connor, the sheriff, had his hoses and police dogs.[15]

---

[13] On the several laws passed to obstruct the civil rights movement, the legislature granted the governor expanded law enforcement authority for "maintenance of public peace and suppression of violence." See Southern Education Reporting Service (SERS 1964, p. 48).

[14] J. P. Strom, interview by South Carolina Department of Archives and History (SCDAH, n.d. [b], p. 29).

[15] Senator Ernest F. Hollings, interview by Synnott (1980, p. 5).

Whereas governors in other states allowed local authorities to react (sometimes brutally) to civil rights activity, Hollings sought to maintain more centralized control over racial contention. Event data appear to validate Hollings's account. Although the arrest of demonstrators was commonplace in South Carolina, not a single report of police brutality resulting in injuries was to be found in the *New York Times Index* during the 1954–65 period.[16]

Third, Hollings sought to control the more volatile segregationists and to keep them away from trouble spots. Although the precise details are unclear, Hollings kept a watchful eye on the Ku Klux Klan. During his administration, Hollings had SLED officers infiltrate the Klan to inform on their membership, meetings, and activities. As Hollings explained, "I was really working more at the time against the Klan than . . . the NAACP" (Synnott 1980).[17] Indeed, Hollings claimed to have substantially reduced Klan membership in South Carolina during his tenure in office.[18]

This policy of monitoring segregationists continued under Governor Donald S. Russell (1963–5). To deter racial violence during the Orangeburg protests in 1963, Russell sent Strom, several other SLED agents, and dozens of highway patrolmen (Cox 1996, p. 436). Also, the governor and SLED officers kept an especially close watch on segregationists during the integration of Clemson College. In a flurry of angry complaint letters to the governor, the South Carolina Citizens' Council's field secretary and the state executive both charged that SLED had arbitrarily detained and questioned the Council field secretary during his visit to the Clemson campus (SCDAH 1963). In reaction to Russell's use of SLED, the head of the state Citizens' Council threatened: "I do not believe the legislature of South Carolina will tolerate much more of this high handed bullying in and about Clemson" (SCDAH 1963). This threat, coming from the head of a feeble organization, proved empty.

---

[16] Of course, despite the lack of reports in the *New York Times Index*, matters may have differed from the perspective of demonstrators. Some reports of the civil rights movement in South Carolina mention the rough treatment of police. Branch (1988, p. 283) reports police use of fire hoses and tear gas.

[17] A skeptical reader might well wonder whether or not there is some revisionism in this historical account.

[18] In a cryptic comment, Hollings indicated that certain individuals were detained so that they could not appear at desegregation events to stir up trouble. In this peculiar statement, the context suggests that Hollings is referring to members of the General Assembly. In this case, "detaining" should be read as "delaying" rather than physically apprehending.

On January 28, 1963, at the moment of critical school desegregation in South Carolina, Harvey Gantt entered Clemson College without violence or public disorder. While Alabama Governor George Wallace pledged "segregation forever," Governor Hollings and his successor prepared a path for calm and orderly integration.[19] Long before the college's integration, its president, Dr. Robert C. Edwards, Governor Hollings, and Strom devised a plan to maintain law and order. A seven-page document described in detail the plan for controlling the campus, handling press coverage, and keeping away potential troublemakers (SCDAH n.d. [a]).[20] In addition, several business leaders and public officials, including the departing and incoming governors and even State Senator L. Marion Gressette of the state's anti-integration legislative committee, urged lawful compliance with the federal court order.

The passage of the Freedom Riders through the state further typified the management of movement–countermovement interactions. Keeping up segregationist appearances, Hollings called for an investigation of the rides and suggested Communist instigation but, equally important, police arrested twenty white "toughs" as they assaulted the riders when they entered the station (*The State* [Columbia, SC], June 8, 1961).[21] Although reports differ on how speedily the police intervened, it is significant that they halted the violence and arrested the white assailants, not the riders. Equally important, during a June Freedom Ride, police escorted the riders as they went unmolested through the state (*New York Times*, June 15, 1961. p. 38).[22]

Although the entrance of Gantt into Clemson did not signal the conclusion of state anti-integration schemes, South Carolina state officials – especially Governors Hollings and Russell – actively suppressed private anti-rights mobilization. Coupled with their tactic of nonviolent legal

---

[19] Although Russell received the credit, the plan for the desegregation of Clemson, discussed previously, was in place *prior* to Russell's inauguration in mid-January.

[20] To learn from the mistakes made in Mississippi, Chief Strom visited the state to meet with Hugh Clay, who was both Director of Training at the Federal Bureau of Investigation's National Academy and vice chancellor of the University of Mississippi. After this meeting, Strom and Gasque made plans to avert a breakdown of law and order. Strom, interview in SCDAH (n.d. [b]), p. 26.

[21] Reports differ on whether law enforcement officers watched the beatings before intervening or promptly took action. See *New York Times*, May 11, 1961, p. 25. Peck (1962) states that the police watched and then intervened. Based on Hollings's statement that the Rock Hill city police were "not good" and "could cause us trouble," it is more plausible that the police did indeed delay before interceding to protect the riders.

[22] Two weeks before, in Columbia, the state capital, African American riders were served at a Greyhound terminal lunch counter without incident (*New York Times*, May 31, 1961, p. 23).

suppression of civil rights mobilization, the judicious use of law enforcement may have weakened the civil rights movement in South Carolina. To the extent that the movement relied upon provoking dramatic confrontations to draw national attention to southern injustice, this strategy of reaction deprived civil rights activists of the means to build the momentum necessary for larger and more ambitious campaigns.[23]

Unlike North and South Carolina, state and local officials in Louisiana refused to articulate a position in favor of law and order or to act against white anti-rights mobilization. This unwillingness encouraged durable contention. Thus, immediately following the integration of two New Orleans schools on November 14, 1960, a mass of working-class white women – dubbed the "cheerleaders" – assembled to accost verbally African American children who might dare to enter. The next night, the White Citizens' Council conducted a mass meeting at which segregationist leaders State Senator William Rainach and Leander Perez instructed their audience of 5,000 to boycott the schools, engage in civil disobedience, and conduct a protest march to the offices of the school board (Keesing 1970, p. 74). On the following day, a demonstration of some 2,000 to 3,000 white youths marched through the downtown, passing through the state supreme court, city hall, the federal courts, and the board of education building. Later, the demonstration went into the business district and "developed into a riot during which thousands of white youths beat up and stoned Negroes and pelted buses and cars with stones and bottles" (Keesing 1970, p. 74). Arresting some 200 black and 50 white teenagers, law enforcement officers quelled the disruptions in the evening only after African American youths started to fight back in retaliation for white violence. In the subsequent weeks, daily white-initiated verbal harassment and sporadic public disorders continued unhampered. Due to the persistent jeering of the cheerleaders and the furor maintained by the Citizens' Councils, the white boycott of integrated schools lasted for the entire school year. During that time, neither state nor city authorities sought to disperse the throng of white anti-rights protesters or to quell the public disorders wrought by the Council, the cheerleaders, and the white students no longer in attendance at the boycotted schools (Bartley 1969; McCarrick 1964, p. 202).[24] Indeed,

---

[23] On this topic, see Barkan (1984).

[24] McCarrick notes that, after initial legislative leadership of the state's resistance, Governor Davis relinquished the direction of the state race policy to the segregationists in the legislature and that the governor opted against "standing in a schoolhouse door" or some other executive-led clash between state and federal authority.

the state legislature even commended the boycotters "for their courageous stand."[25]

While the Louisiana state government mounted a vigorous assault on civil rights organizations, white terrorist groups received different treatment.[26] In April 1965, the Joint Legislative Committee on Un-American Activities (JLCUA) carried out a confidential "survey of operations" of the various Ku Klux Klan organizations in the state. In letters sent to all Louisiana district attorneys, Jack Rogers, the committee's general counsel, explained: "Our information obtained up to this point is inadequate for an honest evaluation of these groups because we do not know to what extent, if any, they have been involved in actual criminal acts" (LSA 1965). The replies presumably vindicated the Klan because, in August, the JLCUA cleared the organization of any criminal activity and described the Klan as a "political action group" with "a certain Halloween spirit" (*New York Times*, August 1, 1965, p. 57).[27] At the same time as this investigation, committee records indicate that Rogers received a letter from J. M. Edwards, Grand Dragon of the United Klans of America, Inc., that opened with the line "Hope this will help" and continued with a list of the identities of local civil rights advocates (apparently members of the Congress of Racial Equality). Though perhaps unsolicited and unwanted, this letter potentially hints at a degree of cooperation between this faction of the Klan and the JLCUA. More important, the general counsel's lack of adequate information on the Klan indicates that state authorities had not infiltrated the white supremacist organization or cultivated informers, as was done in more moderate states.

The weakness of state repression of anti-rights mobilization coincided with intense private resistance to the civil rights movement. Based on the *New York Times Index*, between 1954 and 1965 private citizens initiated

[25] SCR 1 and HCR 1 (Second Extraordinary Session, 1960), quoted in Fairclough (1995, p. 244). Also, SERS, "Statistical Summary," p. 28.

[26] In a perverse fashion, the state government used the anti-Klan laws to attack the National Association for the Advancement of Colored People (NAACP), the most prominent proponent of racial integration. Using these laws, the state attorney general demanded that the organization file membership lists with the secretary of state. After it refused to do so, the state prosecuted the organization and successfully obtained an injunction against NAACP activities, thereby crippling much of the organization. Eventually, the NAACP branches in New Orleans, Lake Charles, and Shreveport submitted their membership lists. The lists were promptly obtained by Rainach and forwarded to the local Citizens' Councils and newspapers (Fairclough 1995, pp. 195–7, 207–11).

[27] According to the *Times*, the committee's report was based on a single public hearing for which no notice was given.

144 anti-rights events, many of which involved disruptive crowd actions, shootings, bombings, arsons, cross burnings, and assaults. Almost 60 percent of all reported private anti-rights events involved violence or intimidation (32 and 26 percent, respectively), resulting in numerous reported injuries and at least four murders.

Under the administration of Governor John McKeithen (1964–72), the state government finally plotted a course toward moderation, though this new direction resulted less from soul searching than from an acknowledgment of the heightened federal commitment to impose greater racial equality on the South as well as the costs of continued opposition. The passage of the Civil Rights Act of 1964 and the Voting Rights Act of 1965 rapidly transformed the political strategies of key state officials. While north Louisiana legislators continued to thwart the civil rights movement, the governor gradually shifted haltingly toward an acceptance of token integration and the diminution of overtly racist appeals to white voters. Also, the eventual mobilization of the national state allowed southern officials to shift the political costs of implementing the unpopular civil rights agenda. Thus, the more farsighted state officials sought calmly to reverse their opposition to greater racial equality as the political gains for defending segregation diminished.[28]

As in Louisiana, state and local officials in Mississippi refused to condemn or suppress white anti-rights mobilization. In the fall of 1962, Mississippi Governor Ross Barnett (1960–4) not only blocked the registration of James H. Meredith at Ole Miss, his incendiary rhetoric and unwillingness to maintain order allowed the eruption of bloody mayhem. At the end of the rioting, 2 men lay dead and over 100 were injured (including 25 federal marshals hit by gunfire). This missed opportunity to contain white violence epitomizes the overall response of Mississippi public authorities to civil rights activities. Recurrent abdication of law enforcement duties allowed private citizens to engage in intimidation and violence against civil rights activists with little fear of legal reprisals.

While other states were crushing or severely limiting the activity of supremacist organizations, the Mississippi government encouraged white countermobilization and generally tolerated those inclined toward violence. The "respectable" White Citizens' Council, born amid the plantations of the Mississippi Delta, benefited from huge monthly donations

---

[28] Yet, even in the late 1960s, Governor McKeithen again expressed opposition to public school integration (Fairclough 1995, pp. 242–4).

from the state government. Between June 1960 and December 1964, the Sovereignty Commission transferred nearly $200,000 to the Citizens' Council Forum to churn out anti-integration propaganda for radio and television (Johnson Family Papers, n.d.; McMillan 1971, p. 336). Indeed, during the Barnett administration, the ties between the Council and the Sovereignty Commission were especially close, as four of the twelve members of the Sovereignty Commission were also members of the Council's board of directors and three others were Council members, including the governor (McMillan 1971, p. 336). The Sovereignty Commission likewise conveyed the message to citizens and law enforcement officials that civil rights activists were "communists, sex perverts, odd balls and do-gooders" dedicated to the destruction of the southern way of life (Johnson Family Papers, n.d.).

Although relations were far from cordial between state officials and the Ku Klux Klan and similar organizations, authorities lacked any eagerness to suppress them; indeed, many Klansmen belonged to local law enforcement organizations. Thus, the notoriously violent White Knights of Mississippi, with dozens of Klaverns and an estimated membership in the thousands, operated without hindrance in the early 1960s. Not surprisingly, in the decade after the U.S. Supreme Court struck down school segregation, the *New York Times* reported over 200 acts of violence and intimidation resulting in at least 75 injuries and 8 murders (not including the injuries and deaths at Ole Miss). Yet, despite violence of this magnitude, authorities rarely arrested or prosecuted white supremacists, and all-white juries even more seldom convicted them.[29] Only after relentless national publicity about vicious and unchecked violence during the 1964 Freedom Summer campaign did state authorities launch a probe of Klan-type organizations and begin to purge the Highway Patrol of their members. That state authorities finally began to crack down on white supremacists after Freedom Summer can be seen in the drop the following year in reported incidents of private anti-rights violence and harassment from 100 to 35, despite comparable levels of pro-rights agitation. This decline is especially telling because it suggests that state authorities had the capacity to reign in white supremacists but opted not to do so. This policy of encouraging anti-rights mobilization and refusing to suppress white violence thus made

---

[29] Although several acquittals were cited, there were no reports of convictions in the *New York Times Index* of a white for anti-rights or racial violence between 1954 and 1965 (Belknap 1987, pp. 128–58; Harding 1987).

the struggle for racial equality in Mississippi particularly contentious and dangerous.

The Politics of Contention

In this examination of movement–countermovement interaction, I have shown that the behavior of state and local authorities fundamentally affected the intensity of anti-rights contention during a period of heightened protest. A comparison of the ostensibly similar cases of South Carolina and Mississippi is especially instructive. As these case studies demonstrate, the governors of both states promised to maintain segregation, but their contrasting strategies helped to produce fundamentally different amounts of countermovement violence. In South Carolina, the governor denounced the forces of racial equality, but he made it plain that anti-rights lawlessness would not be tolerated. The decision to suppress anti-rights mobilization involved inserting state law enforcement personnel into localities to centralize control over police responses to civil rights protests and ensuing public disorders. The suppression of organized anti-rights mobilization further included the infiltration and disruption of Klan-type organizations. Mississippi governors in this period similarly opposed federal intervention and denounced civil rights protests, but, by failing to defend public order, they allowed private anti-rights contention to flourish.

Instead of regarding incidents of private violence against civil rights demonstrators as sporadic manifestations of racial hostility, I have suggested that the pattern of events should be viewed within a larger political context in which state authorities permitted certain forms of contention and not others. Quoting a southern law enforcement officer, George McMillan of the Southern Regional Council argued that

[white anti-rights violence] can be stopped at any time. There is no mystery about how to do it. There is not one single incident of violence in the South that could not have been stopped by the local police if they showed people that they meant business about preserving law and order.... (McMillan 1962, p. E7)

A contemporaneous observation by Deputy Attorney General Nicholas deB. Katzenbach likewise captures the central proposition of this analysis:

the experience of the [Justice] Department in the Oxford, Mississippi, crisis and in the several disturbances in Alabama convinced all those who participated that the most crucial factor in maintaining law and order in a community gripped by racial crisis is the support of State and local law enforcement officers. If they are clearly determined to support law and order, the prospects of violence are considerably reduced. If they encourage violence or abdicate responsibility for law enforcement functions, violence on a substantial scale is virtually certain to occur. . . . (U.S. White House Files 1964).[30]

For reasons such as these, McMillan (1960, p. 32) concluded that the behavior of southern law enforcement personnel was thus properly understood as "an extension of politics."[31] Although state and local officials might not be able to check every incident of racial strife, all articulated (either formally or informally) a policy toward anti-rights activities. By opting not to quell anti-rights mobilization, state actors adopted a de facto policy of intimidation and violence toward an oppositional social movement even though state and local political actors may not have been directly engaged in the planning and execution of anti-rights actions. As Arnold Heidenheimer, Heclo, and Adams (1990, p. 5) note, "government inaction, or nondecision, becomes a policy when it is pursued over time in a fairly consistent way against pressures to the contrary." Even ostensibly private acts of violence might therefore be viewed as logical extensions of state policy carried out by third parties with tacit official sanction.

If state mediation of movement–countermovement interactions should be regarded as a public policy outcome, then explanations for intermovement contention must address the political factors determining the behavior of public authorities. While social movement theorists appreciate the importance of political allies and opponents, they seldom seek to explain why *certain* elites are supportive and others are opposed, and why these elites might change their position over time. Lacking a theory of political behavior, the analysis of movement–countermovement interactions is often limited to vague suppositions that movements will be more or less successful if political elites are more or less amenable.[32]

---

[30] Gurr (1989, p. 207) likewise suggests that Klan activity continued or diminished, depending upon official tolerance or repression.

[31] See also Eichhorn (1954, p. 136). Similarly, Chalmers (1965, p. 376) writes, "The Klan, therefore, has only successfully turned to violence where popular and police sentiment have granted it a high degree of local immunity." On the lack of official sanctions against Klansmen in Birmingham, Alabama, see Corley (1982, p. 180).

[32] While McAdam (1982, pp. 174–9) addresses the interaction among white supremacists, civil rights activists, and the federal government, he does not attempt to explain why certain state and local governments were more or less tolerant of official or private violence against demonstrators than others. In a related way, Burstein (1985, 1998a) has criticized social movement theorists for their relative inattention to how precisely movement activity affects public opinion and political processes.

Although a complete explanation for the shifting posture of state actors toward anti-rights mobilization is beyond the scope of this essay, even a brief exploration of this question suggests that politics matters. In the wake of the Supreme Court's ban on school segregation, the virtual absence of public support for integration discouraged compliance with the Court's ruling. In states such as Alabama and Mississippi, where plantation interests and working-class whites exerted greater leverage within dominant political coalitions, authorities were especially hesitant to deter countermovement activity. During this initial phase of relative tolerance for countermobilization, white agitation was widespread and repeatedly produced civil disorders. In response to the negative publicity and other costs associated with these disorders, key manufacturing and commercial interests as well as middle-class whites came forward to denounce the results of obdurate anti-rights strife. In Virginia and the Carolinas, where these more moderate elements wielded greater clout at the outset, their growing dissatisfaction supplied state and local authorities with an incentive to take a position in favor of law and order. To the extent that officials could effectively claim that the cost of continued intransigence outweighed the value of maintaining the racial status quo, public officials staked out a position in favor of keeping the peace – even if this meant checking white countermobilization.[33] After a period of civil rights mobilization and disruptive countermobilization, then, declining political rewards for supporting resistance caused public authorities to suppress countermovement activity, which in turn reduced the amount of movement–countermovement contention. Even in Mississippi, a fortress of segregationist fervor, heightened political mobilization among elements of the business community eventually prompted state officials to move against the Klan (McMillen 1973, p. 165).[34] While this general political logic is discussed in numerous historical studies of the civil rights movement, the theoretical implications of this political argument have been overlooked in contemporary social movement theory (Ashmore, 1957, pp. 118–21; Bloom 1987; Cobb 1982; Jacoway and Colburn 1982; Nicholls 1960, pp. 114–23).

As the case studies suggest, the behavior of federal and state officials affected the intensity of local contention. The division of authority within

[33] Further, the enactment of the Civil Rights Act of 1964 and the Voting Rights Act of 1965 furnished ambivalent authorities with additional protection from electoral reprisals because the federal government could be blamed for the forceful imposition of change.

[34] For an extended discussion of the politics of southern responses to civil rights mobilization, see Luders (2000).

the American state makes political calculations and competition at multiple levels of government all the more relevant for understanding changing patterns of contention (Meyer and Staggenborg 1996, pp. 1637–8, 1647–8). Federal hesitation to intervene on behalf of civil rights activists gave states considerable latitude in devising a response to civil rights mobilization. State government behavior likewise conditioned what localities could do. In South Carolina, certain localities might have been more intransigent had state law enforcement not intervened at the behest of the governor to limit the actions of local authorities. Conversely, the persistent unwillingness of the Louisiana and Mississippi governments to suppress Klan mobilization allowed bombing, arson, and brutal violence to take place with great regularity.

Not only did business leaders, middle-class whites, and others begin to clamor for greater moderation, elected officials also recognized the political implications of the transformation already underway. The enactment of the Civil Rights Act and the Voting Rights Act, of which stimulated broadening of black enfranchisement, signaled to elected officials that continued resistance to some enlargement of racial equality was inevitable and that resistance to change was no longer a plausible strategy for political success (Black 1976, p. 342). In consequence, even in Mississippi, tacit state support for lawlessness was coming to an end by the mid-1960s (Harding 1987; Landry and Parker 1976, p. 11). Finally, Supreme Court cases that further extended the reach of the Justice Department in prosecuting anti-rights violence made punishment under federal auspices a real possibility.[35] Irrespective of the specific reasons for the behavior of federal, state, and local officials, the point is clear: If these actors regulated the broad contours of movement–countermovement conflict, then explanations for these interactions must be attentive to the political considerations affecting the behavior of public authorities.

Conclusion

In this essay, I have sought to demonstrate five propositions. First, southern state authorities responded to countermovement activity in differing ways. Second, I have shown that the contention accompanying movement–countermovement interactions is not arbitrary but is strongly conditioned

---

[35] *United States v. Guest* (1966) and *United States v. Price* (1966) substantially enlarged federal jurisdiction to prosecute civil rights violations under existing statutory law.

by the behavior of public authorities. Third, to the extent that countermobilization occurs and state actors possess the capacity to govern movement–countermovement interactions, the general magnitude of ostensibly society-centered contention should be regarded as the product of a formal or de facto state policy.[36] Fourth, I suggested that social movement theory must be refined to better encompass the complex relationship among state actors, movements, and countermovements. Specifically, theories that concentrate exclusively on the repressive capacities of state institutions run the risk of ignoring how countermovements may serve as third-party "administrators" of state policies.[37] In this light, the unduly state-centric concept of political opportunity structure is flawed. Even among those who are attentive to movement–countermovement interactions, the political factors shaping the policy decision about the regulation of these interactions are typically overlooked or untheorized. Fifth, by taking seriously the political calculations of elected officials, I offered a partial explanation for the changing intensity of countermovement contention over time. Finally, in addition to these assertions, I suggest that the central insights of this investigation might be extended to comparative studies of ethnic or racial contention. Although the intensity of ethnic or racial conflict often appears to be merely an expression of society-centered hostilities, this research shows that public authorities often possess significant control over the general magnitude of contention. Even though group-based competition for valued resources affects the intensity of ethnic or racial hostilities, I suggest that competitive relations occur on a political field that structures these transactions. Overly economistic accounts of racial or ethnic conflict will be of limited analytic value if they neglect how politics defines the terrain upon which contention takes place. Only by attending to the political mediation of group relations can we begin to account for the historical patterns of racial and ethnic strife or offer prescriptions about how to reduce the intensity of this conflict in the present.

---

[36] While countermovement violence no doubt affects the initial movement, the nature of this influence is complex. In some instances, harsh repression can crush movements; in others, social movements can grow in response to state reprisals. See Gupta, Singh, and Sprague (1993), Gurr (1970), and Lichbach and Gurr (1987). In the case of the civil rights movement, the tactic of deliberately provoking white violence served to advance the civil rights agenda in Congress and disrupt segregationist political alignments. The point is simply that movements must respond to countermovement contention.

[37] Elsewhere as well, in cases such as the former Yugoslavia, East Timor, Northern Ireland, and Colombia, paramilitary organizations operated in this fashion (Cigar 1995; Tesoro 1999; White 1999).

2

State versus Social Movement

FBI COUNTERINTELLIGENCE
AGAINST THE NEW LEFT

David Cunningham

The social movement literature has been most concerned with explaining how individuals come to be participants in movements and how these movements mobilize resources to achieve their goals. A key insight in this literature is that movements are incredibly fragile. Studies that have simulated the growth of movements under various conditions consistently find that small changes in the distribution of interests, the level of connectedness within the targeted population, or the amount of resources held by particular key individuals can drastically alter outcomes (see Granovetter 1978; Kim & Bearman 1997; Marwell & Oliver 1993). It is clear that this fragility is recognized by those who seek to oppose these movements. The fact that these opponents act on this recognition, often with a devastating effect on movements, is most clearly evidenced in totalitarian states by the existence of terror. Modern democratic states engage in repressive strategies as well, though usually more subtly through attempts to disrupt the organizational structure of protest groups.

Despite the important role played by those who oppose movements, social movement researchers have largely ignored this dimension, paying only tacit attention to how repression is allocated (although, for exceptions, see Davenport 2000; Tilly 1978). This essay contends that to capture more fully how repression affects protest movements, we need to understand how authorities organize and allocate repression. The particular context I examine here is the United States between 1961 and 1971. During this time period, the Federal Bureau of Investigation (FBI) operated a domestic counterintelligence program (officially abbreviated to COINTELPRO) directed at Communist, White Hate, New Left, and Black Nationalist/Hate groups. While repressive actions were initiated through other agencies (both at the federal level, through the Central Intelligence Agency, the National

Security Administration, and so on, and at the local level mainly through police departments), COINTELPRO is unique in that it was a program set up solely to "expose, disrupt, misdirect, discredit, or otherwise neutralize the activities" of protest groups that, in their view, engaged in actions that threatened the security of the U.S. government (Memo from Director to all field offices, 8/25/67).

Here, I present a more detailed account of the FBI's COINTELPRO against the New Left and consider perhaps the key question related to the allocation of repression: What was COINTELPRO's impact on the decline of the New Left? The degree to which the FBI was successful in disrupting its targets is visible through the program's outcomes, but it is also important to examine how endogenous organizational processes both facilitated and hindered the overall effectiveness of COINTELPRO. By focusing on the flow of information within the Bureau, I illustrate how a tension between innovation and control at the FBI's center ultimately limited the FBI's ability to achieve its intended goals effectively. More broadly, I suggest that an examination of organizational processes within repressing agencies can move us closer to a full understanding of how repression impacts subsequent protest outcomes.

Repression in the Social Movement/Collective Action Literature

It is widely recognized that increased costs stemming from the expectation of repression can limit a protest group's ability to provide incentives for participation or, more directly, actually create barriers to participation (McAdam 1982, 1996; Klandermans and Oegema 1987; Morris 1984; Tarrow 1998). Repression plays an even larger role when models assume interpersonal influence or when individuals "take account of how much others have already contributed in making their own decisions about contributing to a collective action" (Oliver, Maxwell, and Teixeira, 1985, p. 504). Following this assumption, certain individuals' unwillingness to bear the potential costs of repression influences the decisions of others as well, since both participation and nonparticipation tend to have a "multiplier effect" throughout a group (Oberschall 1994).

However, studies that focus on the repression of social protest tend to deal only with its effect on the protest group's ability to mobilize participants. Opp and Roehl (1990) argue that repression has a negative direct effect on protest (by increasing the perceived costs of protest activity) but that "micromobilization processes" can reverse this effect and even create a context in which protest activity intensifies. This argument stems from a running debate in the literature about how levels of repression influence subsequent waves of protest. Various studies suggest that the perception of repression as illegitimate can create a sense of moral indignation (DeNardo 1985; Gamson, Fireman, and Rytina 1982; Goldstone and Tilly 2001; White 1989) and/or generate further disillusionment with societal political institutions (Opp and Roehl 1990), both of which can lead to increased protest activity. Little consensus on this point has emerged, however, and various analysts have suggested that repression's effect on protest is positive, negative, U-shaped (Gurr 1970), inverted U-shaped (DeNardo 1985; Muller and Weede 1990), lying S-shaped (Neidhardt 1989), or reverse lying S-shaped (Francisco 1995). Until recently, the most notable finding has been the fact that seemingly all possible relationships have been supported by empirical work in this area (see Koopmans 1997; Lichbach 1987, p. 293). Even more recent work by Rasler (1996), which usefully introduces temporal and spatial dimensions to the analysis – finding that repression has a short-term negative effect but a long-term positive effect on protest – contradicted earlier conclusions that repression escalated protest in the short run while often successfully suppressing dissidence over time (see Hibbs 1973).

But regardless of the shape of the posited relationship, these findings view the effect of repression as hingeing on participants' ability to (1) perceive authorities' past efforts to repress and (2) hold expectations about the allocation of repression in reaction to future protest activity. The implicit assumption behind all of this work is that repression is purposively *overt* (and therefore predictable) and that it is initiated by authorities in *response* to protest activity in order to increase the costs of further protest. Correspondingly, repression is generally operationalized in a manner consistent with this assumption. Measuring the number of arrests or formal measures taken to restrict access to protest sites (e.g., Gibson 1989; Opp and Roehl 1990; Rasler 1996) delimits repression to include only its overt forms. It is important to move away from the assumption that covert activities will impact protestors in the same manner as arrests and other overt forms of repression.

As we shall see, many of COINTELPRO's repressive actions were covert and proactive, working behind the scenes to prevent disruptive protest before it occurred. Since we can no longer unquestioningly accept the conclusion that protestors' perceptions of repression matches the authorities' allocation of repression (see Kurzman 1996), the direct relationship between repression and subsequent protest becomes less straightforward. Additionally, covert repression may *indirectly* reduce protest by reducing available resources and breaking down solidarity and trust within protest groups. But since we cannot accurately measure covert repression by examining how protestors perceive the activities of authorities, our focus needs to shift to the study of the repressors themselves.

The Setting: The FBI in the COINTELPRO Years

Between 1956 and 1971, the FBI operated a domestic counterintelligence program, commonly referred to as COINTELPRO. This program was initiated under the direction of J. Edgar Hoover, who held the position of FBI director from 1924 until his death in 1972. The range of groups targeted by COINTELPRO expanded considerably over the course of the program, since as a particular class of groups was defined as a target, a separate COINTELPRO was opened for them. The first COINTELPRO was initiated against the Communist Party–USA in 1956, followed by the addition of COINTELPROs against the Socialist Workers Party (in 1961), White Hate Groups (in 1964), Black Nationalist/Hate Groups (in 1967), and the New Left (in 1968).[1] In theory, these programs could be disbanded if their goals were met (i.e., if the targeted groups were completely neutralized). However, in practice, none of these programs were ever discontinued, even when field offices requested this when targeted groups became inactive for an extended period of time.[2]

Each COINTELPRO was assigned to a Special Agent in Charge (SAC) in each FBI field office (fifty-nine field offices eventually participated in at

[1] These groups were categorized in this manner by the FBI. See the following discussion and Cunningham (2000, chapter 2) for a more detailed discussion of particular groups targeted under the New Left program.

[2] The response to an attempt by the Indianapolis Field Office to disband its COINTELPRO against the New Left is representative of the FBI's reaction to such requests: "every evidence points to the fact that militant leftists are continuing their efforts to disrupt higher education. You should continue to follow the activities of the New Left in your territory through the program and to seek means to neutralize it in accordance with outstanding instructions" (Memo from Director to Indianapolis, 3/16/70). Likewise, a lack of proposals from the Kansas City Field Office (after eight months of reports of inactivity by New Left groups) prompted the following memo from the director (Hoover): "This reflects a very negative approach to this program by your Division. It is to be noted that the best time to attempt to neutralize the New Left is when it is weak and disorganized. Counterintelligence action taken can be decisive and may even result in complete withdrawal of the New Left from these educational institutions" (Memo from Director to Kansas City, 1/23/69).

least one COINTELPRO). This SAC was expected to initially compile a description of all existing target groups and key activists ("those individuals who are the moving forces behind the [target groups] and on whom we have intensified our investigations") and submit general recommendations for effective counterintelligence activity. In the case of the New Left, the director[3] then summarized all of these initial recommendations in a memo to all field offices. SACs were then expected to submit specific proposals for neutralizing groups within their division, and these proposals had to be authorized by the director before the initiation of any action. Often, the director would request revisions to proposals, and it was not unusual for a SAC to submit several iterations of a proposal prior to its approval. Finally, each SAC was responsible for compiling quarterly progress reports summarizing potential and pending actions, as well as any tangible results stemming from past activities.

Though COINTELPRO does not provide a complete picture of the repression faced by protest groups between 1956 and 1971,[4] it does provide an ideal context for examining how a state-sponsored organization allocates repression. Each COINTELPRO was a single organization whose job was to define the field of insurgency and then make decisions about the allocation of repression. The nature of the program ensured that, once the organizational structure of COINTELPRO was authorized and formalized, this decision-making process was purely endogenous. A minimal requirement for the authorization of any counterintelligence action was

[3] Note that, while the title of "director" is almost universally assumed to be equivalent to J. Edgar Hoover, several high-level agents based in the national FBI headquarters in Washington, D.C., were authorized to write under the director heading (see U.S. House of Representatives 1974, p. 22). Thus, throughout this essay, I conceive of the director not as an individual (e.g., Hoover) but instead as a small group of individuals within the FBI who are distinguishable by their central position in the Bureau (as discussed later, they were the only employees of the Bureau who had access to information from all fifty-nine field offices participating in COINTELPRO–New Left).

[4] Other forms of repression (arrests, surveillance, opening mail, etc.) occurred both within other agencies in the federal government and at the local level (especially in police departments and, for student groups, in college and university administrations). Often the COINTEL program facilitated and worked in conjunction with these other organizations, but we should in no way see the FBI as the architect of all repression during this period. In addition, while in operation for only fifteen years, COINTELPRO is really one part of an ongoing institutionalized program that responds to threats to national security, rather than a situationally specific program developed in response to *particular* threats or challenges to the state in the 1950s and 1960s (see Gurr in Stohl and Lopez 1986). In this sense, the FBI engaged in certain types of counterintelligence prior to the mid-1950s as well as later in the 1970s.

that the FBI was not identified as the source of the action, and Hoover battled hard to keep COINTELPRO autonomous from other federal agencies (see Keller 1989, chapters 2 and 3).[5]

The Data

Virtually all transfer of information within COINTELPRO took the form of memos sent between the director's office in Washington, D.C., and field offices located in fifty-nine cities throughout the United States. These memos are accessible by the public through the Freedom of Information Act, and all of the memos that had been released as of 1977 (amounting to approximately 50,000 pages) have been collected on microfilm by Scholarly Resources, Inc. While it is impossible to determine the proportion of memos that have not been released by the FBI, Davis (1997) describes the files released in 1977 as "virtually the entire file" (p. 18), though he does not explain how we might be able to verify this estimate.[6] More encouraging is the fact that, when read together, the files compose a coherent narrative. Since there is a considerable amount of cross-referencing of proposals and actions, the extent to which this narrative emerges in an understandable manner provides a fairly good sense of the overall completeness of the available files. With few exceptions, I have been able to piece together the sequences of information and actions that compose the repressive activity under COINTELPRO. Of course, it is possible that certain (likely severe) activities were not included in the files at all and instead were dealt with face-to-face, over the telephone, or under a different, more highly classified memo heading. However, this possibility is not as likely as it seems, since the FBI was a highly bureaucratic organization and valued the documentation of all actions. And, since the COINTEL program was disbanded prior to the establishment of the Freedom of Information Act, there was no expectation by anyone within the FBI that the public would ever have access to the information in these documents. If such "top-secret" files do in fact exist, there seems to be no obvious way to determine the types

---

[5] However, it is important to clarify that, while the decision-making process was insular, selected *outcomes* of COINTELPRO activities were often used by Hoover (in reports to congressional officials, etc.) to gain political advantage and additional autonomy for the FBI generally.

[6] But note that Linda Kloss, who has worked in the Archival Matters division of the FBI for over twenty years and remembers the release of COINTELPRO documents, confirms Davis's view (personal communication, 1998).

of actions they document or any way to gain access to this information in a systematic manner.

Beyond the potential for unreleased files, the FBI also censored portions of certain files released to the public to "preserve the interest of national security" or to prevent interference with law enforcement proceedings.[7] For certain files, these deletions harm my coding process when they eliminate entire paragraphs that presumably discuss particular actions against targets. More often, however, these deletions only include the names of informants and, in some cases, particular targets (though these targets' group affiliations are generally uncensored). Even in instances where entire paragraphs or pages are censored, it is sometimes possible to re-create the missing patterns of events, since these are generally communicated within multiple memos (in addition to sending proposals and information about specific events related to targets, each field office was required to submit quarterly progress reports summarizing all potential and pending counterintelligence activity, as well as any "tangible results" of previous actions). Often, information that is censored in one memo is included in later summaries.

COINTELPRO–New Left

In the three-year life of the program against the New Left, field offices proposed a broad range of actions against a large number of targeted groups. While the term "New Left" was never formally defined within the FBI, the program was designed to deal with those activists that "urge revolution in America and call for the defeat of the United States in Vietnam" (Memo from C. D. Brennan to W. C. Sullivan, 5/9/68). It was also clear that many of these activists were located on college and university campuses.[8] In their initial summaries of New Left activities, several SACs commented on the difficulty in defining the New Left.[9] Despite this rather vague directive

---

[7] For a full discussion of FBI criteria for deleting information within documents, see Churchill and VanderWall (1990, chapter 1).

[8] Especially since the major event that precipitated the initiation of this COINTELPRO was the student revolt at Columbia University in April 1968 (see Davis, 1997 for a detailed account of the relationship between the Columbia uprising and the establishment of COINTELPRO–New Left).

[9] Most of these SACs cited the dynamic, fluid nature of the movement that made the identification of specific groups and leaders difficult. As a strategy to overcome the nebulous nature of the New Left, the New York Field Office proposed a set of criteria (including age, class background, aversion to work, "Jewish liberal background," and antiestablishment dress and ideology) to identify New Left adherents.

from the FBI (or perhaps because of it), the range of groups eventually targeted was quite broad and included

- *student groups* such as Students for a Democratic Society (SDS) and its various factions (Weatherman, Worker-Student Alliance, Revolutionary Youth Movement I and II, etc.), Youth Against War and Fascism (YAWF), and the Southern Student Organizing Committee (SSOC).
- *antiwar groups*, including the Student Mobilization Committee (SMC) and the New Mobilization Committee (NMC).
- *anarchist groups*: The most prominent example was the Youth International Party (Yippies), initially led by Abbie Hoffman and Jerry Rubin, but several other local, loosely organized hippie-type groups were identified by the FBI as advocating anarchy.
- *groups affiliated with the Communist Party*, including the Young Socialist Alliance (YSA), Socialist Workers Party (SWP), and DuBois Clubs of America (DCA).[10]
- *visible public figures:* These individuals were perceived to have political sensibilities closely aligned with the New Left; many were academics (e.g., Angela Davis, Herbert Marcuse, and sixteen other faculty members at universities across the United States) or individuals who had gained status as activists or revolutionaries apart from their organizational affiliations (e.g., Mark Rudd, Eldridge Cleaver).
- *underground publications:* Many newspapers or other periodicals were self-published and served to connect persons sympathetic to New Left causes. Examples included *Open City* (published in the Los Angeles area), the *San Francisco Express Times* (San Francisco), *Duck Power* (San Diego), and *Rat* (New York City).
- *black protest groups:* Many of these groups were associated with the later civil rights movement, most notably the Student Nonviolent Coordinating Committee (SNCC) and the Black Panther Party. Another set of these groups, which included the Black Allied Student Association and the Black Student Organization, were located only on college campuses.

Fundamentally, FBI repression of these groups and individuals was as much an attempt to resist a challenge to traditional American lifestyles as

[10] Here, the line between the COINTELPRO–Communist Party USA and COINTELPRO–New Left blurred. It seems, however, that Communist groups represented on college and university campuses tended to be dealt with under the New Left banner. In other cases, the groups targeted under this program also overlapped with those targeted under COINTELPRO–Black Nationalist/Hate Groups.

it was about suppressing political gains and minimizing disruption. This concern with the New Left's countercultural values was clearly illustrated by the Cincinnati field office's treatment of Antioch College, a small liberal arts school in Ohio. According to the Special Agent in Charge (SAC) of the Cincinnati office's repression of the New Left, Antioch was "most often run by a small group of militants that are permitted by college authorities to attack every segment of American society under the semblance of being 'highly intellectual.' Anyone visiting the campus doubts its academic scholarly environment *because of the dirty anti-social appearance and behavior of a large number of students, who can be seen to have the fullest beatnik image*" (Memo to Director, 6/3/68; emphasis mine). The Cincinnati SAC reported that, due to the permissiveness of Antioch administrators, no disruptive incidents had occurred at Antioch during the past school year, and furthermore, "there is, in fact, little reason for disruptive activity [in the future] since the students are permitted to do exactly what they want to without interference from college administrators" (Memo to Director, 7/16/68). Despite this recognition, students at Antioch were repeatedly targeted for repression by the Cincinnati office, presumably for their adherence to antiestablishment ideals rather than their potential for any disruptive threat. In this same manner, much of the FBI-generated material against the New Left focused on the "immoral" and "dirty" lifestyles of particular members rather than on their political ideals. The Jackson Mississippi field office even went so far as to *define* New Left members solely by their adherence to a "hippie" lifestyle. Likewise, the SAC in the Newark field office described a New Left newspaper as

a type of filth that could only originate in a depraved mind. It is representative of the type of mentality that is following the New Left theory of immorality on certain college campuses.... The experimental literature referred to in the letter ... contained 79 obscene terms referring to incest, sexuality, and biology, four dozen "cuss" words and a dozen instances of taking the Lord's name in vain. (Memo to Director, 5/23/69)

Thus, political ideology was confounded with a commitment to an alternative lifestyle, with the latter often structuring the FBI's allocation of repression against the New Left.

Toward this end, a wide variety of counterintelligence actions were initiated against these groups. The most comprehensive attempt to catalog these actions was made by Churchill and VanderWall (1988), who list ten "methods" utilized within COINTELPRO. These methods

Table 2.1. *Typology of COINTELPRO Actions against the New Left*

Function	
1	Create a negative public image
2	Break down internal organization
3	Create dissension between groups
4	Restrict access to group-level resources
5	Restrict ability to protest
6	Hinder ability of individual targets to participate in group activities
7	Displace conflict
8	Gather information (intelligence)
Form	
A	Send anonymous letter
B	Send fake (signed) letter
C	Send articles or public source documents
D	Supply information to officials
E	Plant evidence
F	Utilize informants
G	Utilize media sources
H	Disseminate FBI-generated information about targets
I	Interview targets
J	Supply misinformation
K	Make fake phone calls
L	Actively-harass targets
M	Supply resources to anti–New Left groups
N	Send ridicule-type information

(e.g., fabrication of evidence, utilizing infiltrators and agents provocateurs, harassment arrests) represent the *forms* that particular actions take. However, the *function* of each action can vary, even within a single form (i.e., infiltrators can be used to break down target groups' internal organization or to create dissension between groups). I extend Churchill and VanderWall's typology by treating form and function as independent dimensions. Thus, a set of distinct actions (forms) can all be utilized to realize the same goal (i.e., perform the same function). The extent to which forms are distributed across functions, and how this distribution shifts over time, provides insight into the organization of repression within COINTELPRO as well as the learning process that emerged based on outcomes of previous actions.

For the New Left, I have identified eight functions and fourteen forms, which are listed in Table 2.1. Table 2.2 shows how each of the 462 actions initiated within COINTELPRO–New Left were distributed across forms and functions. Note that of the 112 possible form–function pairs, only 35

Table 2.2. *Form–Function Combinations in FBI COINTELPRO Actions against the New Left*

		A	B	C	D	E	F	G	H	I	J	K	L	M	N	Total
							Form									
F u n c t i o n	1	6	0	0	1	–	4	41	16	–	–	–	–	2	0	70
	2	7	11	0	0	1	24	0	10	3	0	0	1	0	5	62
	3	2	20	0	0	0	10	2	0	0	0	0	0	0	8	42
	4	1	0	0	27	–	1	0	0	0	0	0	0	0	0	29
	5	13	0	36	39	–	0	0	1	0	3	1	0	0	0	94
	6	41	0	0	111	0	0	3	0	2	0	0	0	0	0	157
	7	0	0	0	1	–	0	0	0	0	0	0	0	0	0	1
	8	–	–	–	0	–	4	–	–	3	–	–	–	0	–	7
TOTAL		70	31	36	179	1	44	46	27	8	3	1	1	2	13	462

were actually initiated.[11] Of these thirty-five actions, sixteen were utilized in fewer than three instances. In the next section, I will focus on the patterning of each type of action, especially the innovation of new types of action over time. In order to clarify how each form–function pair translates into real activities initiated by COINTELPRO, Table 2.3 summarizes these categories and includes examples of each type of action.

The Impact of COINTELPRO

The FBI's motives aside, COINTELPRO did have a significant effect on its targets. In this section, I explore these effects at two levels. First, the

---

[11] A small number of these action types were logically impossible in the sense that particular forms could not serve specific functions or certain functions could be achieved only through a limited set of forms. The nature of this typology (where form and function are generally independent dimensions) ensures that the number of structurally precluded actions is not large. However, these structural (rather than actual) "zeros" are listed in the cells of Table 2.3 as dashes (–) rather than zeros. See Cunningham (2000a, chapter 3) for a more detailed discussion of each particular structural zero.

Table 2.3. *Typology of COINTELPRO Actions against the New Left*

(1) **Create an unfavorable public image.**
   (A) Sending anonymous letters
   8/2/68 Memo from Detroit to Director
   Proposal to send anonymous letters to local newspapers criticizing the
      upcoming "Convention of Radicals" sponsored by the Peace and Freedom
      Party and the New Politics Party.
   (D) Supplying information to officials
   12/10/69 Memo from San Antonio to Director
   Contacted various officials to spark uproar against planned Vietnam Moratorium
      Committee (VMC) event. This uproar resulted in the VMC's plan to read the
      names of deceased veterans being publicized in a critical manner in the news
      media.
   (F) Utilizing informants
   10/3/69 Memo from Cleveland to Director
   Had undercover agent infiltrating Students for a Democratic Society (SDS)
      make the group seem excessively militant in a television interview.
   (G) Utilizing media source
   1/7/70 Memo from Washington Field Office to Director
   Proposal to publicize "anti-Israel" comments made in Weatherman (SDS
      splinter group) newspaper. Media coverage should "suggest that a nationwide
      educational program be undertaken by the Jewish community to point out
      the evil nature of the politics of the SDS."
   3/31/70 Memo from Philadelphia to Director
   Used ongoing relationship with press contacts to stimulate the writing of
      two articles that clearly illustrate the "interlocking nature of the New Left
      conspiracy and the unhappiness it creates in understandable human terms."
   (H) Disseminating FBI-generated information about targets
   2/7/69 Memo from Chicago to Director
   Proposal to distribute pamphlet portraying SDS as a group of "spoiled
      infants" to responsible, moderate student groups.
   (M) Supplying resources to anti–New Left groups
   2/11/69 Memo from Jackson to Director
   Proposal to assist unknown American Legion member in publishing an
      anti–New Left pamphlet to be distributed to colleges and high schools
      in Mississippi.
(2) **Disrupt the internal organization.**
   (A) Sending anonymous letters
   9/18/69 Memo from Salt Lake City to Director
   Proposal to send an anonymous letter to the SDS president at the University
      of Utah accusing a visible new member of being a federal agent.
   (B) Sending falsified letters
   1/8/69 Memo from Chicago to Director
   Distributed letter (ostensibly from an SDS member) titled "Betrayal at the

SDS National Office," which accused the national officers of SDS of forgetting the ghetto and attempting to organize only blue-collar workers.

(E) Planting evidence

8/31/70 Memo from Director to Los Angeles

Sent altered diary of an unknown Progressive Labor Party member to another member in the hope of creating suspicion that the former member was an informant.

(F) Utilizing informants

10/23/70 Memo from Director to Thirteen Field Offices

Sent informants who were "rank and file members of SDS/WSA [Worker-Student Alliance]" to planned meetings and demonstrations in Detroit and San Jose to "promote factionalism and demonstrate disagreement with [SDS] national headquarters concerning current policies."

(H) Disseminating FBI-generated information about targets

6/29/70 Memo from Cincinnati to Director

Disseminated photos of Jerry Rubin in a "compromising position with the Cincinnati Police Department" in order to create suspicion within the Weatherman organization that Rubin was a police agent.

(I) Interviewing targets

10/28/70 Memo from Director to Fourteen Field Offices

Interviewed individuals who had been contacted in the Revolutionary Union's (RU) nationwide organizing drive in order to make possible affiliates of the RU believe that the organization was infiltrated by informants at a high level.

(L) Actively harassing targets

2/28/69 Memo from New Orleans to Director

Harassed targets through phone calls to targets directly, as well as to their employers, and by following them.

(N) Sending ridicule-type information

1/6/71 Memo from Minneapolis to Director

Proposal to mail copies of cartoon ridiculing "hippies" to New Left members anonymously.

(3) Create dissension between protest groups.

(A) Sending anonymous letters

11/24/69 Memo from New York to Director

Proposal to send anonymous letter to the Student Mobilization Committee in the hope of creating suspicion that the Liberation News Service was working for the FBI.

(B) Sending falsified letters

12/22/69 Memo from New York to Director

Proposal to send a fake letter stating that an unknown sender will no longer provide money for the Black Panther Party (BPP) breakfast program in order to shed suspicion on a BPP member's handling of breakfast money and to widen the split between the BPP and SDS.

(continued)

Table 2.3. *(continued)*

(F) Utilizing informants
6/4/69 Memo from Chicago to Director
Used an informant "close to" Chicago BPP leadership to create a rift
between SDS and the BPP, as well as prepared and distributed a cartoon
"highlighting the supposed subservient role of the BPP to SDS."
(G) Utilizing media source
8/26/69 Memo from Boston to Director
Proposal to furnish information to a media contact to be used in articles
focusing on the rift between SDS and the BPP.
(N) Sending ridicule-type information
2/7/69 Memo from New York to Director
Proposal to distribute anonymously a leaflet ridiculing National
Mobilization Committee leader Dave Dellinger. The leaflet referred to a
"Pick the Fag" contest, with the "winner" designed to be Dellinger.

(4)   Restrict access to group-level resources.
(A) Sending anonymous letters
1/19/70 Memo from Minneapolis to Director
Proposal to send an anonymous letter to a critic of the Young Socialist Alliance
(YSA) conference in the hope that he/she would "apply pressure" to the
board of governors at the University of Minnesota so that the YSA would
not be allowed to use public university facilities for "radical" activities.
(D) Supplying information to officials
6/17/68 Memo from Pittsburgh to Director
Contacted a "cooperative official" at the Mellon Foundation to block a grant
request by Unity, Inc. (a civil rights group).
(F) Utilizing informants
8/6/69 Memo from Columbia to Director
Had informants pick up and then destroy large volumes of the New Left
literature available at a New Left club.

(5)   Restrict the ability of target groups to protest.
(A) Sending anonymous letters
7/26/68 Memo from Chicago to Director
Proposal to send an anonymous letter to the board of trustees at the University
of Chicago to alert them to the "dangers posed by the New University
Conference (NUC)" in order to have them restrict NUC activities.
(C) Sending articles or public source documents
8/12/68 Memo from Director to Ten Field Offices
Sent copies of a *Reader's Digest* article critical of SDS actions at Columbia
University to university administrators "who have shown a reluctance to take
decisive action against the New Left" in order to encourage them to limit the
freedoms of such groups in the future.

(D) Supplying information to officials
10/7/70 Memo from Oklahoma City to Director
Disseminated information to university officials regarding Abbie Hoffman's proposed visit to Oklahoma State University that led to the cancellation of Hoffman's appearance.
(H) Disseminating FBI-generated information about targets
6/18/69 Memo from New York to Director
Proposal to distribute a leaflet designed to disrupt a planned National Mobilization Committee (NMC) meeting.
(J) Supplying misinformation
8/15/68 Memo from C. D. Brennan to W. C. Sullivan
Sent 250 requests for housing for out-of-town demonstrators at the Democratic National Convention with fictitious names and addresses in order to "cause considerable confusion among the demonstrators."
(K) Making fake phone calls
12/28/70 Memo from Los Angeles to Director
Made irate phone calls ostensibly from parents of UCLA students criticizing Angela Davis.

(6) **Hinder the ability of individual targets to participate in group activities**
(A) Sending anonymous letters
11/25/68 Memo from Cleveland to Director
Proposal to send an anonymous letter to parents of two targets informing them of their children's fasting in opposition to the war.
(D) Supplying information to officials
1/6/69 Memo from Los Angeles to Director
Contacted official to ensure that a targeted individual would not be hired to teach at San Fernando Valley State College.
(G) Utilizing media sources
4/1/71 Memo from Miami to Director
Furnished information about Weatherman fugitives to local media sources, which was used in articles about fugitives and, in turn, generated a number of leads about location of fugitives.
(I) Interviewing targets
3/30/70 Memo from Richmond to Director
Interviewed members of the Radical Student Union (RSU) in an effort to locate SDS fugitives and to discourage others from joining RSU.

(7) **Displace conflict.**
(D) Supplying information to officials
12/23/69 Memo from Albuquerque to Director
Had officials from the Environmental Health Service harass the Student Organizing Committee for selling food not meeting health standards in order to generate conflict over this minor issue.

(continued)

Table 2.3. *(continued)*

(8)	**Gather information (intelligence).**
	(F) Utilizing informants
	2/14/69 Memo from Washington Field Office to Director
	Circulated petition at an SDS meeting for the purpose of obtaining members' handwriting specimens, addresses, and other information.
	(I) Interviewing targets
	7/1/69 Memo from Norfolk to Director
	Interviewed unknown college professor, an "admitted former member of the Communist Party," to learn about protest activity on campus.

immediate "tangible results" of particular COINTELPRO actions were documented by SACs in their quarterly progress reports to the directorate. While only a fraction of their actions had known results, the patterning of these results gives us some insight into the FBI's reaction to the distinct types of threat posed by the New Left. Additionally, these results provide one source for evaluating the real effect of COINTELPRO on its targets. However, since these reports reflect the perceptions of particular agents obviously invested in the process of generating results, they certainly do not constitute an unbiased account. To supplement the FBI's records, I also develop an account of the role of COINTELPRO in the downfall of the movements associated with the New Left. While the decline of social movements is an exceedingly complex issue not easily attributable to a small number of causes, I discuss the role of particular types of FBI actions in the eventual disintegration of targets such as SDS. As we will see, repression had a direct effect on the ability of protest organizations to mobilize resources, and also more indirect long-term effects on the very psyche of those most closely tied to these movements.

FBI-Reported "Tangible Results" of COINTELPRO Actions

Measuring the effectiveness of COINTELPRO requires knowledge of the results of actions initiated within the program. While it is impossible to always understand the true effect of particular actions on protest targets, SACs were required to report their perceptions of the "tangible results" of actions in each quarterly progress report submitted. From these reports, we can gain some sense of each SAC's evaluation of his field office's actions, as well as the directorate's perception of the effectiveness of particular action types across field offices. Unfortunately, the results of the majority of the actions initiated against the New Left were never included in progress reports, making it difficult to gain a full picture of the outcomes of COINTELPRO actions. For results that were reported, I have coded each as either a failure or a success based on information included in the memo describing the outcome(s) of a specific action. In all cases, the reported results clearly fit into one of these categories; I can only assume that ambiguous results went unreported. Of the 463 actions against the New Left, 85 (or 18.4 percent) have known results, these reported successes greatly outweighing reported failures (77 to 8). It may be that agents were more willing to report successful actions for career advancement purposes; it would not have been difficult to treat failed actions as perpetually incomplete and therefore never reportable as a tangible result. However, most of the reported successes were very tangible – ranging from arrests, to protest participants losing their jobs, to protest organizations being refused access to public meeting places – and were likely not the sorts of outcomes that agents could have convincingly exaggerated to enhance their own reputations. To provide a sense of the range of documented successes, Table 2.4 lists all such recognized results in COINTELPRO–New Left.

The range of results listed in Table 2.4 is quite broad. Seven of the eight functions the FBI sought to achieve (see Table 2.2 for the full range of functions associated with COINTELPRO actions) were realized in some tangible form. The most commonly achieved result was the successful breakdown of organization within targeted groups. In various ways, the FBI was also frequently able to create and/or sustain a negative public image of various targeted groups. To a lesser extent, COINTELPRO actions successfully created dissension between targeted groups, restricted access to resources (financial or otherwise) sought by targeted groups, and restricted the ability of both targeted groups and particular individuals to participate in protest activity.[12]

The patterning of successes is determined in large part by the types of actions that were proposed and carried out. In general, agents tended to propose actions that were easily carried out on a regular basis. That is, in order for an agent to demonstrate that he (at that time, all SACs were men) was taking the counterintelligence program seriously, he needed to propose actions frequently (failure to do so often led to the imposition

---

[12] One additional function – displacing conflict – was never acknowledged as yielding a tangible result. However, this type of action was initiated very rarely (only once in COINTELPRO–New Left).

Table 2.4. *Reported Successful Results of COINTELPRO–New Left Actions*

Result	No. of Occurrences
Conflict and/or disorganization created within target organization	9
Target fired from job	9
Legislators and/or university administrators increased penalties associated with student protest	7
Target(s) arrested	7
Conflict created between targeted organizations	6
Member(s) forced to leave target organization	6
Newspaper article published using FBI-supplied information	4
Increased the financial costs associated with target organization's activities	4
Caused target organization to lose access to meeting place or headquarters	4
Member(s) of target organizations wrongly suspected of being informants	3
Target organization disbanded	3
Target eliminated from consideration for job	2
Caused target to drop out of school	2
Target left United States due to perceived pressure from the Immigration and Naturalization Service	2
Effectively created negative public image of target	2
Target organization's phone service disconnected	1
Disrupted target organization's attempt to coordinate protest	1
Television program aired using FBI-supplied information	1
Target organization not allowed on campus	1
Caused target organization to alter plans at considerable financial cost	1
Caused target to be harassed by the Internal Revenue Service	1
Restricted the sale of target organization's publication	1
TOTAL	77

of organizational controls, generally in the form of scalding memos from the director). The majority of these actions were thus those that could be easily achieved. While utilizing a media source to create negative publicity and supplying information about targets to officials were often not the most sophisticated, innovative, or even effective actions, they could be carried out consistently with a minimum of advance planning and little expenditure of resources. These "generic" activities also did not require the targeted group to behave in any particular manner, and they were never subject to cancellation based on the target's activities. Consequently, these types of actions tended to overwhelm more sophisticated proposals that expressly reflected the overall strategy of each COINTELPRO. The desire to initiate actions regularly constituted one disincentive to proposing innovative action types; later, I discuss additional internal barriers to effective COINTELPRO action.

COINTELPRO and the Decline of the New Left

At the time of the counterintelligence program's disbanding in 1971, major New Left targets had either disappeared or ceased to hold any real promise for mass appeal. SDS, easily the central target of COINTELPRO–New Left, was close to 100,000 strong in 1969 (Sale 1973, p. 664) but had been reduced to a set of bitterly militant factions separated by an inability to agree on often arcane points of leftist revolutionary ideology. Weatherman, the best known and longest-lasting of these factions, went entirely underground in early 1970 and by 1971 existed as a number of isolated small cells. Total membership in these cells never exceeded 200 (Sale 1973, p. 651), and Weatherman (later changed to the less sexist Weatherpeople or Weather Underground) thereafter proceeded to protest various political injustices through sporadic symbolic bombings. Though they succeeded in bombing several courthouses and police outposts, as well as the U.S. Capitol and the Pentagon, arguably their most visible feats were the engineering of drug culture guru Timothy Leary's escape from a minimum-security prison in California and the accidental death of three of their own members while manufacturing bombs in a Greenwich Village townhouse. While Weather Underground actions reached mythical proportions in some circles, the hoped-for resulting call to arms among the masses never became a real possibility. By 1972, their organization, as well as the other remnants of SDS (controlled by the Progressive Labor Party faction), ceased to exist in any significant sense. Apart from SDS, campus insurrection dropped sharply in the fall of 1971, though protests against the Vietnam War – by this time almost entirely detached from issues of race, poverty, or a radical critique of the establishment – continued into the mid-1970s. With the ending of draft calls and the continuing withdrawal of troops from Vietnam, these protests gradually lost their urgency and finally their raison d'être.

Of course, the fact that the organizations associated with the New Left were in significant decline by the early 1970s does not necessarily mean that COINTELPRO was responsible for this decline. Churchill and

VanderWall (1990) do argue that COINTELPRO played a central role in the downfall of its targets, and even go so far as to see the FBI as the root cause of the New Left's late 1960s shift toward violence and revolution, with the recipe for violence in this case being "rage at the violently physical form assumed by the repression (beatings, shootings, gassings), coupled to a consistent official policy of lying, victim-blaming, and other misrepresentation in the media; and an increasing belief – often fostered by agents provocateurs – that some form of violence might in itself serve to rectify the situation" (p. 228). But clearly, a complex set of factors contributed to the collapse of the New Left. Oberschall (1993) acknowledges the role played by repression (conceived broadly to include FBI "dirty tricks," as well as judicial action and brute force by police and National Guardsmen) but also identifies two additional factors: organizational weaknesses within the protest groups themselves and their success in achieving their central goals. He concludes that repression likely had some effect on the decline of 1960s social movements, but that this effect was small compared to the role played by "factionalism and organizational weaknesses" (p. 287). However, it is important to understand that the central accomplishment of COINTELPRO was its demonstrated ability to itself disrupt its targets' internal organization. The use of informants and the introduction of misinformation generated mistrust, paranoia, and internal conflicts that served to contribute greatly to the factionalism and disintegration of various groups in the New Left. Weakness in internal organization was certainly not a sole product of FBI activity – many New Left groups, with their focus on participatory democracy and unclear, ever-shifting goals, were especially susceptible to internal dissension – but the direct cumulative effects of FBI infiltration cannot be disregarded. Despite limitations created by the structure of the FBI itself, the sheer number of repressive actions that were carried out under COINTELPRO–New Left played a central role in the creation of the repressive climate that contributed to the splintering of the New Left by the end of the 1960s.

The toll of constant covertly repressive activities was evident among movement members. Retrospective accounts by former New Left leaders frequently focus on the exhaustion created by constantly feeling watched and never knowing whom to trust, as informants inevitably infiltrated almost all prominent New Left groups. Tom Hayden, an early president of SDS and a longtime FBI key activist designate, spoke of the paranoia associated with participation in underground groups, closely associated with the knowledge that groups like the FBI could kill targets given the opportunity: "Whether you engaged in 'armed struggle' or not, the chances were good that you would not be treated politely if caught; more likely, you would be shot in your bed like Fred Hampton"[13] (Hayden 1988, p. 422). Antiwar activists Rennie Davis and Dave Dellinger speak of similar feelings of exhaustion and paranoia (see Dellinger 1975; Hayden 1988, pp. 461–4).

By the end of the 1960s, the dialogue emerging within the larger New Left seemed equally pessimistic. Consider the account of Yippie cofounder Jerry Rubin, in his "letter to my movement friends" published in the SDS newspaper *New Left Notes* in January 1969. In the letter, Rubin laments the depression and demoralization that have replaced the "euphoria [and] over-flowing optimism" that, in his view, had prevailed within the larger New Left movement just three years earlier. While he still views the movement as vibrant in many ways – "the most exciting energy force among whites in the nation" – its effectiveness had come to be severely limited through, basi-cally, a systematic program of state repression that has "bottled up resources, sapped energy, and demoralized the spirit." What forms of state repression were perceived as responsible for this downturn in energy (that, as we know, would never reverse its course)? Rubin points to the plainclothes police of-ficers who were watching his activities basically twenty-four hours a day, the undercover agents who served as provocateurs within the movement, and especially arrests on trumped-up charges that led to lengthy and ex-pensive court battles. The intersection of these state tactics emerges within two incidents that Rubin saw as illustrative of life in the American "police state." In his own words, the first involved

three New York narcotics detectives, carrying a mysterious search warrant, stormed into my Lower East [sic] apartment, angrily tore a Castro poster off the wall, and arrested me for alleged possession of three ounces of marijuana. They spent 90 min-utes in my apartment questioning me about Yippie plans for Chicago [related to the upcoming Democratic National Convention] and going through my personal papers and telephone book. The search warrant claimed that [three days earlier] an informer was in my apartment with me and he saw dangerous drugs there.

---

[13] Hampton was a leader of the Illinois chapter of the BPP and was killed in a police raid in the early morning hours of December 4, 1969. Both the FBI and the Chicago police were unquestionably involved in what was basically an assassination. The police fired close to 100 rounds at several Panthers present in Hampton's apartment, killing both Hampton and BPP leader Mark Clark. It is also likely that FBI informant William O'Neal, who had risen in the BPP ranks to become Hampton's personal bodyguard, had drugged Hampton to ensure that he would not wake during the attack.

The second incident stemmed from Rubin's actions at the DNC, when an undercover Chicago police officer infiltrating the Yippies claimed that Rubin had used a bullhorn to incite a crowd to "kill the pigs" at a clash in Grant Park. The accusation had led to Rubin's being held on a $25,000 bond (higher than the amount set for the average accused murderer at the time) and an order to not leave the state of Illinois prior to his trial. Such potentially dire consequences for actions that may not have even occurred had, as Rubin recognized, served to effectively fragment the predominantly white New Left, as "the casualties of the last battle [were left to] their own individual fates as [the movement] moved on to the next dramatic action," forcing "many activists . . . to turn to their parents for help, rather than to the movement which is trying to overthrow their parents' institutions."

In his plea for financial assistance to offset his mounting legal fees, Rubin was prone to making sweeping claims about "the criminal conspiracy to deprive him of his civil rights." If anything, however, it seems that Rubin actually underestimated the extent to which he was targeted by state agencies as a subversive threat. While his complaints were understandably rooted in the immediate events that led to his arrest and upcoming trial, the FBI was simultaneously engaged in a massive information-gathering process that yielded a detailed account of Rubin's political and financial activity since early 1968. The compiled summary, dated September 9, 1969, was ten single-spaced pages in length and included all activity on bank accounts linked to Rubin as well as an accounting of his financial returns from all speaking engagements. The comprehensive nature of the information clearly illustrated the FBI's connection to bank officials (who provided presumably confidential account information), as well as its dense network of developed informants (who were even able to estimate the amount of money informally donated to Rubin after particular campus lectures). Such intelligence activity was a key, if generally unperceived, component of the increasingly connected repressive apparatus; the information gathered by the FBI could, in turn, be used as evidence of tax fraud for the Internal Revenue Service or of conspiratorial activity in court. The result was an ever-encroaching repressive climate; as Rubin puts it: "When cops first come on campus, the liberals scream – but gradually the liberals get tired and go to sleep. Cops and courts never sleep."

So, by the end of the 1960s, there was a growing sense across the larger movement that their actions had activated a significant reaction from the authorities. At times, the shape of the repressive beast was clearly perceived.

Generally, however, it was articulated as a ubiquitous juggernaut: Given the impression that they were isolated, defenseless nails, everything seemed to take on the form of a potentially fatal hammer. In one sense, then, the massive mobilization by the FBI, combined with other police and judicial activity, created a climate of repression that provided a strong disincentive for individuals to continue to participate in protest activity. Quite apart from the form that COINTELPRO actions took, their ability to sustain a ubiquitous presence ensured some degree of success.

But it is clear that the form of COINTELPRO actions was important – some actions were clear successes, others clear failures – and it would be a mistake to view all actions as equivalent. To capture the extent to which the FBI capitalized on effective actions, it is important to move beyond the somewhat self-serving reports of FBI agents and anecdotal accounts of the FBI's targets, and instead focus on the organizational processes that defined the FBI's allocation of repressive activity. Such endogenous processes serve as one measure of the extent to which the state's repressive apparatus was indeed successful in its efforts to disrupt its intended targets. In the next section, I deal more directly with the inner workings of the FBI itself and illustrate how internal information flows restricted its ability to maximize its effectiveness.

Organizational Learning and the FBI's Effectiveness

An examination of the FBI's effectiveness with its counterintelligence programs should account for evidence of a learning process that led to evolving repressive forms, as well as processes and structures that constrained the ability of the organization to revise its assumptions and initiate effective actions. Here I present evidence of a macro-level learning process within the FBI and then show how the structure of the Bureau itself, in some instances, served to restrict its ability to innovate in response to shifts in the protest field.

On July 5, 1968, each of the FBI's field offices received a memo from the director listing twelve suggested actions against New Left targets. This memo summarized responses from agents to an earlier request for "suggestions for counterintelligence action against the New Left" and presented the set of actions that the director felt "[could] be utilized by all offices." These actions ranged from "instigating conflicts . . . between New Left leaders," to using articles from New Left publications to "show the depravity of . . . leaders and members," to disseminating misinformation to

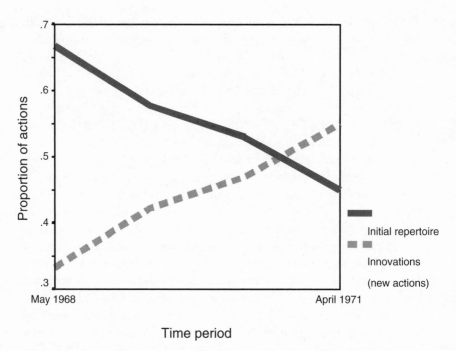

Initial repertoire

Innovations
(new actions)

Time period

Figure 2.1 Innovation in FBI COINTELPRO actions.

disrupt planned protest activities. The memo served as a representation of the initial repertoire[14] of actions against the New Left, and I have placed each of these twelve action types into the form–function framework discussed earlier (and summarized in Table 2.1). Figure 2.1 illustrates how the proportion of repressive actions fitting into the FBI s initial repertoire changed over time. I conceive of all actions that were not part of the initial repertoire as innovations or new action types (differing from those in the initial repertoire in form, function, or both). The figure clearly shows that the use of actions that fit into the initial repertoire decreased over time as new types of actions emerged. The emergence of innovation, in this case, provides at least preliminary evidence of a learning process. The new actions that appeared over time may have been a result of old actions proven to be ineffective or outliving their effectiveness or a reaction to shifts in the field of protest. But the key to the FBI's maximizing its effectiveness through the introduction of these new actions lay in the *patterning* of these

---

[14] See Tilly (1978) for a general discussion of repertoires.

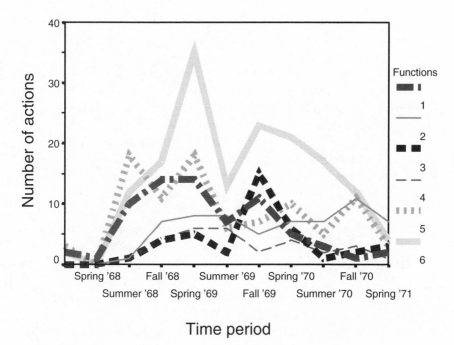

Figure 2.2   Changes in FBI COINTELPRO actions over time.

innovations at the national level. To what extent did innovations diffuse through the organization so that effective actions in one territory could be applied in other territories as well? I return to this question in the next section.

Figure 2.2 illustrates the distribution of function types over time. I divide each calendar year into three time periods (spring, summer, and fall), which roughly correspond to time breaks in the academic calendar: the fall semester (September–December), the spring semester (January–May), and summer recess (June–August). These time periods are significant since they represent a conception of periodization that the FBI considered meaningful in terms of campus-based protest. The fall was a period of mobilization when existing campus organizations attempted to convince students (both new and returning) to become involved with various issues and causes. The spring then became a time in which protest activity would peak, since the ongoing mobilization between September and December could be effectively translated into action. Protest then would disappear almost completely during the summer as the vast majority of students moved away from campus. As there was a high degree of student turnover from one school year to the next, this process repeated itself during the following school year.

Two patterns are clearly evident in Figure 2.2. First, function 3 (creating dissension between protest groups) exhibited a marked increase during the fall of 1969. This increase was due to the impending alliance between SDS (the primary campus-based group targeted by COINTELPRO–New Left) and the Black Panther Party (or BPP, which was the primary target of the Black Nationalist/Hate Group COINTELPRO). Given the high level of repression faced by both of these groups in all time periods, the FBI was understandably concerned about the possibility of this alliance. When a rift seemed to be developing between the groups, the director sent out a general request for proposals that would serve to "exacerbate this recent split" (Memo from Director to 16 Field Offices, 8/20/69). Three weeks later, the director ordered these same field offices to use informants in both groups to "take action that would expand the rift between these two organizations and irrevocably block any possibility of a reconciliation" (Memo from Director to 16 Field Offices, 9/8/69). The authorization of many of the resulting flurry of proposals accounts for the increase in actions that created dissension between groups during this time period, and this type of action decreased soon thereafter, as the alliance between SDS and the BPP did indeed collapse.

Second, the use of function 6 (hindering the ability of individual targets to participate in group activities) was initially high and decreased sharply after the beginning of 1969. This shift reflected the director's recognition of a significant change in the protest field, namely, the increasing militance of protest groups and their increased willingness to use violence to achieve their goals. As a result of this increased radicalism, the FBI felt that many New Left organizations had lost their mass appeal, and the earlier concern with the mobilization potential of particular groups disappeared. Therefore, the director no longer saw the repression of individuals who were not central to their organization (i.e., those who were not leaders) as effective, and proposals that did not significantly impact the organizational structure of the protest group were generally rejected after the first part of 1969.

In both of these instances, shifts in the allocation of repression were driven by *key events*, or events defined as important at the national level (e.g., by the set of central actors in the FBI based in Washington, D.C.). The importance of key events – what distinguished these events from others – was that they were recognized by the director, who then disseminated information about these events to all of the field offices in a position to act on them. Thus, information about key events was always shared by all concerned actors in the FBI. In Figure 2.2, we see no clear patterning of innovation at the national level in the absence of key events. To understand why, we must look at how information flows through the organizational structure of the FBI.

Constraints on Innovation

One of the many consistencies within COINTELPRO memos is the emphasis on finding new and creative ways of arresting the attacks by the New Left (see, e.g., Memo from Director to Knoxville, 7/8/69). Innovation was always highly valued within the organization; new ideas about repressing target groups were always "appreciated," even if these innovative proposals were ultimately rejected by the director. In several cases, the director criticized agents for following the "Bureau line" too closely and not applying knowledge of local New Left organizations to specific proposals. An exchange between the director and the Minneapolis field office ended with the director berating the Minneapolis SAC for "relying so heavily" on an FBI-generated pamphlet and suggesting that the Minneapolis office "seek local examples" that could serve as the basis for innovative repressive actions (Memo from Director, 1/29/69). However, despite this emphasis on innovation, the director's actions often limited the emergence of new actions. Over the course of COINTELPRO–New Left, the director rejected eighty-six proposals from field offices. Through these obtrusive controls on proposals, the director significantly limited the *range* of actions that entered the FBI's repertoire. Table 2.5 presents the distribution of rejected proposals in COINTELPRO–New Left. Shaded cells indicate form–function combinations that were never carried out within this COINTEL program. We see that twelve would-be innovations were rejected by the director, which would have increased the number of action types in the FBI's repertoire by 35 percent. Through this control over the types of actions that were deemed acceptable, the director significantly limited the emergence of innovation in COINTELPRO–New Left.

More significantly, the director's actions also limited the ability of innovations to diffuse through the FBI. Table 2.6 lists the innovations that emerged during the three-year life of COINTELPRO–New Left. In this program, the directorate authorized twenty-six types of innovative actions

Table 2.5. *Rejected Proposals for FBI COINTELPRO Actions against the New Left*

Function	Form															Total
	A	B	C	D	E	F	G	H	I	J	K	L	M	N	O	
1	6	2	4				7	3					3			25
2	2							2							1	5
3	1	5	3					3					1			13
4		1	1													2
5	6		2	4						1				2		16
6	5		2	10			1	1	1			2				24
7																0
8							1									1
TOTAL	20	8	12	14	0	0	9	7	3	1	0	2	4	2	1	86

(e.g., form–function pairs that were not part of the initial repertoire from Figure 2.1). Of those twenty-six forms, seventeen were used four or fewer times, and each of these seventeen remained local; they were used only by a single field office. The key question here is: Why did these innovations (which were constantly encouraged within the structure of the FBI) rarely diffuse through the Bureau in a manner that allowed the ideas of one field office to be utilized by other offices?

To answer this question, we need to think about the organizational structure of COINTELPRO itself. As described previously, all interactions involving proposals or information about local New Left targets were dyadic exchanges between the director and individual field offices. On certain occasions, the director solicited other field offices for further information or advice concerning a proposal, but in no instances did an agent from one office contact another office directly. In this way, the director had access to information from *all* offices and controlled the flow of information between offices. We can visualize this structure as a star with the director in the center and field offices each at the end of a set of unconnected branches. This structure has long been recognized as an ideal context for central actors to

Table 2.6. *Innovative Actions*

(1)	Create an unfavorable public image.
	(A) Sending anonymous letters (6)
	(D) Supplying information to officials (1)
	(F) Utilizing informants (4)*
	(M) Supplying resources to anti–New Left groups (2)*
(2)	Disrupt internal organization.
	(A) Sending anonymous letters (7)
	(B) Sending falsified letters (11)*
	(E) Planting evidence (1)*
	(F) Utilizing informants (24)*
	(H) Disseminating FBI-generated information about targets (10)
	(I) Interviewing targets (3)*
	(L) Actively harassing targets (1)*
(3)	Create dissension between protest groups.
	(A) Sending anonymous letters (2)
	(B) Sending falsified letters (20)*
	(F) Utilizing informants (10)*
	(G) Utilizing media source (2)*
(4)	Restrict access to group-level resources.
	(A) Sending anonymous letters (1)
	(D) Supplying information to officials (27)
	(F) Utilizing informants (1)*
(5)	Restrict the ability of target groups to protest.
	(A) Sending anonymous letters (13)
	(H) Disseminating FBI-generated information about targets (1)
	(K) Making fake phone calls (1)*
(6)	Hinder the ability of individual targets to participate in group activities.
	(G) Utilizing media sources (3)
	(I) Interviewing targets (2)*
(7)	Displace conflict.
	(D) Supplying information to officials (1)
(8)	Gather information (intelligence).
	(F) Utilizing informants (4)*
	(I) Interviewing targets (3)*

Note: Actions with asterisks indicate forms that are not part of the initial repertoire (for any function).Parenthetical counts indicate the number of times action types were carried out.

maintain a high level of control within an organization. In Ronald Burt's (1992) language, this structure allows the director to fill the "structural holes" that exist between field offices within the organization. A structural hole can be thought of as "the separation between nonredundant contacts" (Burt 1992, p. 18), similar to what Mark Granovetter (1973) thought of as a weak tie, or a tie that tends to bridge otherwise unconnected social worlds. Generally speaking, persons whose networks are rich in structural holes enjoy benefits in information access as well as control gained through the brokering of relations between other persons. Thus, a person in an "optimal" structural position has ties to diverse pockets of persons who are not strongly connected to each other. Such persons will "enjoy higher rates of return on their investments because they know about, have a hand in, and exercise control over, more rewarding opportunities" (Burt, 1992, p. 49). In the case of the FBI, filling a structural hole allows the director to have access to all information stemming from each field office as well as to broker all lines of communication within the organization. Thus, if this structure is perfectly maintained, no actor in a field office will be able to receive information that does not first reach the director.

At the organizational level, one implication of this structure is that information about new types of repressive actions was often not diffused to other field offices; most ideas about repressing the New Left remained local. Often, this lack of diffusion led to redundant sets of proposals from field offices unaware of each other's ideas. After the SDS-led uprisings at Columbia University in the spring of 1968, *Barron's* printed an article titled "Campus or Battleground?" that was highly critical of the SDS presence on college campuses throughout the nation. Between June and August 1968, no fewer than ten field offices informed the FBI of the publication of this article, with each office suggesting that the FBI reprint and disseminate it to campus administrators. While the FBI did carry out this action in August 1968 (see Memos from Director to 35 SACs on 7/29/68, 8/2/68, and 8/12/68), this redundancy well illustrates the extreme limits on information flow between field offices participating in the COINTEL program.

The director's control on information flow is perhaps clearest in the few instances in which field offices attempted to interact with each other concerning particular repressive actions. Even these interactions were brokered by the director; comments intended for another field office were actually placed in memos to the director and prefaced by statements such as "for the information of the New York office." One such example of this sort of indirect interaction occurred between the New York and San Antonio offices in early 1971. The sequence of memos in this interaction was as follows:

1/26/71 Memo from SAC, San Antonio, to Director:
Proposal to furnish public source information about a Student Mobilization Committee (SMC) conference at Catholic University to Catholic officials. The goal is

to withdraw archdiocese money generally used to support Catholic University in reaction to the university's failure to restrict New Left activity on campus.

2/1/71 Memo from SAC, New York, to Director:
In response to the director's request for recommendations regarding San Antonio's proposal, the New York office states that they doubt the effectiveness of the proposal. The SAC also includes a comment about the historical role of radical philosophies in religious life as an apparent attempt to belittle the San Antonio SAC's ideas.

2/2/71 Memo from Director to SAC, San Antonio:
Despite the New York office's reservations, the director authorizes this proposal.

2/4/71 Memo from SAC, San Antonio, to Director:
San Antonio informs the director that information provided by New York on 2/1/71 is not suitable for dissemination, and also includes a response to the New York field office's criticism of San Antonio's proposal:

> With respect to New York's patronizing comments that various forms of radical philosophy have found their adherence at all levels of religious life, San Antonio is fully aware of this situation. This attitude espoused by New York tends to indicate a fait accompli complex. However, New York should be aware that there is a great number of Catholics, both religious and laymen, who do not subscribe to this radical philosophy. It is strongly felt that at the emergence of the so-called permissive attitude that if effective counterintelligence actions had been taken, the Bureau's investigation in New Left and other such matters would not have been as great as it is today. For additional information of New York, through counterintelligence efforts of the San Antonio office ... [lists notable accomplishments].... As a result of the above, at the present time institutions of learning in San Antonio proper are free of any radical elements and organizations.

2/10/71 Memo from Director to SACs, New York and Washington:
Director acknowledges San Antonio's comments from 2/4/71 and instructs both the New York and the Washington, D.C., field office (WFO) to submit public source information related to the SMC conference to San Antonio, as well as to submit suggestions for additional counterintelligence techniques surrounding SMC conference. The memo states:

> Comments of New York and San Antonio noted at Bureau. It is opinion of Bureau that decisive, aggressive, timely, and well-organized counterintelligence operations are invaluable in disrupting or altering, to our advantage, activities which are clearly against US public interest. Major and overriding concern, or course, is providing full security to insure Bureau is protected as source of action.

2/11/71 Memos (Two) from New York to Director, and SACs, San Antonio and WFO:
Includes information about the planned upcoming SMC conference and various items that San Antonio can furnish to sources.

3/19/71 Memo from SAC, San Antonio, to Director:
Update on actions against SMC. The memo also includes the following statement illustrating the degree of control exhibited by the director within this organizational structure (compare wording to that of the 2/10/71 Memo from Director):

> San Antonio strongly feels that *decisive, aggressive, timely, and well-organized counterintelligence operations are invaluable in disrupting, or altering, to our advantage, activities which are clearly against US public interest.* San Antonio feels that the COINTELPRO–New Left Program is one of the most vital aspects of the Bureau's operation and the Bureau can be assured that this matter is closely followed. (Emphasis added)

Notable is the indirect manner in which the offices communicate, addressing all comments to the director, as well as the degree of control exhibited on the ideas of SACs in each field office. It should not be surprising that the general phrasing and perspective of memos composed by SACs are similar to the director's, but the 3/19/71 Memo from San Antonio to the Director includes a verbatim quote (italicized) taken from the earlier director's memo. While imitating the director may be perceived by agents as an effective career-advancement strategy, we would expect this sort of homogeneity of ideas in a structure that is so strongly regulated by a central set of actors.

Returning to our earlier question of why innovative ideas rarely diffused through the FBI, one way to view the director is as a strategic actor who maximized control of the center of the FBI by controlling the information that flowed to and from peripheral actors in the organization. Thus, the director had two goals that became contradictory: the desire to maximize control within the FBI and the desire to effectively repress organized protest. The latter goal required a repertoire of repressive actions that was flexible enough to respond to shifts in the protest field, but the former constrained the flow of information within the FBI, limiting the ability of each field office to learn from the others. In the absence of key events that led to the director's coordination of field office activities through the transmission of information to multiple offices, the learning process remained local. This limited the ability of SACs to take advantage of other offices' innovations and ultimately hindered the FBI's ability to maximize the effectiveness of its actions.

Conclusions

I began this essay with the assertion that social movement research generally suffers from a weak understanding of the role of repressive activity in contentious politics. This weakness has several origins, ranging from a focus on the protestors themselves, to the implicit assumption that all repression is overt and reactive, to the difficulty of obtaining data that capture a range of repressive acts. These issues have resulted in an inability to understand adequately how repression impacts subsequent protest. Here, I have argued that an understanding of the effects of political repression necessarily involves an understanding of how repressive activity is allocated. While repression invariably has a tangible effect on the ability of challengers to win concessions and mobilize participants and other resources, its allocation is only indirectly related to the characteristics of protest targets themselves. Political repression does not appear out of a vacuum; it is always initiated through some type of organization, often (though not always) affiliated with the state. Using COINTELPRO as a vehicle to understand the impact of repression on its targets, I have reached two conclusions. First, the FBI's activities certainly had a significant effect on the New Left. According to field office reports to FBI national headquarters, we see that only a minority of COINTELPRO activities led to any tangible results. However, while the targets of the FBI's activities were not often cognizant of particular repressive actions, the effectiveness of COINTELPRO seems to lie in the fact that it was able to operate within a context that allowed its activities to contribute to a perceived repressive climate. That is, the program worked precisely because its targets expected repression to exist and thereby altered their activities and behaviors accordingly.

Second, beyond the perception of effectiveness by FBI agents or their targets, we can gain insight into the effectiveness of a repressive apparatus by examining processes endogenous to the repressing organizations. Here, I analyzed the patterning of communication within the FBI and found that, in the case of COINTELPRO, the unique structure of the FBI itself (shaped by the director's desire to maximize control) placed severe constraints on information flow, thereby limiting the FBI's effectiveness in allocating repression. While this conclusion is specific to the FBI itself, it does illustrate the fact that a fuller understanding of the impact of repression needs to account for processes within repressing organizations as well as within the targeted groups themselves.

3

Setting the State's Agenda

CHURCH-BASED COMMUNITY ORGANIZATIONS IN AMERICAN URBAN POLITICS

Heidi J. Swarts

On June 5, 1991 in San Jose, California, 800 church members attended a "prayer service" whose special audience was Mayor Susan Hammer. Amidst incense, candles, religious music, and prayers to "free the oppressed of our city, especially our youth," the 800 faithful watched their leaders propose a range of programs, a comprehensive antidrug master plan, and a long-range plan to divert San Jose Redevelopment Agency funds to youth services. Instead of the threatened $2.8 million cut to neighborhood services, the mayor offered them a five-year $6 million set of programs designed and funded as they had proposed.

On September 28, 1997, in St. Louis, 750 church members sacrificed their Sunday afternoon and a St. Louis Rams home game to attend a "Public Meeting on Smart Growth" in the echoing gymnasium of the University of Missouri at St. Louis. The roll was called with nine church denominations represented. Black and white children gave prayers for their future. In a "reflection," Monsignor Ted Wojcicki recalled the church's commitment to "the poor and marginalized" and reminded the crowd that "the Book of Nehemiah says 'Come let us rebuild the wall of Jerusalem!'" The Rev. Sylvester Laudermill, Jr., African Methodist Episcopal, thundered, "We demand smart growth in the St. Louis region! Are you with me?" to applause; "Are you with me?" More applause. Attached to the program everyone received was a "Theological Statement on Smart Growth."

Neither of the foregoing sounds like a conventional description of agenda setting and policymaking in American politics. Yet federations of churches such as these are among the few vehicles mobilizing and training low- to middle-income Americans across neighborhood, race, and class lines to promote their agendas in city politics. Sometimes they win and manage to play an integral role in urban policymaking. What factors explain their varying strategies and results? The literatures on social movements and on agenda setting in American politics have seldom overlapped. Thus they provide little help in answering such questions.

This essay argues three main points: (1) Concepts developed in the so-cial movement literature – political opportunity, mobilizing structures, and framing – can help illuminate the agenda-setting process. (2) The results of the two cases analyzed in this essay (San Jose and St. Louis, taken from a larger study) suggest conditions and strategies that lead to success or failure for citizens' organizations seeking to influence urban politics. Specifically, a centralized rather than a fragmented governmental structure open to influence through district council elections may provide better leverage to grassroots organizations. While St. Louis's fragmented and widely dis-persed authority may have offered more points of access to challengers than San Jose's, no single entity could address critical regional issues affecting the city. San Jose's more centralized government, once persuaded of a course of action by a citizens' movement, could act to implement it. Moreover, the type of issue selected is critical and interacts with political opportunity, mobilizing capacity, and issue framing to influence success. Not only are redistributive issues difficult to undertake at the city level (Peterson 1981), regulatory issues that enhance central city economic capacity *in the long run* may be harder to advocate than allocational issues that elites perceive will improve economic capacity in the short run. (3) Further, community orga-nizations can significantly influence urban agendas even when their issues fail. Perhaps most important, even limited successes in winning resources or influencing policy send vital encouraging signals to participants, which encourages further civic activism.

There has recently been much discussion of civil society and the role of voluntary associations in democracies, in particular in American poli-tics (Putnam 1993, 1996, 2000; Skocpol 1996; Skocpol and Fiorina 1999). However, knowledge of grassroots citizens organizations is very limited. The rise of the religious right in American politics has made social sci-entists aware of evangelical and fundamentalist church activism. The devolution of social services to the states, particularly due to the 1996 Personal Responsibility and Work Opportunity Reconciliation Act, as well as President George W. Bush's controversial faith-based community ser-vices initiative of 2001, made the role of churches in providing social services visible. Scholars have treated American mainline Protestant and Catholic church involvement in *national* left-of-center activism on hunger, global human rights, Central American solidarity, and antinuclear advo-cacy (e.g., Meyer 1990). But left-of-center church efforts to train mem-bers in pragmatic political skills and build locally active organizations of low- and middle-income citizens are virtually invisible in discussions of civic associationalism and urban politics alike.[1] This is unfortunate since one recent survey estimates that approximately 3 million Americans are directly or indirectly involved with church-based community organizing (Hart 2001).

One reason for the invisibility of such local grassroots organizations is that scholars focus overwhelmingly on the national state. However, particularly in federal systems, there are many loci within "the state" where policies are made. Social movement organizations do not always aim at national or even state governments. Thus, although not highly visible, policy shifts affecting large numbers of people can occur when protest groups target state or local agencies or officials. This is not to say that local decisions are isolated from national policy or global economic trends – indeed, quite the opposite is true. However, major areas of policy are formally controlled by, and offer targets at, the state and local levels: marriage and family policies, economic development, education, law enforcement, social services, and parks and recreation, to name a few. Some movements choose to target city governments in a long-term strategy to build power for a national movement: For example, gay rights organizations demand domestic partner benefits, and labor/community coalitions demand "living wage" ordinances city government by city government. Community organizations such as those in this study tend to focus on local, and occasionally statewide, political action as their primary arena. While this scope of activity clearly limits their potential for influence, it fits their resources and probably offers the best possibility for gaining visible results. The focus on local governments also provides the most opportunities for members to develop political skills and experience success – and leaders consider developing feelings of political efficacy among poor and working-class citizens to be one of their most important goals.

This essay examines major campaigns of two community organizations, one in St. Louis, Missouri, and one in San Jose, California.[2] Each is an independent ecumenical association of churches, Roman Catholic and Protestant, organized into a federated citywide structure. Further, each

---

[1] For example, in their major study of American political participation, Verba, Schlozman, and Brady (1996) were surprised to discover the major role churches play in providing civic skills, especially to blue-collar persons with little chance to learn them at work. But this should not be surprising given the dominance of the Christian church in American social movements and voluntary associations since the founding of the nation.

[2] This essay is drawn from a larger study of both religious and secular community organizations in urban politics.

citywide group is part of a national organization that provides staff and leadership training, consultation, and ongoing coordinated strategic planning. Each city organization is active at the neighborhood, city, and regional levels.

I will briefly review the related social movement and agenda-setting literatures before tracing each campaign. Then I will discuss the campaigns' efforts in light of three themes drawn from recent work in the political process approach to social movements: political opportunities, mobilizing structures, and cultural framings (McAdam 1982; McAdam, McCarthy, and Zald 1996; Tarrow 1998a). The invisibility not just of church-based community organizations but of most grassroots citizens' organizations hampers our understanding not just of local politics and policymaking, but of such organizations' *potential* to increase participation among the politically inactive and provide new channels for democratic influence in policymaking. While their role may be small compared to that of business lobbies and government bureaucrats, ignoring them or comparing them naively to social movements of the 1930s and 1960s promotes the simplistic notion, on the one hand, that ordinary citizens are powerless to influence public policy, and on the other, that they *could* wield major influence if only these organizations would do something different. Their successes and failures illustrate the sobering limitations – and real achievements – of grassroots mobilizing without the aid of a larger mass movement culture.

Movements: Protest versus Policymaking

The U.S. federal system has many venues for policymaking. The devolution of national authority over social welfare and other policies suggests that state, city, and regional governing bodies have increasing opportunities for policy innovation. City- and state-level organizations and movements are probably better positioned to influence agendas that are determined locally rather than nationally.[3] However, the literatures on social movements and institutionalized policymaking seldom intersect. Agenda setting as a critical aspect of policymaking is typically conceived as a narrow process of competing national interest groups and elites. Studies that consider interest groups

---

[3] I am using the definition of "movement" put forward by Meyer and Tarrow (1998a, p. 4): "collective challenges to existing arangements of power and distribution by people with common purposes and solidarity, in sustained interaction with elites, opponents, and authorities."

usually consider national specialist organizations of experts (Baumgartner and Jones 1993; Kingdon 1984). They exclude the complicated local and state-level struggles that influence city and state agendas, and interact with other forces to form national agendas.

For their part, social movement scholars don't usually conceive of grassroots movements and organizations as regular participants in the policy-making process. They are seen as challengers that extract concessions from policymakers in nonroutine, noncooperative, often disruptive processes (Tarrow 1998b).[4] This is understandable, especially for scholars whose frame of reference is the 1960s, ethnic nationalism, revolutions, or other disruptive movements. Of course, both contentious mass movements and more decorous voluntary associations have long contributed significantly to the American political agenda – not just by blocking policies but by proposing new ones (Sanders 1999; Skocpol 1992). Nevertheless, the literatures of policymaking and social movements have remained separate and distinct in focus and assumptions.

Some recent contributions to the agenda-setting literature do consider the role of citizens' organizations (Baumgartner and Jones 1993; Berry, Portney, and Thomson 1993; McCarthy, Smith, and Zald 1996).[5] These tend to make large-n cross-sectional comparisons of different organizations or of organizations under different conditions. Such comparisons are essential for making general claims. However, they are unable to illuminate the *processes* that cause some organizations and movements to achieve more success than others in bringing issues to agendas and winning desired results.[6] By examining the processes and results of two citizens' campaigns, I identify how the elements of political opportunity, mobilization capacity, and issue selection and framing influenced organizational success or failure.

The Literature on Agenda Setting

When Cobb and Elder (1972) wrote their influential book on agenda setting, it was against a backdrop of fractious mobilization, violent clashes, and cities in flames. Their intervention in the debate on participation

---

[4] A valuable exception is Costain and McFarland (1998). See Katzenstein (1998) for an insightful critique of the social movement literature on this point.

[5] Baumgartner and Jones's (1993) ambitious study fruitfully combines various methods, including large-N comparisons and specific historical case studies.

[6] But see Clemens (1997) for a study of the historical process of Progressive interest group development.

82

responded to this context. It argued for the possibility of social change that neither suppressed dissident voices nor endangered the stability of democratic government:

If a democratic system is to survive and major changes are to occur short of full-scale revolution, the principal forces for change must participate in shaping the agenda of legitimate controversy. (1972, p. 166)

Their work was also a response to the pluralist-elitist debate in democratic theory. Elite theorists saw agenda setting as an integral part of democratic participation (Bachrach and Baratz 1962; Schattschneider 1960). Cobb and Elder intended their agenda-building perspective to describe why some social groups succeed and others fail in gaining representation, including those whose issues never reach the agenda.

Agenda building focuses on the widespread, open contention over issues *before* they reach the public agenda. It may be more important to the long-run stability of the system than electoral participation: While elections may fortify the short-term stability of a system, over the long run formal (governmental) agendas in a democracy should reflect and respond to the systemic (public) agenda (Cobb and Elder 1972, p. 164).

The years since Cobb and Elder's 1972 contribution have been relatively quiescent in the United States, a time of abeyance for left-of-center social movements. Yet as left-wing mobilization has declined, the number of scholars writing about it has increased. Partly this is because scholars responded to the 1960s by revising their understandings of American politics to include social movements as rational actors that mobilized resources (McCarthy and Zald 1977) in response to changing political contexts (McAdam 1982; Tarrow 1998a; Tilly 1978). Yet the role of social forces and movements in influencing agendas has been largely ignored in the literature on agenda setting in American politics. For example, in his study of federal policymaking (1984), Kingdon argues that "visible" participants such as elected officials, media, and political parties set agendas; "hidden" participants such as specialists, academics, and consultants propose specific alternatives. Experts generate specific proposals, while interest groups "affect the governmental agenda more by blocking potential items than by promoting them" (pp. 21, 71). Yet we know, for example, that the Progressive Era program took shape around earlier demands of the agrarian and populist movements, that the civil rights movement produced the landmark legislation of 1964–5, and that the feminist, environmental, and consumerist movements resulted in important new laws (Costain 1992; McAdam 1982; Sanders 1999). Has the nature of policymaking changed? Or is much of the action of generating proposals dispersed, only gradually bubbling up through elite channels such as think tanks and congressional staff?

Many studies of agenda setting similarly emphasize the role of elites. Baumgartner and Jones's more recent study of agendas and policy change (1993) does acknowledge the role of citizen mobilization, especially the growth of citizens' interest groups and their role in bringing pressure *against* nuclear power, pesticides, and other potential threats. However, in both Baumgartner and Jones's and Kingdon's narratives, the actors are public officials and other elites, and the action takes place in formal government settings.

Scholarship on agenda setting tends to focus on national politics and thus has limited relevance to city or regional-level agenda setting. Kingdon argues that the abundant resources available to national policy entrepreneurs allow them to develop solutions to problems, which then sit on the shelf until factors combine to form a favorable opportunity: A recognized problem, an available solution, and the right political climate ultimately open a "policy window" (1984, pp. 114ff). In response to Kingdon's argument that policy entrepreneurs develop solutions to problems and wait for an opportunity to propose them, Berry et al. note that a city government cannot support an infrastructure of policymakers: "a local government is like a third world country in comparison to the federal government in terms of resources available" (1993, p. 117). More often, solutions to urban problems aren't waiting on the shelf but are developed ad hoc for the problem at hand – or not at all. This may provide opportunities for citizens' organizations to propose alternatives.

A few studies treat agenda setting at the local level (Berry et al. 1993) or focus on groups of mobilized citizens (McCarthy et al. 1996). Berry et al. (1993) included agenda setting in their study of city-sponsored citizen participation programs in the United States. However, this study is seriously limited, as it operationalizes agenda setting as the concurrence of individual citizens' attitudes with individual officials' attitudes. Data on individual citizens and officials can tell us how well their attitudes and actions correspond, but they miss the essential role of organizations in mediating and shaping individual attitudes. They cannot measure the role of organizations in helping frame or construct issues, nor can they describe the process by which they go about it.

McCarthy et al. reviewed data on five kinds of social movement organizations to investigate which repertoires of tactics emerge in specific contexts when organizations attempt to influence policy (1996, p. 292).[7] The framing literature has heretofore emphasized how movements' choices in framing issues influence success. The authors' goal is to bring social context into discussions of framing issues and setting agendas. A comparison of tactics that are used most commonly in the *public, media, electoral,* and *governmental* (local, state, and national) arenas reveals some general patterns – for example, that groups with fewer resources tend to use outsider tactics (demonstrations, civil disobedience), while those with more resources tend to use insider tactics (lobbying, legislation). They find that poor-empowerment groups such as church-based community organizations tend to use a mix of both.

McCarthy et al.'s cross-sectional study primarily considers comparative tactics rather than comparative success. It does not trace comparisons over time, reveal the process of grassroots agenda setting, or assess the results of such attempts. I apply their useful distinctions among agenda-setting arenas in a comparison of how two grassroots campaigns attempted to influence agendas, and how differences in political opportunity, mobilizing structures, and framing influenced success. Elements of political opportunity will be identified. By "mobilizing structures" I refer to the range of organizational forms by which people are organized and mobilized – ranging from the family, workplace, congregation, school, and association, to other social networks, to formal organizations. "Framing" refers to the strategic construction and presentation of problems and solutions (Goffman 1974; Snow et al. 1986). Actors frame issues in ways that they hope will resonate with larger publics and thus appear on agendas.

A review of the literature on agenda setting tells us little about how the voluntary sector might influence urban agendas. Baumgartner and Jones's discussion of urban policy analyzes the brief moment when it appeared on the federal agenda, ending in the 1980s (1993, chapter 7). According to this literature, when citizens' organizations *do* attempt to influence agendas, we would expect them to do so primarily by blocking other initiatives, not by proposing their own (Berry et al. 1993; Kingdon 1984).

The two cases that follow describe how some local citizens' organizations have attempted to influence their city and regional agendas. They show that to understand urban, regional, and state politics in the United States today – increasingly where decisions about social welfare and other policies

---

[7] The types of organizations are empowerment of the poor, peace, anti–drunk driving, environmental, and established public interest groups.

are made – it is not enough to consider *national* actors. Nor is it enough to consider *established* political elites. We must look to organized bodies of citizens, their limitations and their potential, as a source of political innovation. Furthermore, to understand an important source of citizen participation in agenda setting, we must look to the churches (Verba, Schlozman, and Brady 1996).

Two Church-Based Community Organizations

This essay compares the attempts of two multi-issue federations of churches to influence their city and regional agendas. Both groups organize at the neighborhood, city, regional, and state levels. The first is PACT (People Acting in Community Together), a seventeen-church federation in San Jose that mounted a campaign for a five-year integrated youth services program. It put its issues on the mayoral, city council, and redevelopment agency agendas and won new city programs. In addition, it created a precedent for diverting redevelopment agency funds, albeit a small fraction, from downtown development to neighborhood services.

The second is MCU (Metropolitan Congregations United for St. Louis), a sixty-one-church organization that has pursued an ambitious long-term campaign against urban sprawl in the St. Louis region. While its members were unable to win their initial regional campaign, they played a key role in placing sprawl on the public, media, electoral, and governmental agendas.[8]

In the 1970s and 1980s, church- or congregation-based organizing was developed by Saul Alinsky–style organizers as a strategy for building lasting organizations, which they thought were necessary for a long-term political presence (Campbell 1986; Ramsden and Montgomery 1990; Reitzes and Reitzes 1987). In church-based organizations (CBOs), individual congregations address their own community issues and come together to work on citywide issues. CBOs do not provide services but organize grassroots issue campaigns. Most congregation-based organizations are members of coalitions called "networks," which create organizations and provide extensive staff and leadership training.

The CBOs draw on the Alinsky organizing tradition but differ. First, CBO organizers are often people with strong personal faith commitments

---

[8] Data were obtained during six months of fieldwork in each city. These include extensive observation of organizational processes; numerous interviews with staff, city officials, and other informants; fifty interviews with leaders; and organizational files, newspaper articles, and other records.

and a biblically based vision of social justice.[9] Second, some CBOs view strengthening congregations and their members' individual capacities as ends in themselves. A longer-term perspective on change leads to an emphasis on political education, training, and civic responsibility as much as immediate political victories. Organizers train local people to organize by conducting one-to-one interviews with church members, conducting research, designing campaigns, and negotiating with decision makers. The one-to-one interviews are essential in identifying concerns and recruiting participants. Third, this emphasis on building leadership and organizational capacity results in distinctive organizing practices that can be described as a "relational" style of organizing (Appleman 1996; Swarts 2001).

Like most CBOs, PACT and MCU are multi-issue, citywide action organizations. They endorse not politicians but issues, although they may hold candidates' nights and mobilize voters. Tactics vary both among organizations and within the life of one organization, but a staple tactic is the mass "accountability session," where officials or decision makers are asked to make specific commitments in front of a crowd and are pressured by "pinners" to give a "yes" or "no" answer. Politicians new to this format typically react with hostility, as it is designed to demonstrate power and demand respect from officials. When politicians realize that CBOs will retaliate if ignored but can provide resources (issues, publicity, and votes) if respected, and that their rules and behavior are consistent and predictable, they frequently pursue collaborative policymaking relationships with CBOs.

San Jose PACT: An Incremental Agenda of Neighborhood Youth Services

The sun-belt city of San Jose is a boomtown that has styled itself "the capital of Silicon Valley." The population is 30 percent Hispanic, 25 percent Asian, 4.5 percent African American, and most of the rest white. Because its area aggressively expanded decades ago through annexation, it has been

---

[9] Whether this is a significant factor in congregation-based organizing is unclear, since religious people have always been attracted to community organizing. Saul Alinsky's earliest major funders were religious denominations, and his successor, Ed Chambers, was a Benedictine seminarian. CBO is the dominant form of community organizing today, so it may simply draw the best organizers. A goal of the larger study from which this is taken is to distinguish such structural and cultural aspects of CBOs as factors influencing their effectiveness.

able to capture taxes from its population boom. Yet the city is not immune to problems. Its pro-growth coalition has channeled vast sums into downtown redevelopment projects, while in some neighborhoods, streetlights are obscured by trees untrimmed in forty years (Castillo 1998). State budget cuts seriously damaged the public schools. The dropout rate for Asian and Hispanic students ranges from 30 to 60 percent. Drugs are a persistent problem, and crime plagues low-income neighborhoods. PACT was founded in 1985 by Catholic priests who invited the Industrial Areas Foundation network of organizations to help start a church-based organization. PACT, whose membership varies from fourteen to seventeen churches, belongs to the Pacific Institute for Community Organization (PICO) network of organizations.[10]

In 1988, the issues emerging in its one-to-one interviews and research led PACT to focus on "the drug epidemic and the associated pain and violence touching the vast majority of South Bay families." Every spring, PACT holds its largest annual event, a citywide mass meeting organized as an "accountability session." PACT pressures either the mayor or, in an election year, candidates for mayor, to seek adoption of its agenda for the year. In election years the meeting precedes the Democratic primary; in nonelection years, it precedes the city's budget proposal and adoption.[11]

In 1989, meetings with city officials culminated in that year's mass meeting with Mayor Tom McEnery in June. The day before his meeting with PACT, McEnery announced Project Crackdown, a $1 million multipronged neighborhood effort to fight drugs in neighborhoods. At the meeting with over 1,000 PACT members, the mayor agreed to make the drug policy a priority during the coming year. Project Crackdown was widely seen as a victory for PACT.

The next year, 1990, was an election year. At that year's mass action, PACT got commitments from the three mayoral candidates for delivery of a comprehensive antidrug plan within six months of election. After Susan Hammer was elected mayor, PACT established a negotiating relationship with her.

---

[10] There are currently four major CBO networks: the Industrial Areas Foundation (IAF), founded by Saul Alinsky in 1940, with sixty member organizations; the Gamaliel Foundation, with forty organizations; PICO, with forty-one organizations; and DART in Florida, with seventeen organizations. The Industrial Areas Foundation pioneered the church-based model in the 1970s.

[11] In this predominantly Democratic city, the winner of the November election is typically decided in the Democratic primary, held in June.

Meanwhile, the city of San Jose had embarked on an ambitious program of downtown development. Through tax-increment financing, the city's Redevelopment Agency was heavily subsidizing large downtown building projects. PACT members perceived the city as "putting in statues and palm trees, and yet they didn't have money for neighborhood services." [12] PACT made its programs to prevent and arrest juvenile crime, dubbed San Jose BEST (Bringing Everyone's Strengths Together), central to its 1990 agenda. It pursued BEST by targeting the ten-person city council district by district. [13] Individual PACT churches were located in six of the ten districts, and local church organizing committees launched individual campaigns to gain their council member's support.

In 1991, the recession in California led the city to threaten a $2.8 million cut in neighborhood services. [14] PACT demanded priority for a comprehensive five-year plan for "youth and the drug epidemic." It proposed that the mayor unveil such a plan at PACT's annual all-city action in June and negotiated with the mayor's office for five months to develop the plan. PACT's more ambitious proposal was to fund programs from San Jose's Redevelopment Agency. The agency funded only major building projects concentrated in downtown, never neighborhood services. Although the mayor had confirmed in writing her support for Redevelopment funding, at the last minute the powerful Redevelopment Agency head fought back, claiming that the fund diversion was illegal. [15]

PACT thus entered the June 5 meeting with the mayor unsure of her support. At the meeting, held in the city's Catholic cathedral, 800 PACT members participated in a "prayer service" and an accountability session with the mayor. PACT framed the issue as a double standard in the city budget: one five-year $96.4 million budget for redevelopment and building projects and a one-year operating budget for everything else. PACT proposed programs and a long-range plan to divert Redevelopment Agency funds to youth services. Leaders were delighted when the mayor responded with a five-year $6 million plan of programs diverting redevelopment monies for Project BEST and a rehabilitation center for youth. Although PACT

---

[12] Interview, PACT officer, January 27, 1999.

[13] The ten-person city council has been elected by district since 1988.

[14] At the same time, the mayor supported a cost overrun of $25 million or more to the San Jose Sharks arena, and was pursuing a major league baseball stadium and team.

[15] Los Angeles implemented this strategy legally, and PACT proposed the same method: Find city budget items that Redevelopment could legitimately fund, use Redevelopment money to fund them, then reallocate that portion of the regular city budget to the new programs.

failed to win significant future allocation of redevelopment funds for youth programs, BEST and Project Crackdown have been extremely successful. PACT's strategy has been to initiate specific agenda items and, once proven effective, push the city to expand them and make them ongoing. Project BEST is now in its twelfth year and Project Crackdown in its fourteenth.

The PICO network structure builds in opportunities for diffusion of issues, strategies, and tactics. The latest addition to PACT's neighborhood youth services agenda has been city-funded "homework centers." In 1993, one PACT church learned about the homework centers that a sister PICO organization in San Diego had won. The centers provide afterschool child care, tutoring, and safe spaces away from gang activity during the time of day that most juvenile crimes are committed. The church worked with two city council members to fund five homework centers in public schools in its neighborhood. What began as a one-time city expenditure is now a permanent budget line item that funds 135 afterschool homework centers, each with a paid director. The centers are extremely popular with parents and teachers. Although a large percentage of students they serve are from low-income families, homework centers are a universal, not a need-based, program and attract broad support. They have become a winning issue for the mayor and city council members.

As part of the fourteen-organization PICO California Project, PACT also helped raise education issues at the state level. In 1998, the project brought 2,500 members to a Sacramento town meeting with twenty state legislators to push for the state's largest-ever school facilities bond act ($9.5 billion) and a bill providing statewide funding for afterschool programs (both passed). PACT helped reshape the afterschool legislation more in the image of its homework centers rather than as a recreation program.

In summary, during the 1990s, PACT successfully put neighborhood anticrime and youth services on the city agenda. Through identifying issues of concern to members, research, negotiations with the mayor and city council members, and mass meetings with these officials, they pressured the city to institutionalize innovative programs for neighborhood drug prevention (Project Crackdown), antigang and antidrug youth programs (San Jose BEST), individual neighborhood recreation centers and programs, and homework centers in all San Jose public middle and high schools. They also established important political capital in their collaborative policymaking relationship with city officials. They failed to institutionalize ongoing reallocation of a significant portion of the Redevelopment Agency's budget. However, their local policymaking efforts influenced other city agendas and the state agenda: They modified state legislation, and programs they successfully proposed have been replicated in other cities. Homework centers are now a staple agenda item for other PICO California organizations, and Project Crackdown is credited as the model for the national Weed and Seed neighborhood anticrime program.

MCU for St. Louis: Agenda Building for Fundamental Reform

The St. Louis church-based organization Metropolitan Congregations United for St. Louis (MCU) includes three allied organizations with a total of sixty-one churches. It is affiliated with the Gamaliel Foundation of some thrity-eight organizations, concentrated in the Midwest. MCU includes churches in areas that are predominantly white and blue-collar, black low-income, and racially mixed, including both city and inner-ring suburbs.

While the eleven-county St. Louis region remains roughly constant in population, the once-bustling city of St. Louis is losing population rapidly to the suburbs.[16] Because, as in many midwestern cities, the city has lost middle-class population (and votes), top Gamaliel Foundation staff concluded that regional federations bringing together city and suburban churches were needed to solve inner-city problems. In 1996, MCU began to form as a metrowide organization of the three separate St. Louis organizations.

St. Louis has a partisan mayor and board of aldermen. Despite the city's 59 percent population decline since 1960, there are still twenty-eight aldermen, leaving each with a district of less than 15,000. While St. Louis has historically had a strong-mayor form of government and San Jose a city manager–council government, San Jose's mayor is in a stronger position. This is partly because St. Louis's power is extremely fragmented, not only within the region but also within the city itself.[17]

---

[16] The eleven-county St. Louis region's population has remained steady at 2.5 million, but outlying St. Charles County grew 22% in population since 1990, while St. Louis County grew only 1.5%. The City of St. Louis's population declined from 850,000 in 1950 to 350,000 today and is declining faster than that of any other large U.S. city. Both 1998 and 1999 Sierra Club studies rank St. Louis second only to Atlanta in having the worst urban sprawl in the nation.

[17] When St. Louis "seceded" from St. Louis County in 1876, it gained its own structure of "county" functions separate from city offices (Glassberg 1991). The president of the Board of Aldermen and the city controller jointly control the city budget, and the police department is state controlled (a legacy of the Civil War).

Through the Gamaliel network, MCU learned of urban policy consultants David Rusk, Myron Orfield, and others.[18] MCU consulted with them and began to research the causes of St. Louis's decline, including urban sprawl. St. Louis has a hypersegregated population that is 47 percent African American. Black inner-city poverty is highly concentrated (Rusk 1995). The exacerbation of problems related to poverty, drugs, crime, and poor schools has spurred the loss of the middle class; in turn, sprawl further isolates and impoverishes the inner city. Not only did urban sprawl and the loss of businesses and residents reduce the local tax base, city services, and housing values, it affected the churches. Rather than invest in their existing infrastructure, they were forced to build new facilities as their population moved outward.

Rusk argues that community development in blighted neighborhoods fails to reverse concentrated poverty and city decline. Only "elastic" city boundaries make this possible by expanding to recapture the suburbs, either through extensive annexation or city-county consolidation. While San Jose increased its territory and control through annexation in the 1960s, St. Louis's city charter mandates strict boundaries that preclude capture of the suburban tax base. Rusk argues that sprawl also fuels St. Louis's racial segregation and concentrated poverty. Since local governments almost never initiate regional growth management, revenue sharing, or equitable housing policies, state legislatures are the preferred arena for major reforms such as these. MCU leaders decided that urban growth boundaries were the best, if not the only, solution.[19]

In 1996, MCU began a series of three "learning summits" and nine "town hall meetings" featuring public officials and Rusk and Orfield, that targeted their constituents, the media, and the public. Newspaper coverage recruited allies. Following other regions, MCU framed the issue positively as "smart growth." MCU worked with state legislators to draft legislation, and a representative from a district that included some MCU churches introduced it in 1997.[20] The bill failed to get a committee hearing, but it got publicity in St. Louis. MCU sought a broader base by pulling together a "Smart Growth Alliance" of environmentalists, transportation policymakers, mass transit advocates, and St. Louis county municipal officials.

[18] Rusk is the former mayor of Albuquerque, and Orfield is a Minnesota state legislator. Both are consultants in urban planning and policy.

[19] Growth boundaries have been successfully implemented in cities such as Portland, Oregon, and San Jose, California.

[20] The representative, Ron Auer, was himself a member of an MCU church.

In 1997, the issue assumed more prominence on the city agenda. First, MCU held a citywide "public meeting on smart growth" in September. Turnout was 750 instead of the hoped-for 2,000, and the mayor and county executive were absent (ironically, out of town at a meeting addressing the same issue). There, MCU announced two goals: their "smart growth boundary" legislation and $20,000 of city and county funding for a report on the costs of St. Louis urban sprawl. The issue of sprawl exploded onto the media and public agendas when a state assembly committee organized by Rep. Ron Auer held public hearings on the issue in St. Louis. Mayor Clarence Harmon testified in favor of measures to halt sprawl. This widened the conflict by drawing the mayor into contention with outlying St. Charles County officials.[21]

In 1998 the sprawl debate crystallized around the Page Avenue Extension, a long-pending state- and federal-funded $550 million highway extension and bridge that would add ten freeway lanes from St. Louis County to St. Charles County.[22] Opponents saw the Page Avenue Extension as a costly boondoggle that would facilitate the further loss of St. Louis population to outlying suburbs. Supporters, chiefly developers, road builders, and local business, framed the project as necessary to ease traffic congestion and enhance economic development. MCU helped put a referendum blocking Page on the November 1998 St. Louis county ballot. The coalition of environmentalists, MCU, and others provoked a countermobilization of suburban developers, big business, road builders, construction unions, and real estate, financial, and other suburban interests. The anti-Page forces, including MCU, were outspent eight to one.[23] The referendum to block the Page Avenue Extension was defeated by a 60 percent majority in November 1998.

Prior to its campaign against urban sprawl, MCU had successfully undertaken many neighborhood and citywide campaigns, such as preserving public schools and an inner-city post office, and helping establish the city's

---

[21] One official on the hearing panel invited Mayor Harmon, who is black, out to St. Charles, "where he'd feel safe." This incited the charge of coded racism, since St. Louis's crime is typically asociated with its high black population.

[22] Sixty percent of St. Charles County residents work outside their county, helping create a demand for the highway extension, which would be funded by federal and state highway trust funds raised by gasoline taxes.

[23] According to one leading activist, the vote would have been close, perhaps 50–50, but freeway advocates had over $800,000 compared to Taxpayers Against Page Freeway's $160,000. Telephone interview, January 9, 1999.

only vocational high school and a major new inner-city shopping development center. However, it never attempted a coordinated regional campaign. Issues it had previously selected tended to have public appeal and little entrenched opposition. MCU lacked experience assessing political opportunity at the state level and did not realize that urban growth boundaries were unwinnable in Missouri's conservative state legislature.[24] Legislators and planners finally convinced MCU to back off on the growth boundaries issue or be ignored.

The Page Avenue fight helped MCU clarify the identity and strength of their opponents. Perhaps most significantly, they learned that St. Louis's business elites refuse to oppose unplanned growth. Civic Progress, the powerful organization of forty individuals that includes CEOs of twenty-six top corporations, supports downtown preservation and mass transit, but it also supports infrastructure development in general and donates heavily to the pro-Page Avenue side.[25] The chamber of commerce follows suit because many of its members rely on suburban growth.

In addition to powerful vested interests, development policy reform faces what many describe as a "lack of civic leadership."[26] This is linked to politicians' electoral calculations. Local officials such as the St. Louis County executive, a congressman, and a local mayor all planned campaigns for higher office from this sprawling suburban Republican area. Donations from the county executive's campaign chest to Democratic officials all over Missouri help ensure their loyalty.[27]

Even civic leaders with less to lose have not taken a leadership position.[28] Retired Senator Jack Danforth heads St. Louis 2004, an elite-driven effort

---

[24] The state legislature is traditionally hostile to regulatory policies such as urban growth boundaries. Conservative rural interests have historically been hostile to St. Louis, and the eastern Missouri representative to the highway commission has always been a homebuilder. Interview with St. Louis County Municipal League member, January 1999.

[25] A partial list of campaign donations supporting Page, in order of magnitude, includes builders and developers, $231,650; major corporations that are members of Civic Progress, $175,092; other St. Charles interests, $157,755; road builders, engineers, and unions, $136,600; miscellaneous others, $116,335; and real estate and finance interests, $10,950. The total is $828,382. Figures compiled by the St. Louis County Municipal League, December 20, 1998.

[26] Interview, anonymous *Post-Dispatch* reporter, January 1999.

[27] Efforts at statewide campaign finance reform have repeatedly been thrown out of the courts for technical reasons.

[28] Of two prominent retired U.S. senators, Tom Eagleton and Jack Danforth, Danforth supported the Page Avenue Extension, while Eagleton claimed he opposed it personally but wanted to avoid controversy. Telephone interview, anonymous local activist, January 1999.

aiming at no less than "a rebirth in the St. Louis region" that is essentially a free-market approach to making the city competitive with the suburbs by improving urban conditions without regulating growth. It is well funded by the same major corporations that, in their guise as Civic Progress, oppose regulating development.[29]

The defeat of the referendum to stop the Page Avenue Extension was a benchmark in the debate on urban sprawl. The *St. Louis Post Dispatch's* editorials against sprawl added a note of urgency: For the first time, the essay spoke favorably of urban growth boundaries, noting that "this region needs to put the idea on the front burner for consideration." For its part, MCU retreated from the growth boundaries issue and repositioned itself for a much longer campaign.[30]

In summary, MCU played an important role in helping place sprawl on the St. Louis regional agenda. Its selection of the urban growth boundaries issue was a triumph of public policy analysis over pragmatic political calculations. MCU's political climate provides many barriers to successfully addressing fundamental causes of urban decline – barriers that include fragmented political authority, entrenched opponents, racial polarization, and the difficulty of explaining to voters the causes of and solutions to urban sprawl. However, the effects of sprawl (if MCU succeeds in portraying them this way) are widely felt across race and class lines among residents of the urban core. Successful campaigns on this issue depend on many factors, including sprawl opponents' organizational strength and the appearance of sprawl on the national political agenda. While successful outcomes have eluded MCU on the issue of sprawl, there can be no doubt that it influenced the public, media, electoral, and governmental agendas. Its leadership learned hard political lessons and, through coalition building with municipal officials, environmentalists, and transit advocates, laid the groundwork for a much longer struggle.

What can we learn from these cases about the ability of grassroots community organizations to influence urban agendas? The factors that led to

---

[29] St. Louis 2004 has ambitious goals and some impressive achievements. One 2004 initiative has raised $751 million for a project to revive eleven targeted low-income neighborhoods and make them sustainable. Critics see this effort as ultimately futile, since it leaves intact the sprawl that is killing these impoverished communities: "That's kind of like putting an elderly person on life support and making them comfortable while they suck the blood out of them." Telephone interview, member, St. Louis County Municipal League, January 8, 1999.

[30] Telephone interview, MCU staff organizer, January 1999.

differing results can be usefully described in terms of differences in political opportunity, mobilizing structures, and strategic framing of issues.

Political Opportunity

For many scholars, political opportunity includes these elements: the opening up of political access, unstable alignments, influential allies, and divided elites (McAdam 1996; Tarrow 1996). An additional factor is government capacity: the power of the state to repress and to implement policies (McAdam 1996, p. 27). As applied to San Jose and St. Louis, "state capacity" refers to the ability of local government to make and implement policy for the metropolitan area. In liberal democracies such as the United States, unstable alignments take the form of electoral instability (Tarrow 1996, p. 55). Division among elites suggests that allies might be available, including actors in local government, business, the media, and others.

Opening of Political Access and Electoral Instability

The "opening of political access"[31] refers to the formal institutional aspects of political opportunity, while "electoral instability" refers to the opportunity to influence political candidates. In San Jose, city council district elections, won in 1988, allowed PACT to mobilize effectively in districts where a PACT church was located. Political opportunity interacted with PACT's ability to mobilize during the late 1980s, when mass meetings forced Mayor Tom McEnery to respond to its demands with a new city program. This, in turn, opened access to the mayor's office, and with this political capital, PACT maintained access to McEnery's protege, new Mayor Susan Hammer.

PACT has taken advantage of election cycles by mobilizing large numbers of likely voters to pressure candidates. As in St. Louis, in San Jose significant electoral competition takes place within the Democratic Party rather than between the two major parties. PACT provides a large organized grassroots constituency for mayoral as well as city council candidates. San Jose politicians have frequently emerged through neighborhood activism, and bringing neighborhood issues to the electoral agenda can provide a resource for political entrepreneurs seeking to differentiate themselves from other candidates.

---

[31] These two elements seem so closely related in these cases as to be worth considering jointly.

In contrast, MCU's campaign on urban sprawl is a case of trying to create opportunities where few exist. While widely shared grievances related to sprawl[32] impelled MCU to select this issue, few discernible openings appeared in the political context. MCU had access to the mayor, some aldermen, a few state legislators, and a host of bureaucratic allies; however, St. Louis city officials and a handful of state legislators lack the power to address this regional issue.

In St. Louis and the State of Missouri, electoral competition did not provide opportunities for smart-growth advocates to pursue their agendas. In the conservative Missouri climate, officials from suburban areas seized the opportunity to oppose measures that smack of regulation – even freeway carpool lanes. In the state legislature, smart-growth advocates are hugely outnumbered. The appearance of urban sprawl on the national agenda, for example, during the 2000 presidential campaign may increase its visibility in Missouri.[33] For example, in the November 1998 elections, a full 85% of 150 measures across the nation to combat sprawl passed. However, as of July 2002, no measures related to growth regulation (even studies) had been passed by the Missouri legislature.

Influential Allies

At a minimum, church-based organizing is designed to gain the visible support of church dignitaries, and both organizations have done so. PACT allies also included politicians whose agendas may be furthered by PACT's support; constituencies of the programs it initiated, including public school teachers and administrators; occasionally the San Jose *Mercury News*; and, on quality-of-life issues, the powerful Silicon Valley business interests that share PACT's goal of preparing youth for Silicon Valley jobs. While these business interests would oppose PACT's challenges to Redevelopment Agency priorities, they support PACT on campaigns that would enhance San Jose's economic capacity: housing, education, and transportation (Peterson 1981).

---

[32] These included middle-class population loss, church membership loss, decline in home values, loss of tax revenues and consequent decline in schools and public services, diversion of public monies to build costly new infrastructure, and increased poverty and crime due to middle-class flight.

[33] As early as 1998, Al Gore came out against "the ill-thought sprawl hastily developed around our nation's cities." *St. Louis Post-Dispatch*, February 20, 1998.

MCU's allies included local planners, municipal officials, environmental organizations, several state representatives, the mayor, and the daily newspaper. These were insufficient to take on the majority of local business and political leaders. The St. Louis *Post-Dispatch*'s leadership was cautious: The essay presented sprawl as a technical rather than a political problem, clearly spelling out its costs but unwilling to identify those that profit from sprawl.[34]

Divided Elites

On their most fundamental challenges – passing urban growth boundaries, and reallocating 30% of the Redevelopment Agency budget to youth and neighborhood-serving programs – MCU and PACT, respectively, discovered that elites were unified against them. When the Redevelopment Agency and the mayor's office split on the issue of a small one-time reallocation of funds, the mayor sided with PACT. But as for major reallocations of resources, PACT ran aground on San Jose's powerful progrowth coalition (Mollenkopf 1983).

The St. Louis region's progrowth coalitions have shown no significant cleavages thus far. Local public officials have refused to limit development based on their electoral calculations and their suburban constituents' interests. While business interests support the antipoverty and antiblight measures that would benefit them or their workforce – school desegregation, better education, urban revitalization, and mass transit – they refuse to support restrictions on development.[35] As the debate continues, a cleavage between downtown and suburban business interests could develop but is unlikely, not only because of business's stronger impulse to ally against restraints, but also because businesses and individual businesspersons' interests are often divided between downtown preservation and suburban growth.

[34] This is partially because suburban readers are a growing market for newspaper subscriptions. The newspaper refused to print a list of the donors to the pro–Page Avenue extension campaign. However, the essay came out against the Page Avenue extension. Telephone interview, Repps Hudson, reporter, *St. Louis Post-Dispatch*, January 1999.

[35] While Civic Progress, the organization of St. Louis's most powerful corporations, strongly supported a school tax measure, it also supported the Page Avenue Extension. Interview, Tim P. Fischesser, January 8, 1999.

Government Capacity

This factor differs significantly for the San Jose and St. Louis city governments. While San Jose's large area is governed by one city government, the St. Louis metro region is carved into ninety-two local governments. Even within the City of St. Louis, power is fractured and widely dispersed. The Board of Aldermen represents twenty-eight wards, while San Jose's city council represents only ten districts. On its own, the City of St. Louis lacks the governmental capacity to restrict sprawl. Any campaign for growth restrictions must be regional, including both Missouri and Illinois suburbs. St. Louis and its inner-ring suburbs face an uphill battle to enlist suburban allies and are outnumbered in the state legislature.

In sum, for both PACT and MCU, the five aspects of the political opportunity structure – opening of political access, electoral instability, influential allies, divided elites, and government capacity – can be collapsed to three. Formal political access is related to both electoral instability and governmental capacity. Political access includes the governmental structure and rules for electing city council members. Both PACT and MCU have some version of geographic representation in the city council, and some access to the mayor, but San Jose's political structure gives PACT two advantages over MCU. First, San Jose's ten-council-member system makes it much easier for PACT to influence a council majority of six. St. Louis's highly dispersed twenty-eight-member Board of Aldermen requires MCU to woo and win fifteen elected officials to achieve a majority. Second, a key to political access is the number of city governments that control a given territory. While San Jose controls a large area due to annexation, St. Louis's city charter restricts it to a small area. It was not enough for MCU to gain the St. Louis mayor's or any number of city aldermen's allegiance, since the decisions that affected the city's economic growth were dispersed among ninety-two local governments (as well as among businesses and state and national governments).

The dimensions of influential allies and divided elites are also hard to separate in city politics, since elite allies become available when elites are divided. While elites in both cities were unified against both organizations' most far-ranging reform proposals (ongoing reallocation of Redevelopment Agency funds and urban growth boundaries), PACT had elite support for specific issues perceived to reduce crime or improve education for urban youth.

This suggests that political opportunity must be considered *relative to* the issue pursued. Note that the substantive choice of issue is different from how the issue is framed. The urban sprawl issue, particularly the strategy of urban growth boundaries, meant that MCU had chosen an issue over which political elites regionally were divided – with city and inner-ring suburban officials in favor of restricting sprawl but business elites unified in opposition. MCU and its allies were not strong enough to counter opposition from business and the state legislature. PACT, in contrast, selected allocational rather than regulatory issues that its local progrowth coalition understood as advantageous.

Mobilizing Structures

Churches are unique mobilizing structures in the United States. Their resources include formal and informal networks, as well as shared language and values whose salience in members' lives is exceeded by few institutions (Reitzes and Reitzes 1987; Verba et al. 1996). Churches' potential resources include denominational funding, ongoing formal and informal networks, social legitimacy, pastoral and lay leaders, and shared language and beliefs. PACT and MCU gained these resources from their member churches, and also from the congregation-based organizing networks of which they are members (PICO and the Gamaliel Foundation, respectively). Both provide resources peculiar to this organizational structure, including national leadership training sessions, staff training, ongoing consultation, network-wide strategy, and staff recruitment.

In PACT, shared Christian faith helps bring together very-low-income Hispanic Catholics with middle-class Anglo Protestants. MCU must surmount greater divisions. Its sixty-one churches pull together residents of racially divided north and south St. Louis, as well as north St. Louis County. Black pastors' fear of white control has reduced MCU's ability to recruit black churches. Nevertheless, it is unclear that any institution offers more potential to unite St. Louis's diverse residents than the church. Neither PACT nor MCU had the staff, budget, allies, or mobilization capacity to take on fundamental regulatory or redistributive reforms, although they raised such issues on local agendas. Both had adequate resources to win allocational gains (Peterson 1981) with a small redistributive effect.[36]

---

[36] These include leading successful efforts to keep open an inner-city post office and schools, build a new inner-city supermarket and shopping center, open the only vocational school in the City of St. Louis, and open new city-funded youth and recreation centers in low-income San Jose neighborhoods, new housing units, and the like.

While both PACT and MCU gain similar resources from their base of churches, PACT is part of a fourteen-organization statewide coalition, which gives it much more clout at the state level. MCU is the only Gamaliel affiliate in Missouri; the CBO in Kansas City belongs to the PICO network, and organizations from rival networks rarely collaborate. Yet a campaign on urban sprawl could clearly benefit from coordination with the other largest city in Missouri. This lack of network cooperation reveals a weakness in CBOs' ability to mount statewide and national campaigns. Because the diminished resources for grassroots activism force organizations and networks to compete for scarce funding, they have an incentive to distinguish themselves from the others rather than to collaborate.

PACT had approximately double the budget and staff of MCU. This had direct effects on mobilization capacity. MCU launched a state legislative campaign without this infrastructure and got predictably poor results. MCU seeks to form a much broader coalition of churches: Expansion beyond the inner-ring suburbs would also insulate MCU from being painted as a special interest group defending particular neighborhoods. Their church base allows them to recruit suburban churches on the basis of both long-term self-interest (efficient use of taxes, reduced congestion, preserved open space) and ethical and religious appeals to social justice. MCU will need more financial and political capital to move urban growth boundaries onto the electoral and governmental agendas with any chance of success. This is also true for PACT if it seeks to undertake more far-reaching regulatory or redistributive challenges, for example, of the Redevelopment Agency.

To sum up, both organizations profit from the church-based structure of this organizing model. They gain structural resources such as church and denominational funds, social networks, and leaders. Membership in a network of similar organizations provides access to trained staff, ongoing consulting, and networkwide training for local leaders. Finally, they have cultural resources such as a strong Christian collective identity and shared language, values, and rituals. While stubborn barriers of race, class, and interest (urban/suburban) challenge these CBOs, they take advantage of what is probably the most versatile institutional base for community organizing. Among CBOs, to be sure, the level of resources differs: PACT had a larger budget and therefore more organizers per church; thus, with fewer than one-third of MCU's churches, it can mobilize as many people.

Because CBOs are members of networks, they can join together on larger campaigns, as PACT has begun to do in the PICO California Project.

However, because these networks compete for funding and churches, they forfeit other opportrnities to join forces, especially at the national level.

Framing

In organizing parlance, specific issues are "cut" from general problems. The hallmarks of a good issue are that it is concrete, specific, and winnable. Once an issue is selected, it must be "framed" in ways designed to win constituents' and allies' support.

As church-based organizations, both PACT and MCU frame and experience their issues as "values-" and "faith-based" no less than the Christian Coalition does, and they use prayer, music, and other liturgical elements. Both PACT and MCU use the CBO method of identifying problems by employing a bottom-up process of one-to-one interviews with church members. This process is designed to ensure that issues will be widely shared across race, class, neighborhood, and denominational lines. Issues are then chosen with the top-down help of organizers and senior network staff, who ideally consider the strategic context.

Both organizations' framing strategy has included the use of expert knowledge. PACT and MCU, like most CBOs, strive to be (and appear) credible and well informed by conducting research on issues and educating their members to present the research convincingly. Funding a study of the costs of sprawl is not only geared to getting information, but is a cultural strategy designed to gain legitimacy and win allies among middle-class suburbanites.

In one respect, PACT and MCU differ strongly in their ability to frame their campaigns. In pursuing distributive programs *for* youth, families, education, and neighborhoods and *against* drugs and gangs, PACT could present them as "valence issues." A valence issue has only one legitimate side, elicits "a single, strong, fairly uniform emotional response and does not have an adversarial quality" (Nelson 1984:27). PACT demanded programs to address "the drug epidemic and the associated pain and violence touching the vast majority of South Bay families." Californians of all races and classes felt the impact when the state's educational ranking declined from number 1 to number 49. Because homework centers are spread throughout diverse areas, they are easy to support.

Meanwhile, MCU took on the highly complex regulatory issue of urban growth boundaries. Its difficulty in promoting the issue of smart growth supports findings that easy-to-understand issues are more successful on media and electoral agendas than complex ones (Carmines and Stimson 1989 and Nelson 1984 in McCarthy et al. 1996:309; Cobb and Elder 1972). There are many facets of urban sprawl: race, economics, the environment, responsible planning, special interests, highway congestion, and tax increases. Both sides can emphasize quality-of-life issues: For example, during the Page Avenue battle, proponents of Page Avenue claimed that it was necessary to *prevent* traffic congestion, while opponents made the more difficult argument that ultimately it would *produce* congestion. To frame sprawling development as dangerous requires a long-range perspective. One local planner notes:

The pro-sprawl people say I can make money building highways, have a nice new 3,000 foot home . . . anti-sprawl people say we'll ruin the environment, lose wetlands, and cause problems down the road. One reason the issue is so contentious is people are talking at different temporal levels.[37]

As they pursue the issue among the middle class in a politically conservative climate, MCU leaders have considered coopting the language of "property rights" from the other side and applying it to property owners in the region's older areas whose investments are threatened by unchecked sprawl.

In sum, PACT and MCU had the advantage of being able to tie the issues they select to faith, religion, and morality. However, their issues differed in complexity and the ability to be framed as a valence issue with universal appeal. For MCU the choice of issue may be more important than how it is framed. The urban growth boundaries issue is not *inherently* antigrowth, although it is inherently regulatory. Its relationship to economic development depends on the temporal context in which it is framed. Advocates make a powerful argument that, over the long term, growth boundaries would enhance the city's and the regional core's growth. These areas' municipal officials are convinced of this fact and embrace measures to combat sprawl. However, the business factions that profit directly from sprawl oppose such measures, while other business factions' interests are divided between the city and its suburbs. Even if growth boundaries are successfully framed as essential to the St. Louis urban core and therefore essential to local business in the long term, it is difficult to convince a business audience that restraints on growth are beneficial. The issue's complexity also makes it difficult to

[37] Interview, Mark Tranel, University of Missouri at St. Louis, January 20, 1999.

frame for ordinary citizens, so MCU has a challenge in building wide public support.

Conclusion

In the shared context of left-of-center movement demobilization, both PACT and MCU needed to forge a coalition of working- and middle-class members to win concessions that would benefit not only these constituencies but also low-income people. Both groups selected issues that had the potential to unite all these constituencies. However, PACT used a piecemeal rather than a fundamental reform strategy and won incremental outcomes that it institutionalized in the city's budget. MCU pursued urban growth boundaries on the basis that this issue was fundamental even though it was not winnable, and they learned from its failure to adopt a more incremental approach.

In both PACT and MCU, a mass base – mobilization – was a necessary but not sufficient condition for placing items on the governmental agenda. The organizations faced very different cities, but both cities competed hard for economic development (Peterson 1981). In both, developers and their allies were among the most powerful interests. Both PACT and MCU took on these interests. However, PACT selected a distributive issue, fighting for a small share of resources that nevertheless would significantly benefit its constituency. While it threatened the redevelopment agency's hegemony (in terms of precedent more than actual cost), it did not threaten development and business interests, but appealed to their interest in education and safe neighborhoods. MCU, on the other hand, took on business interests with an ambitious regulatory issue and had few resources or powerful allies. It was unable to win urban growth boundaries, but it succeeded in putting the issue of urban sprawl on the media, public, and governmental agendas.

Independent citizens' organizations based on churches can perform an agenda-setting function that heretofore has not been visible in discussions of agenda-setting, participation, or related literatures. The agenda-setting literature has a national bias, and expert policy entrepreneurs are much scarcer in local than in national government (Kingdon 1984). City agendas are more accessible than state and national agendas, allowing local organizations not only to veto proposals but to launch positive campaigns and generate proposals that can benefit thousands of constituents. Citizens' organizations thus can help make urban policy. The practice of identifying issues from the bottom up helps motivate wide participation and inoculate participants against strategic framing attempts by media or opponents.

Are church-based community organizations a social movement? Perhaps they are better understood as locally based interest organizations (Karapin 1994). The answer may be that grassroots citizens' organizations take on a form specific to liberal democracies (Meyer and Tarrow 1998a; Tarrow 1998b). Ongoing resources and accommodation by the state have fostered their professionalization (McCarthy and Zald 1977). In a context where movements are accommodated – perhaps pacified – how are we to judge whether they have won meaningful access or been coopted? I suggest that judgments about cooptation cannot be made without considering the political opportunity for a given movement (see Katzenstein 1998; Swarts 2001). Reforms are most likely when "a system is challenged fundamentally by a range of social movements" (Tarrow 1996:60). This is the *opposite* of the current American context for left-of-center social movements. We should therefore expect significant concessions for urban community organizations to be rare and extremely hard won. Most church-based organizations, including PACT and MCU, must regularly demonstrate their ability to mobilize large numbers just to command regular access to top officials.[38] Even relatively limited distributive issues are won only with laborious mass mobilization and careful issue selection and framing. For example, just to get one city council member to support a drug treatment facility, one PACT church's organizing committee knocked on 400 neighborhood doors to gain local support and mobilized 200 people to meet with the council member.[39] Redistributive and regulatory issues are even harder to undertake (Lowi 1964; Peterson 1981).

PACT and MCU share a process, language, and set of strategies with about 150 similar organizations in the United States. They place a heavy

---

[38] Church-based organizations that gain more institutionalized access to and the right of consultation with officials have often demonstrated greater mobilization capacity than PACT or MCU – for example, 6,000 to 8,000 members. PACT and MCU have ongoing consulting relationships with city council members and specific allies, but have thus far not mobilized the numbers to command ongoing access to the mayor's office, regardless of occupant. CBOs are more vulnerable than more powerful interest groups to changes in administration: For example, PACT had regular access to Mayor Susan Hammer and her budget director but had to reestablish this access with her successor, Ron Gonzalez, elected in 1998.

[39] Yet just one initiative of the well-connected, elite-led St. Louis 2004 initiative raised $751 million for a major community development project. This project, of course, does nothing to affect the ongoing structural forces creating misery in such neighborhoods.

emphasis both on democratic process and civic skills training and on getting political results. This dual focus on democratic education and pragmatic results is unusual in contemporary American voluntary associations and is worth examining for its advantages and drawbacks. As social policy-making is increasingly devolved to the state and city levels, we need to better understand how such locally based organizations succeed and fail at influencing it.

4

State Pacts, Elites, and Social Movements in Mexico's Transition to Democracy

Jorge Cadena-Roa

Theories of democratic transitions as pacts among elites build on the elite paradigm and on theories of the authoritarian state. Juan Linz (1975) conceived of the authoritarian state as a type of political regime intermediate between democracy and totalitarianism. Authoritarian states have limited, nonresponsible political pluralism and no independent political mobilization (Linz 1975, p. 264). State elites are considered the main, if not the only, consequential actors. They are responsible for limiting pluralism by de facto and de jure means, controlling, demobilizing, and repressing challengers. From that perspective, it is not surprising that the "pact school" (Burton and Higley 1987; Diamond and Linz 1989; Higley and Gunther 1992; O'Donnell and Schmitter 1986; Przeworski 1990, 1991) explains democratization as a result of pacts among elites – the main, if not the only, consequential actors. Thus, analysis of rational decision making among elites suffices for the interpretation of contentious events and makes irrelevant the study of social movements since they are either inconsequential or manipulated.[1]

The Mexican transition to democracy departs from the pact-school model in a number of ways. Transitions have usually been from nonelected authoritarian governments to elected representative governments, but Mexico's transition to democracy did not mean merely the establishing or reintroduction of parties and elections: Elections for president and Congress have taken place regularly since 1920. Transitions have usually been sudden events, but the Mexican transition has been a gradual and

---

[1] The pact school includes elite-centered and rational-choice models of consensual transition that highlight the construction of elite "pacts" (or "transitions from above" or "elite settlements"); see Edles (1995, p. 355).

erratic process; it started in the 1970s and it took almost three decades to come to term. The Mexican transition was not triggered by the death of an aging dictator, overthrow of a rigid dictatorship, overwhelming division within the elites, insurrection by a large movement demanding radical political change, or any other major threat to elites' tenure, interests, or resources capable of forcing them into quick action. Democratic transitions have usually been analyzed as elite-centered processes, but in Mexico social movements and popular protests have been crucial to the democratization process. The Mexican transition has taken place without elite pacting,[2] without drafting and ratifying a new Constitution, and without a change in the party controlling executive power prior to December 2000.

Drawing evidence from the Mexican case, this essay argues that social movements do have significant consequences in democratization processes. In place of an elite-centered approach to democratic transitions, this essay calls for an approach to transitions sensitive to the interweaving of contentious movements and routine politics.

There are many competing definitions of democracy and different sequences of democratization. Charles Tilly (1998, p. 3) argues that "a regime is democratic in so far as it maintains broad citizenship, equal citizenship, binding consultation of citizens at large with respect to governmental activities and personnel, as well as protection of citizens from arbitrary action by governmental agents." Tilly calls net shifts in all these factors "protected consultation," and democratization consists in any net shift toward protected consultation. Democratization requires, McAdam, Tarrow, and Tilly (2001) claim, that some groups (governmental elites, counterelites, people demanding it for themselves, a combination of these) want such a shift to take place and are willing to make efforts to effectuate it, while others who see their vested rights and privileges threatened oppose it. Thus, "democracy results from, mobilizes, and reshapes popular contention" (McAdam et al. 2001, p. xx). Accordingly, this essay considers democratization as any net shifts in protected consultation, including those that result from popular contention.

In Mexico's democratization process, different groups built alternative and independent networks of trust (social organizations and parties) and urged a legal-institutional framework to protect citizens' rights. The pact

---

[2] There was an elite pact in 1928–9 that cemented the "revolutionary family" and excluded other elite factions – the Catholic Church, business, and the emergent middle class (Knight 1992).

school considers alternation in power and drafting and ratifying a new Constitution as hard evidence that this transition has taken place. Only the first had occurred as of December 2000, but compared to the 1970s, 1980s, and early 1990s, there have been clear shifts toward protected consultation. This essay examines how these net shifts took place and demonstrates the critical impact of popular actions in that process.

Multiple paths to democracy arise because transitions are path-dependent processes: Where you can get to depends on where you are coming from. Thus, the analysis of the Mexican transition to democracy begs the question: Transition from where? After answering this question, I analyze Mexico's "social movement for democracy" through some of the key contentious events that pushed people to forge independent organizations and forced parties to change their situation.

Transition from Where?

The contemporary Mexican state was formed by the military and political leaders of the popular revolution that defeated the regime of Porfirio Diaz (1877–1910). The revolutionary state swept away the Porfirian oligarchy and army, and enacted a political program that stressed social justice and included a developmental state, land reform, labor protection, public education, and welfare policies (subsidized staple foods, health services, etc.). The legitimacy of the postrevolutionary state came from popular support for the revolutionary project, not from democratic processes.

Mexico's remarkably prolonged political stability during the twentieth century is well known in Latin American countries, most of whose political regimes during the 1960s and 1970s were characterized by instability, frequent coups, barrack rebellions, and periods of indiscriminate violation of human rights.[3] In these decades, Mexico had a salient place among developing countries as a "soft," even "benign," authoritarian state. Although a single party controlled the political system, private enterprise flourished, elections for president and Congress took place regularly since 1920, and Mexico's presidents served strictly limited terms.

It is not easy to briefly describe the Mexican state without attaching to it a label that might obscure rather than illuminate its most important features. The Mexican state has been described both as a *demodura* (a combination

---

[3] The last military rebellion that led to the fall of a constitutional government in Mexico was in 1920. The last – unsuccessful – military uprising was in 1929.

of *demo*cracia [democracy] and dicta*dura* [dictatorship] – in Spanish *dura* also means "hard," "tough") and as a *dictablanda* (a combination of *dicta*dura and *blanda*, which means "soft"). These puns allude to the fact that the Mexican state and political system are complex hybrids that up to the 1970s combined several disparate elements:

(*a*) *A Presidential System of Government.* Despite the Constitution, which established a republican system with checks and balances, the legislative and judiciary branches were not truly independent of the executive branch, which concentrated power in a single person, the president of the republic. The president could appoint and remove without almost any restriction all the cabinet members, including the attorney general and the regent of the Federal District. The president has been head of a strong executive branch, commander in chief of the armed forces, and leader of the state party during his term (Carpizo 1978; González Casanova 1970). The president serves a six-year term with no possibility of reelection.

(*b*) *A Highly Centralized Regime.* On paper, Mexico is a federal republic with thirty-one formally sovereign states and one Federal District. In practice, the president has controlled the selection of candidates for elective office, including members of Congress, state governors, and the president's successor. The president can remove governors and members of Congress through impeachment. The states reproduce internally the same centralized structure: The governor dominates the state judiciary and legislative branches and has significant leverage in the selection of candidates for state offices.

(*c*) *Subordination of the Armed Forces to Civilian Control through the President and No Military Participation in Politics* (Camp 1992; Rondfeldt 1984). The military has been out of direct power since 1946, when the last military general elected president left his seat to an elected civilian.

(*d*) *A State Party Whose Primary Function Has Been to Bring Together the Main Factions of the "Revolutionary Family," That Is, the Social Forces That Participated in the Revolution and Therefore Felt the Right to Intervene in Mexico's Political Affairs.* The party opened a space where the revolutionary elites could negotiate to avoid open divisions and strife. President Plutarco Elías Calles called for the formation of the National Revolutionary Party (PNR 1929) as a coalition of military, political, and social forces.[4] President

---

[4] In 1928 President-Elect Alvaro Obregón was assassinated, leading to a sharp division in the revolutionary elite. Outgoing President Plutarco Elías Calles called for the foundation of a "party of parties" and political notables. The nature of this party "would not be to compete

Lázaro Cárdenas reorganized it into the Mexican Revolution Party (PRM 1938), and President Manuel Avila Camacho turned it into the Institutional Revolutionary Party (PRI 1946), as it is known today. The party has been adaptable and pragmatic (Anderson and Cockroft 1972) within two limits: maintain social order and promote capitalist development (Reyna 1977). The party has served as the electoral organ of the state, uses the national colors in its emblem, and has depended on the state for its financial resources.

(e) An Electoral System That Was Not Free, Impartial, or Fair. The 1946 Federal Electoral Law regulated electoral matters. According to it, all males twenty-one years of age and older, and married males eighteen years of age and older, had the right to vote. Women's right to vote and be elected in municipal elections was granted in 1947 and extended to national elections in 1953. In 1969 the law was amended to grant all persons eighteen and older the right to vote. To have their names printed on the ballot, candidates must be nominated by a party. Parties were required to be national and registered before the secretary of interior – proscribing, in practice, independent candidates and regional parties. To obtain registration, parties had to prove that they had at least 2,500 members in two-thirds of the federal entities and no fewer than 75,000 members nationwide. The organization and supervision of all federal elections were centralized in the Federal Electoral Commission (created in 1951), which was chaired by the secretary of the interior. The government and the PRI together had a majority vote in the Commission. The National Electoral Register, a federal office, was charged with defining district boundaries and compiling voter registration lists. The Chamber of Deputies, where the PRI had the majority vote, was responsible for approving the results of presidential and congressional elections.

(f) A Noncompetitive Multiparty System. There were only four registered parties that could participate in elections: the National Action Party (PAN), the Institutional Revolutionary Party (PRI), the Popular Socialist Party (PPS), and the Authentic Party of the Mexican Revolution (PARM). In election times the PRI received resources, personnel, and information from the government and, with the complicity of the government, used fraud to manipulate electoral results (Craig and Cornelius 1995; Molinar 1990).

with other parties for the taking and preservation of power, but rather the establishment of a mechanism by which existing sharp controversies within the governing group could be peacefully resolved, particularly those revolving around the transmission of power nationally or locally" (Meyer 1977a, p. 14).

(g) *Corporatist Organizations Affiliated with the State Party That Secured Political Control of Peasants and of Blue- and White-Collar Workers.* Corporatist organizations' leaders represented the interests of the government (and ultimately those of the president, who could arbitrarily remove them), their personal and group interests, and, last *and least*, the interests of their rank and file (Meyer 1977b). Union leaders (particularly those of large national unions) usually had congressional seats subject to party discipline.

(h) *A Process of Negotiation and Bargaining between Governmental Agents and Challenger Groups.* This process often assumed the form of clientage, delivering concessions and benefits in exchange for political support (Cornelius and Craig 1991, pp. 40–1) and cooption, that is, accommodation of challengers' demands in exchange for subordination to the government (Anderson and Cockroft 1972, p. 232).

(i) *A Developmental Mission That Eventually Should Have Led to Social Justice and Equitable Development.* Following 1940, Mexico went through several decades of sustained economic growth (over 6% annually on average) that transformed the country from rural to urban and from agrarian to semi-industrialized, meeting the economic expectations of broad sectors of society. Yet promises of further economic growth and social justice were shaken in the 1970s by budget deficits, inflation, capital flight, and peso devaluation. In the 1980s and 1990s, hopes for economic progress turned into external and domestic debt, budget austerity, diminishing real wages, cuts in consumer subsidies, and structural adjustment policies. The end of sustained economic growth damaged one of the pillars that provided legitimacy to the authoritarian regime.

(j) *A Repressive Response to Political Opposition.* When representation, participation, negotiation, patronage, and cooption failed, dismantling of challenging organizations and repression of individual leaders – which sometimes included gross violations of human rights – appeared as the state's last resource for monopolizing power. There is no question that repression has always been a feature of the Mexican state's domination, but it has not been its main component (Concha 1988). Like any other authoritarian state, the Mexican state has been highly intolerant of the formation of independent centers of political dissidence. Even when the state makes concessions on particular demands, it never fails to "discipline" the mobilized groups (Purcell 1977).

Given these characteristics of the Mexican state, democratization in Mexico could not mean simply the reintroduction or creation of parties and elections in some kind of pacted "big bang." Transition to democracy from an authoritarian postrevolutionary state required the formation of an institutional framework to support a truly competitive multiparty system with free and fair elections; an institutional framework to protect citizens' rights from arbitrary action from government agents; and limits to governmental unresponsiveness and unaccountability.

The Emergence of the Social Movement for Democracy

A series of contentious events from the 1940s on, and especially their collective interpretation by elites and ordinary Mexicans, changed the meaning and significance that leaders, organizations, and common people attributed to the postrevolutionary state. This interpretation resulted from and amplified a process of "cognitive liberation" (McAdam 1982) that tended to erode the symbolic capital of the postrevolutionary state, to diminish its legitimacy, and to increase the number of protest events that could not be resolved within the prevailing political arrangements. This process produced an anticooptation ideology that rejected the government's disposition to accommodate challengers' demands in exchange for their subordination or at least their partial support for the state party. The emergence of uncooptable leaders, groups, and networks expressed itself in demands for organizational autonomy and independence from the state and the PRI. The spread of stubborn leaders and organizations in which the anticooption ideology prevailed started to make the state rely far more on the use of repression.

For brevity, I shall label as the "social movement for democracy" the emergence, diffusion, and knitting together of uncooptable leaders, groups, and networks that shared the interpretation of the postrevolutionary state as one with an increasing antipopular bias.[5] According to their interpretation, this antipopular bias was manifest in the delays in completing the revolutionary project, in the neglect of the demands of the classes that made the revolution, in the ineffectiveness of legal and institutional channels to make the state responsive to popular demands, in the policies that favored business over the people, and in repression of peasants and labor.

---

[5] The social movement for democracy is an *analytical category* to describe a broad and diffuse movement that includes organizations from different social groups encompassing "the actions of organizations and their members [and] the actions of nonmembers in activities that organizations have nothing to do with, and may even oppose" (Oliver 1989, p. 1). Empirically, the social movement for democracy comprises several networks of popular, cadre, and religious organizations, networks of leaders, and pockets of aggrieved populations.

Many of the movements we are about to refer to did not consider themselves as struggling for democracy; often they mainly sought specific rights or better treatment for particular groups. Nonetheless, all these movements (and many others) demanded net shifts toward protected consultation. Thus, if only in retrospect, they may be seen as having pressed the state to move toward greater democracy.

Previous accounts of popular protest in Mexico have rarely looked for the threads of the networks that compose the social movement for democracy in Mexico. Due to the clandestine, informal, or discreet nature of most popular, cadre, and religious organizations, there are no systematic records of their activities and trajectories. Save a few notable exceptions, most secondary sources assumed that mobilization was a nonproblematic response to grievances caused by structural factors. Thus, they rarely paid attention to the role of leaders and organizations and the complex linkages among them. Notwithstanding these limitations, the following sections attempt to document the emergence of the networks of popular, cadre, and religious organizations, and their linkages with pockets of aggrieved populations, that I refer to as the social movement for democracy.

The Popular Challenge – Peasants, Workers, and Teachers

Beginning in the 1940s, several groups challenged the corporatist and authoritarian features of the postrevolutionary Mexican state. The perception that the governments following the Lázaro Cárdenas administration (1934–40) were delaying the "revolutionary project" written into the 1917 Constitution, and neglecting state compromises with peasants, started taking root. The Agrarian Code was reformed in 1942 and 1946, with the result that "protection [of large landowners from peasant land claims] was easier to obtain, while public investment in irrigation works and rural infrastructure and preferential credit were targeted [for] large-scale agro-export enterprises in the north-west" (Harvey 1990, p. 10). Many peasant organizations interpreted the Agrarian Code amendments not as the end of land reform but as the beginning of a full-scale agrarian counterreform. This interpretation suggested that peasants could have their just demands met only through increased contention and independent organization and action.

Around 1943, Rubén Jaramillo, a former Zapatista revolutionary fighter and Protestant minister (Macín 1985), frustrated by the slow pace of agrarian reform, started a guerrilla war in the state of Morelos. The government gave him amnesty, and in 1944 Jaramillo returned to legal political activities. He founded an independent political party that ran candidates for governor in 1945 and 1952, losing in rigged elections (Ravelo 1978). An invasion of agrarian land and the defense of it pushed Jaramillo again into a guerrilla movement; in 1962, a paramilitary group murdered him and his family (Jaramillo and Manjarréz 1967). This case is emblematic of many other peasant movements: "Most of these actions [invasion of agrarian properties exceeding the legal limits] were carried out by groups of peasants who had gone through all the legal procedures to obtain the land, [and] though legally entitled to it, had never received it.... To them, invading is the logical continuation of ineffective legal procedures" (Montes de Oca 1977, p. 58). Invasions of agrarian land and armed defense of what the peasants considered themselves entitled to were "politics by other means" (McAdam, McCarthy and Zald 1988), the means used when routine, legal, and electoral channels were ineffective.

In 1958 several labor unions sought increases in wages and benefits. What started as a labor–management conflict about economic demands turned into a political conflict in which the workers challenged the tight relation among corporatist union leaders, the PRI, and the government. Oil industry workers demanded the derogation from union ordinances of mandatory collective affiliation with the PRI (Pellicer 1968). A telegraph union strike was followed by railroad and teachers' union strikes that had been organized at the grassroots level, outside the control of the progovernment union bosses and in opposition to them. In early 1958, railroad workers demanded a wage increase. The union bosses sought and obtained less than the rank-and-file workers demanded. A movement repudiating the bosses and calling for a democratized union took off. The Ministry of Labor declared illegal the new union committee. In 1959, army troops were sent to guard rail installations, and the dissident leaders were taken into custody and held incommunicado. The strike was finally broken, and the dissident leaders were sentenced to sixteen years in prison on the charge of "social dissolution" (Alonso 1972; Stevens 1970, 1974). Around 1960 the leader of the teachers' union was also put in jail on the charge of social dissolution, and the movement was repressed (Loyo 1979). This period of repression of independent unions was interpreted as proof that unions were not conducive to the representation and promotion of workers' interests but were instead means for controlling labor and enriching corporatist union leaders.

Memories of these struggles and their outcomes were ever-present in later episodes of contention.[6]

After these events, several groups concerned with governmental policies toward labor and peasants united in 1961, under the auspices of former president Lázaro Cárdenas, in the National Liberation Movement (MLN). The Cardenistas (the PRI's left wing), independent intellectuals, the Mexican Communist Party (PCM), the PPS, and many peasant, labor, student, and women's organizations joined the MLN. The MLN raised nationalist and anti-imperialist banners, called for solidarity with the Cuban revolution, and demanded respect for constitutional rights, freedom for political prisoners, the continuation of agrarian reform, and the democratization of labor and peasant organizations. In the wake of the 1964 presidential election the MLN split: The Cardenistas and the PPS supported the PRI's presidential candidate, while other groups formed an electoral front and ran a Communist peasant leader for president.

Many social and political leaders and intellectuals met in the MLN, facilitating communication and interaction among them and the groups they represented. The MLN had a strong influence on the formation and amplification of the social movement for democracy. Many of their members founded political parties, supported social movements, and became faculty members, editorialists and writers, guerrilla fighters, and government officials (Maciel 1990).

Besides the nationwide processes of contention reviewed previously, there were several more at the local level. One of them was staged in Guerrero by students, faculty, and graduates from teacher training colleges (*normalistas*) frustrated with the poor results of peasant and labor struggles. The police repressed a peaceful meeting called by the Civic Association of Guerrero (ACG), causing several casualties. The Federal Congress unseated the governor, the state congress appointed an interim governor, and the ACG was allowed to participate in a number of city councils. In 1962 the ACG decided to run independent candidates in the municipal elections, but local hardliners rigged the elections. The ACG called fraud and a meeting was violently repressed. One of the leaders, schoolteacher Genaro

---

[6] Stevens reports that "several of the most articulate informants, while discussing the impact of their activities, referred repeatedly to the railroad strikes of 1958–1959, which they described as the first widespread protest movement of Mexico's post-Revolutionary period. Indeed, the occurrence of the railroad strikes and their eventual outcome was seen by these informants as a conclusive answer to the often-posed question: 'Is the Mexican revolution dead?'" (Stevens 1974, p. 16).

Vázquez, was charged with being responsible for the shootout and arrested in 1966. In 1968 an armed commando freed him from jail, turning the local, legally oriented ACG into a guerrilla organization that was active until 1972 (Estrada 1986, 1994).

In 1967, in Atoyac, Guerrero, the police repressed a peaceful demonstration demanding the resignation of an elementary school principal; several demonstrators were killed. The leader of the movement, schoolteacher Lucio Cabañas, was charged with the casualties. Cabañas fled and started a guerrilla movement that was active in Guerrero between 1967 and 1974.

Cabañas's story parallels that of Vázquez. Both were elementary school teachers who had studied in the Escuela Normal Rural de Ayotzinapa (with a socialist tradition dating from the Cárdenas administration). Both had been active in the teachers' union's struggle for democratization, in the MLN, and in the popular movement against the governor of Guerrero (Castillo 1986; Ortíz 1972; Suárez 1976). Due to the harassment and repression of their legal activities, they turned to armed movements. These parallels suggest that routine and nonroutine politics are extremes of a continuum rather than unrelated poles (Goldstone 1998). The closure of legal channels for raising popular demands pushed leaders out of legal (but not tolerated) protests and into illegal ones.

In the northern state of Chihuahua, a movement demanding the division of a large landholding failed to get a satisfactory response from the authorities. A small guerrilla group composed of students, *normalista* teachers, and peasants attacked the army barracks. The guerrilla leaders were members of the PPS and former leaders of a student strike at the National Polytechnic Institute (IPN) that was broken in 1956 by army troops. The attack on the army barracks occurred on September 23, 1965, the anniversary of the army occupation of the IPN. Most of the guerrillas died (Guevara Niebla 1988; Rascón and Ruíz 1986). The governor, a fighter in the Mexican Revolution of 1910 under Pancho Villa (Camp 1995), ordered his troops to bury the guerrillas' bodies in unmarked graves without coffins. "They wanted land, give it to them until they are satisfied," he reportedly said. To add a dramatic touch, the dead soldiers were buried with military honors (Hirales 1982; Lau 1991).

Such barbaric acts radicalized many people. This radicalization also affected Christian groups, both Catholics and Protestants. Around the mid-1960s, after the changes set in motion by the Second Vatican Council (1961–5), structures and practices of the Catholic Church all over the world were reformed. In Latin America, these changes received a significant impulse

117

after the resolutions of the Second Latin American Episcopal Conference, which many Catholics interpreted as legitimizing their participation in popular movements aimed at establishing the reign of Christ on earth. Christian base communities (CBCs) that had embraced Liberation Theology and the Preferential Option for the Poor moved into popular neighborhoods and indigenous areas with the idea of sharing "poor people's misery and suffering" (Concha, Gary, and Salas 1986, p. 309). They created coops, literacy projects, and workshops and developed communitarian and democratic practices. Some CBC members became popular leaders, while others joined left-wing parties and organizations. A radical tendency began to emerge among priests close to student and labor organizations. A whole array of religious organizations, centers of Christian theological reflection, publications, and nonprofit organizations providing professional and technical services inspired by Liberation Theology were founded (Carr 1992; de la Rosa 1985; Nuñez 1990).

State repression, discretionary use of law, and electoral fraud confirmed these challengers' most somber perceptions about the state's antipopular bias. Within a few years, *normalista* schools and most public universities and polytechnic schools became centers of diffusion of the anti-PRI and anticooption ideology. *Normalista* students denounced the government's failure to enforce the Constitution and the revolutionary program, especially regarding agrarian reform and political rights. Polytechnic and public university students were particularly radical, many embracing Marxism and attempting to establish links with industrial workers (Orozco 1976).

Schoolteachers and polytechnic and university students and faculty knitted together loose networks connecting leaders of social movements and political organizations with pockets of aggrieved populations all over the country. The formation and amplification of these networks and the changes in the interpretive understanding of the state's responses to popular movements were simultaneous processes. More precisely, they were interactive, derived from debates over movements' goals and state responses, reactions to state responses, and so on.

Student Movements, 1960–1968

The student movement proved to be crucial for the amplification of networks that constituted the social movement for democracy and for the diffusion of the anticooption ideology. From 1960 on, public university students all over the country supported local popular movements and demanded autonomy and reforms of university ordinances. Around 1963, the PCM sponsored the creation of a broad front of student organizations (Guevara Niebla 1988).

In Mexico, as in other countries, a large student movement emerged in 1968. It started as a protest against riot police brutality in police actions to stop a street fight between rival high school students. The movement got the support of authorities at Mexico's largest university, the National Automous University of Mexico (UNAM), who were appalled by police brutality and the violation of the university's autonomy. Over ten weeks, the protest evolved into an impressive student movement urging respect for citizens' rights and accountability of state authorities. The movement council made seven demands: release of all political prisoners (including prisoners from the 1958–9 labor strikes charged with social dissolution), resignation of police chiefs, abolition of the "grenadiers," abolition of the riot police corps, repeal of the infamous social dissolution law, compensation to the victims of repression, and investigation of those responsible for repression and violence against students. The students tried to mobilize support from the population of Mexico City with increasing success. The movement was brutally repressed on October 2, 1968, leaving several hundred students and bystanders killed in Tlatelolco Square. Many more were arrested and held incommunicado. The Congress applauded the army intervention and condemned the students' pacific meeting as "a subversive action . . . perpetrated by foreign elements" (Stevens 1974, p. 238). After faulty trials, sixty-eight persons were found guilty on counts such as incitement to riot, sedition, property damage, homicide, looting, illegal possession of arms, and attacks on agents of public authority. The sentences ranged from three to seventeen years in prison (Guevara Niebla 1978; Poniatowska 1975; Stevens 1974).

Despite being just one more in an already long list of repressive actions demonstrating that legal action and the courts failed to protect citizens' rights from governmental abuse, the Tlatelolco massacre was constructed as the watershed that divided Mexican postrevolutionary history. It took place in the country's capital at a moment when "the whole world was watching," just ten days before the inauguration of the nineteenth Olympic Games, which Mexico was hosting. It severely damaged the state's legitimacy and alienated intellectuals, faculty members, and several cohorts of students from public universities and colleges. The interpretation of the Tlatelolco massacre influenced all debates on the means and goals of social change in Mexico.

119

By the end of the 1960s, the redefinition of the postrevolutionary state had extended beyond the realm of ideas. This redefinition had multiple organizational expressions whose identity was based on the anticooption ideology. I call these organizational expressions social movement for democracy, suggesting that they all pursued increased protected consultation. In the course of the following decades, these organizations converged into several networks.

Transition to Democracy

The transition to democracy in Mexico did not start with any obvious structural weakness in state power. There was no death of an aging dictator, no collapse of a rigid dictatorship, no overwhelming division within the elites, no insurrection by a large movement demanding radical political change, or any other major threat to elites tenure. By the late 1960s, the state apparatus was strong, the elites backed the president, and challengers were isolated and repressed without further noticeable consequences. But the state's symbolic capital and underlying political myth were eroding quickly. Why did the postrevolutionary state systematically repress groups from the revolutionary classes that demanded the enforcement of the revolutionary project? Well, it was widely said, maybe the state was no longer revolutionary.

Arguably, the Tlatelolco massacre ended one cycle of contention in Mexico in which peasants, workers, teachers, and other grassroots groups had appealed to the revolutionary state for aid and met unexpected repression. Yet following Tlatelolco there began a new cycle, based on a strong oppositionist identity and anticooption ideology showing that the delegitimization of the postrevolutionary state was a given among numerous popular groups. Thus, in the early 1970s, Mexico's transition to democracy from an authoritarian postrevolutionary state began with efforts to create an effective opposition to the government and the PRI that controlled it. At the same time, the PRI government itself tried to head off such efforts with liberalizing reforms.

The Democratic Opening

Lame-duck president Gustavo Díaz Ordaz accepted full responsibility for the Tlatelolco massacre, paving the way for his handpicked successor in office, Luis Echeverría. During his campaign, Echeverría distanced himself politically from Díaz Ordaz and, once in office, he adopted a neo-populist, nationalist, and reformist discourse. The Echeverría administration started a liberalization process (the "Democratic Opening") aimed at legitimizing the regime and reconciling the state with popular groups. The problem for the governmental elites was legitimacy, not democracy. Liberalization aimed to incorporate popular organizations in the polity while keeping them subordinated to elite interests, not to set the conditions for elite replacement or to indiscriminately open the polity.

The administration introduced some reforms in response to the student movement. In 1970, the Congress repealed the social dissolution law and passed an amnesty law for prisoners convicted on charges related to political activities – two demands of the student movement. Minor reforms of the electoral laws were passed as well. The Echeverría administration made a point of coopting intellectuals and young professionals into the government. These policies caused serious tensions between the new administration and PRI's hardliners, the "emissaries of the past," as Echeverría himself derided them.

At the time, several public high schools, universities, polytechnic schools, and teacher training colleges had come under left-wing influence. Students in the public education system were the main targets of left-wing recruiting and mobilizing efforts.[7] The dramatic increase in the number of college students during the late 1960s and 1970s increased the pool of individuals with structural availability for political mobilization.[8] In many public universities, student movements sought participation in university government.[9] In

---

[7] This confirms Klandermans and Oegema's (1987, p. 526) finding that "it is not that the more highly educated individuals who are sensitive to political or economic developments create new mobilization potentials but that these individuals are more connected with social networks engaged in recruitment."

[8] The total number of registered college students rose from 75,300 in 1960 to 129,100 in 1966 (a 71.5% increase), to 177,400 in 1968 (a 37% increase compared to 1966), and to 271,200 in 1970 (a 52% increase compared to 1968). By 1980 the total number of registered college students had increased to 838,000 (a 309% increase over the decade). Along with this quantitative change, the composition of the student body also changed dramatically. The increase in female over male students, of first-generation college students over students with college-educated parents, of low-income compared to medium- and high-income students, and of part-time, working students over full-time students were all significant (Casillas 1987).

[9] In the Autonomous University of Puebla (UAP), a student and faculty movement promoted a model of the "popular university": public universities closely linked with popular movements of peasants, street vendors, and urban settlers. Their motto was "For a critical, scientific, and popular university," in which "scientific" stands for "Marxist." The students provided

response to leftist activities on campus, a peaceful student demonstration was repressed by a secret paramilitary group in June 1971, killing about fifty students in Mexico City's streets. The authorities claimed that two antagonistic student groups had clashed, denying responsibility for the massacre (Guevara Niebla 1988). There was no inquiry into the crimes, and no suspect was ever brought to justice.[10]

This episode produced an impasse for the student movement because it showed that repression of peaceful demonstrations would persist despite the Democratic Opening. Legal and institutional protection of citizens' rights against arbitrary action from governmental agents and governmental accountability were seen as null amid the campus flowering of Marxist culture, unparalleled in Latin America (Carr 1992), that already had established prolific means to influence public opinion. Numerous books, magazines, and other forms of propaganda made Marxist views and class analysis perspectives ever-present in most debates. It was widely believed that repression came not from a revolutionary state but from a reactionary and bourgeois state. According to this interpretation, repression of students without further consequences was possible because of students' lack of links to, and support from, popular groups. Thus, establishing links with popular groups (building a "popular base") became the top priority of radicalized student organizations (Bennett 1992).

Maoist groups arguably became the most influential (but not the only) groups in the formation of autonomous social movement organizations with nonnegotiable autonomy from the government and the state party. The Maoist response to the bizarre debates that plagued and divided the Mexican left wing[11] was the "massline:" to confront pressing questions

free legal advice, health services, and support in mobilizations. Several public universities adopted similar processes, embracing populist and sometimes radical positions at the cost of academic studies. Besides the UAP, the most notorious were the autonomous universities of Sinaloa, Sonora, Nayarit, Oaxaca, Guerrero, and the Agriculture School (Guevara Niebla 1988).

[10] Nobody, civilian or authority, was brought to justice for these crimes. Both the regent, Alfonso Martínez, and the chief of the police, Rogelio Flores, were politically rehabilitated shortly thereafter. The PRI made Flores governor of Nayarit for the period 1975–81 and Martínez governor of Nuevo León for the period 1979–85.

[11] The Mexican left wing had agreed by then on the need for a socialist revolution but differed on matters such as the following: Which class should lead the revolution, peasants or workers? What should be the role of intellectuals – should they lead or follow? What should be the relation between party and masses – Leninist "democratic centralism" or the Maoist "mass line"? Who were the enemies, imperialism, the state, the bourgeoisie, reformers? Which enemy should be fought against first, the domestic bourgeoisie or imperialism?

with a practical criterion of truth. As the CBCs had done before, Maoist organizations moved many cadres into poor urban neighborhoods and rural communities with the purpose of addressing their most immediate needs. Despite the Maoists' revolutionary rhetoric and rejection of institutional politics, their practical orientation led them to avoid direct confrontation with governmental authorities. Two Maoist cadre organizations, composed of radicalized faculty and students, had the greatest influence: the Popular Politics Group and the Companion Revolutionary Organization. The rising cycle of popular movements from the 1970s on was closely linked with the presence of interconnected radical cadre organizations that rejected open political participation, criticized registered parties, and called for nonparticipation in electoral contests (Bouchier 1988).

The Echeverría administration tried to strengthen the populist features of the state and announced "Shared Development" policies. A Tripartite National Commission, a corporatist consultation commission with representatives from business, labor, and the administration, parallel to Congress and the party system, was created to strengthen the state and the office of the president as the ultimate arbiters of social conflict. The economic elites opposed state intervention in the economy and the president's populist rhetoric, which they said encouraged extremists and discouraged investment. After bitter confrontations with business leaders, the administration dropped a tax reform. Despite fiscal constraints, the administration expanded state spending, created a large number of commissions and councils, and enlarged the state-owned economic sector. These policies created a huge budget deficit that, despite being balanced with foreign debt, raised inflation. The economic elites responded in 1975 by founding the Business Coordinating Council, an independent high-level coordinating board to oppose governmental policies.

On November 18, 1976, twelve days before finishing his six-year term, in response to peasant land invasions, President Echeverría decreed the expropriation of 100,000 hectares of highly productive irrigated land in Sonora and Sinaloa that were turned into *ejidos* – a form of peasant communal property (Robles and Moguel 1990). This unilateral decision showed the lack of checks and balances on the executive branch and was strongly resented by the economic elites.

Despite its efforts at reform, the Echeverría administration was a complete failure. Economically, it was unable to secure a sound fiscal basis for state revenue; at the same time, it increased the budget deficit, foreign debt, and inflation. This situation, along with the distrust by economic

123

elites, provoked capital flight and the first devaluation of the peso since 1954. Politically, the administration first encouraged union insurgency, to the despair of the traditional union leaders, but when the conflict with the economic elites grew, the administration leaned on PRI's labor sector. Corporatist labor organizations affiliated with the PRI became the most conservative sector of the ruling coalition (Craig and Cornelius 1995). After the 1976 expropriation of agrarian land, the business sector broke with the administration. The Democratic Opening produced no real changes in the party system; an increase in the number of party deputies in 1972 affected the already registered parties. The "dirty war" against urban and rural guerrillas, including the use of paramilitary forces and violent repression, caused human rights abuses. The Shared Development plan thus led to an economic crisis.

The Political Reform

Despite the political turmoil just described (union independence, urban and agrarian land seizures, urban and rural guerrilla actions, a split between the economic and governmental elites) and the economic crisis aggravated by the administration's populist policies, the world of parties and elections remained undisturbed. Together, the government and the PRI controlled the Federal Electoral Register (which defined district boundaries and compiled voter registration lists) and had a majority vote in the Federal Electoral Commission (which organized and supervised federal electoral contests) and in the Chamber of Deputies (which approved election results). Besides, the government was a zealous gatekeeper of the party system through the secretary of the interior (who granted, denied, or canceled party registration). In the 1976 election, not only did the number of registered parties remain the same as in 1970 but, even worse, only the PRI ran a presidential candidate. The PPS and the PARM supported, as they had since 1958, the PRI's candidate. Due to internal disputes, the PAN, a Catholic, conservative party associated with business, failed to nominate a presidential candidate. The PCM ran a presidential candidate, but since this party was not registered, his name did not appear on the ballot. The political opening did not open a thing and even damaged the façade of representative democracy and competitive elections that the postrevolutionary elites had built.

The administration of José López Portillo (1976–82) called for an "Alliance for Production" in an attempt to reduce labor militancy and restore business sector confidence. The administration launched a stabilization plan that included wage restraint and budgetary austerity. But these economic policies did not last long. Once oil was discovered in the southeast of the country, the administration embarked on a high growth program sustained by large deficits and foreign debt that used the oil as collateral. The state-owned economic sector continued to grow,[12] while the private sector received fiscal breaks, subsidies, and protection from foreign competitors. As a result of the Alliance for Production, the relations between the economic and governmental elites improved considerably and the economy grew rapidly again between 1978 and 1981 (8.2% annual average).

The administration announced a "Political Reform" to cool off the political turmoil inherited from the Echeverría administration. In fact, 1977 started a slow and erratic process toward the opening of the party system, the establishment of competitive elections, and the opening of the legislative branch to the opposition. The administration passed a new electoral law – the Federal Law of Political Organizations and Electoral Processes (LFOPPE). This law made registration of opposition parties easier and created incentives for their participation in elections. The LFOPPE almost doubled the size of the Chamber of Deputies (from over 200 to 400 seats) and introduced a mixed electoral system (300 seats were filled with deputies elected in single-member districts and 100 with deputies elected by proportional representation). In practice, this reform meant that the PRI would retreat to a comfortable majority, giving up at least 25% of its seats in the Chamber of Deputies to a more independent (though fragmented) opposition. Under the LFOPPE, three new parties (PCM, the Mexican Democratic Party [PDM], and PST) were registered for the 1979 federal elections, adding up to a total of seven registered parties.

The Political Reform aimed at incorporating dissident groups into a controlled electoral arena and channeling opposition representatives to a weak and subservient legislative branch. The reform had the unintended effect of redefining the relations between parties and movements. The demands of electoral politics and the crowded electoral calendar[13] shifted cadres and

---

[12] From 1970 to 1982 the number of state-owned enterprises rose from 272 to 1,155 (Rogozinski 1993).

[13] In a six-year term 1 president, 31 governors, 32 senators, and 600 deputies were elected in single-member districts, 200 deputies elected by proportional representation, 62 state legislatures (with a variable number of deputies), and about 4,800 mayors. To the strains of the electoral calendar should be added an increasing number of cases in which protests against fraud and manipulation of results followed election day.

leaders from the social movement sector to the institutional politics sector. Once a party obtained registration, it focused on keeping it. Since parties had to be national by law, they started to look for alliances with local movements. Local movements, for their part, looked for alliances with registered parties that could raise their demands before a national audience and nominate their leaders in local elections.

Once the PCM obtained registration, the likelihood of isolation and even repression of radical cadre organizations increased. These organizations believed that the Political Reform was an attempt to divide the left wing from the grass roots and prevent it from organizing a truly revolutionary party. For them, democracy (a change in the political regime) could only be achieved through a socialist revolution (through complete economic and social change). Thus, they decided not to participate in electoral politics.

With the withdrawal of the radical left from electoral politics, a more unified, more moderate, and less ideological left wing emerged. The Mexican Unified Socialist Party (PSUM) replaced the PCM in 1981, and the Mexican Socialist Party (PMS) replaced the former in 1987. In the radical left there were important coalitions too, like the National Union of the Revolutionary Left (1985) and the Federation of Parties of the Revolutionary Left (1987).

In the 1976 presidential election there were four registered parties and only one presidential candidate. As a result of the Political Reform, for the 1982 election, nine registered parties ran seven presidential candidates (the PPS and the PARM supported the PRI's candidate). The seven parties that participated in the 1979 midterm elections achieved definitive registration and two new parties got conditional registration.

The Alliance for Production restored business confidence but proved far too expensive for the country. The sand castle built on tax breaks for business, rising fiscal deficits and foreign debt,[14] unplanned growth of the state-owned economic sector, and lack of productivity in overprotected private industries tumbled when oil prices began to slide. By mid-1981, the country was plunged into a deep economic crisis. Capital flight placed strong pressure on the peso until it was devalued.

Lame-duck President José López Portillo blamed the business sector for the economic disaster, while business leaders blamed the government. The outcome of this dispute between economic and political elites was

---

[14] According to the Economic Commission for Latin America (ECLA), Mexico's foreign debt went from $33,946 billion in 1978 to $72,007 billion in 1981.

the secretly prepared nationalization of the private banks, announced by President López Portillo during his last State of the Union address on September 1, 1982. For the economic elites the nationalization of the banks proved, even more dramatically than the nationalization of agrarian land in 1976, that the Mexican authoritarian state, and the excessive and unchecked concentration of power in a single person, the head of the executive branch, could eventually turn against their interests. The breakdown of elite consensus was severe. In different ways, 1968, 1976, and 1982 dramatically showed the lack of protection of citizens' rights and the lack of consultation before making decisions that affected lives, property, and civil liberties. After 1982, accountability and protection from arbitrary action from governmental officials became a major goal for economic elites as well as popular and opposition groups.

The Break with the Past

President Miguel de la Madrid took office three months after the nationalization of the banks. It seemed that with the nationalized banks the government would have greater leverage over credit, investment, and production. But at the moment, the economy was in very bad shape and relations between the economic and governmental elites were profoundly damaged. Capital flight, investment strikes, resistance to tax reform, and foreign debt put the incoming administration in a feeble position. The government was under pressure on three fronts – the business sector, international banks, and popular movements.

With the business sector (which resented the nationalization of the banks as authoritarian and socialistic and as affecting the whole private sector, not only financial capital), the new administration tried to restore confidence. A few days after de la Madrid took office, the government passed a constitutional amendment limiting the expropriation powers of the executive. Later, the government paid in advance the compensation for the bank expropriation, gave incentives for the development of alternative financial brokers, and privatized or closed hundreds of state-owned companies. These market-oriented policies represented a decisive break with the past. They marked the end of populist, nationalist, protectionist, and state-led development. But for the private sector these measures were not enough. The state, and particularly the presidential system, had proved unreliable. Businesspeople and members of the Catholic Church began to increase their support for the PAN. A radical cohort of PANistas – some of whom had been personally affected by Echeverría's and López Portillo's erratic policies – took over the PAN. They were less compromising on electoral matters, more confrontational, and prone to use civil disobedience and contentious tactics (Loaeza 1999).

To restore the confidence of the international banks and keep the international markets open for Mexico, the administration signed a stabilization plan with the International Monetary Fund (IMF). The plan promoted market-oriented policies, liberalized international trade (Mexico signed the General Agreement on Tariffs and Trade [GATT] in 1986), reduced real wages, canceled subsidies for consumer products, and cut welfare spending.

Popular movements showed their discontent with the economic adjustment and the deterioration of their living conditions through increased protest activity. The "Plan de Ayala" National Coordinating Committee (CNPA), the National Coordinating Committee of the Urban Popular Movement (CONAMUP), and the National Coordinating Committee of Workers in Education (CNTE) got together in the National Front for Defense of Wages, Against Austerity, and the High Cost of Living. This front, along with the National Committee for the Defense of Popular Economy, formed the National Popular Assembly of Peasants and Workers. The assembly called for national civil strikes in 1983 and 1984. From then on, protest activities against price hikes and austerity policies lost their impulse, and protest activities related to electoral contests increased.

In 1983, the PAN won the mayoral elections in the largest and richest municipalities in Chihuahua and Durango. Giving up 25% of a subservient Chamber of Deputies in a bicameral legislative branch didn't seem a bad gambit to legitimate the authoritarian state – after all, the Senate was firmly closed to the opposition. But giving up city halls and governorships was a completely different story. In most states, protest activities related to electoral contests increased dramatically. Strong civil movements and parties with elite support (from the business sector, the Catholic Church, and the middle class) had taken the liberalization of the authoritarian regime seriously and wanted their votes to count. Violence erupted in numerous cases focused on electoral complaints.[15] Through noninstitutional means, civil movements demanded the enforcement of the rules of institutional politics.

---

[15] In 1985, protests against tallied elections included the blockage of international bridges in Acuña and Piedras Negras, the burning down of the municipal palace in Piedras Negras, and roadblocks on highways. In that same year, protestors in San Luis Rio Colorado, Sonora, set afire a police station and several squad cars and blocked border crossings. In Nuevo León the government repressed protests at the main gate of the government palace. In

In several places, coalitions between local organizations and national political parties were formed to defend the vote, despite their differences in
policy matters.

In Chihuahua, where the PAN had won important city halls in 1983
and increased its vote in the midterm 1985 elections, the PRI-dominated
legislature reformed the electoral law to make it easier to rig the 1986
election for governor. The PANista mayors of Ciudad Juárez and Parral instituted a twenty-two-day hunger strike against the reform and announced
that an electoral fraud was in the making. They got thousands of signa-
tures demanding the dropping of the reforms. Protest increased: acts of
civil disobedience, blocking of international bridges, a rally in Mexico City.
Peasants, teachers, the PSUM, the PMT, and CBCs formed the Electoral
Democratic Movement. The archbishop and several bishops condemned
the electoral fraud. The PANista mayor of Chihuahua staged a hunger
strike in the state capital's main square demanding respect for the popular
vote. Protests against electoral fraud gained the attention of national and international media. After rigged elections, the Catholic Church announced
the suspension of church services. The pope intervened to call off the religious protests (Presidencia 1987). The secretary of the interior reportedly
justified the fraud as "patriotic" because the opposition represented a right-
wing coalition (businesspeople and the Catholic Church) in a border state.
In September 1986, over 500 civil organizations and the main opposition
parties formed the Real Vote National Forum demanding clean elections
and electoral reform.

Protests continued. The PAN filed a formal complaint before the Inter-
American Commission for Human Rights (operating under the Organization of American States [OAS]) against Mexican authorities for violations of
human and political rights in the 1986 elections for governor and deputies
in Chihuahua and for city mayors in Durango. After the investigation, the
Inter-American Commission found that the law failed to protect citizens'
rights and observed that since Mexico was an OAS member, it was obliged
to protect the free and full exercise of political rights. Thus, it recom-
mended that the Mexican government protect the rights and liberties recognized by international treaties signed by Mexico (Acosta and Castañeda
1994). Three weeks after the Inter-American Commission made public its

1986 the municipal palace in San Luis Potosí was burned down; a few months later, the
governor resigned. There were many more instances of violence and repression related to
electoral contests (Cadena-Roa 1988).

recommendations, the administration of Carlos Salinas created the Human Rights National Commission (CNDH). Thereafter, many protest activities increasingly adopted a human rights framework. Protests against electoral fraud were conceived as part of the defense of universal human rights. After the Inter-American Commission's recommendations, opposition parties and citizens found international allies and legal institutional means of protection against human rights abuses.

In 1985 two major earthquakes in Mexico City destroyed hundreds of housing units and buildings, leaving an indeterminate number of casualties and homeless persons. Before the earthquakes, many neighborhoods had been organized for different ends (to prevent evictions, to demand services, etc.). Leaders involved in the labor movement, in parties, and in cadre organizations lived there. After the earthquakes, the preexisting organizations engaged in rescuing, helping, and reconstruction tasks and established links among themselves. The earthquakes revealed (even to the groups' members) the thick organizational fabric that had been knitted in the neighborhoods. The earthquake victims' organizations negotiated successfully with the government for a reconstruction program, and many tenants became owners of their reconstructed housing units. Many of the earthquake victims' demands were met but an important sector decided not to demobilize, pressing for a more responsive government for Mexico City.

The administration called for public hearings to reform the government of the Federal District, which includes most of Mexico City, whose executive was a presidential appointee and whose legislative arm was the Chamber of Deputies. In 1987 a constitutional amendment was passed to create the Assembly of Representatives of the Federal District, which was elected for the first time in 1988. The emergence of the Cardenista coalition and the formation of the Partido de la Revolución Democrática (PRD) turned one sector of the earthquake victims' movement into a political force with representatives, after the 1991 midterm elections, in the Assembly of Representatives and the Chamber of Deputies.

Popular contention pushed democratization. The de la Madrid administration calculated that if expanding the Chamber of Deputies to increase participation by opposition parties had worked before, perhaps it could work again. The administration passed a new electoral law, the Federal Electoral Code, that increased the size of the Chamber of Deputies from 400 to 500 seats, raising from 100 to 200 the number of seats filled by proportional representation. The law limited the size of the majority to

70% of the seats, thus increasing from 25% to 30% of the Chamber the minimum percentage of seats available to the opposition. But overall the 1987 Federal Electoral Code was a setback for opposition parties. The code dropped the conditional party registration (the way newly registered parties had obtained registration since 1978), introduced a "governability clause" that ensured a majority party in the Chamber of Deputies even with 35% of the national vote, and kept the Federal Electoral Commission under PRI and government control.

While the administration's structural adjustment policies reassured the economic elites, they caused a split within the governmental elites. A "Democratic Current," led by Cuauhtémoc Cárdenas (former governor of Michoacán, son of revered former president Lázaro Cárdenas) and Porfirio Muñoz Ledo (former PRI president, secretary of labor, secretary of education, and Ambassador to the United Nations) was formed within the PRI. The Current opposed the administration's neoliberal policies of reducing wages and welfare spending and complying with other IMF-sanctioned policies, concurring instead with popular movements' demands. They argued that those policies deviated from the "revolutionary project," letting down popular groups, and that the traditional method of nominating the PRI's presidential candidate (handpicked by the incumbent president) only ensured the continuity of neoliberal policies. The conflict within the PRI turned out to be about who was the legitimate heir of the Mexican Revolution. Cárdenas accused the government of being counterrevolutionary. President de la Madrid rebutted that Cárdenas was a populist and, ultimately, a reactionary. The president handpicked the designer of the administration's structural adjustment program, Carlos Salinas, as the PRI's presidential candidate.

The Current split from the PRI and ran Cárdenas for president. His campaign transformed the whole party system and built coalitions with independent social movements under the National Democratic Front (FDN), a left-of-center nonsocialist coalition. Cárdenas's campaign took advantage of the hardship caused by the adjustment program and the cycle of protest created by the earthquake victims and continued by the student movement at the National University. Beneficiaries of the land reform carried out in the 1930s by Lázaro Cárdenas supported his son. The FDN turned out to be the largest coalition of parties and movements outside the PRI in recent history. The FDN represented a broad and diverse coalition that included whole parties (PARM, PPS, PMS, and the Party of the Cardenista Front of National Reconstruction (PFCRN) and party splinters (the PRI and the PRT). The FDN "presented itself as a progressive force that could occupy the political space traditionally claimed by the PRI. In many ways, it presented itself as the 'authentic' PRI – or as a kind of reembodiment of the PRM: a national, populist movement that included the left and reproduced the PRM coalition, the heir to the Mexican Revolution that was concerned with social justice, and the vehicle that was capable of giving expression to the democratic yearnings of a newly awakened political society" (Collier 1992, p. 124). For the first time since 1952, the PRI's candidate was supported by the PRI alone.

Despite the backwardness of the 1987 Electoral Code, the 1988 presidential election turned out to be extraordinarily competitive. From 1929 to 1982, the PRI and its predecessors had won every presidential election, with percentages ranging from 71% to 100% of the votes. This time, the PRI's candidate, Carlos Salinas, received only 51% of the vote; Cuauhtémoc Cárdenas, the FDN candidate, received 31% and PAN's candidate, Manuel Clouthier, 17%. The election was stained with fraud (González Casanova 1990), and many believed (but could not prove it because the government controlled the whole electoral process) that the election was won by Cárdenas (Barberán et al. 1988). In the election for Congress, the PRI held the majority vote but did not achieve the two-thirds vote required to amend the Constitution. In the Senate, traditionally closed to the opposition, the PRI lost four seats to FDN candidates.

Deepening the Break with the Past

Carlos Salinas took office after one of the most controversial and least credible elections in Mexican history. All opposition parties condemned the 1988 election as fraudulent and manipulated. But even in these dire circumstances, the regime did not break down and there was no institutional paralysis. The incoming Salinas administration (1988–94) seemed to be up against the wall, but the new president took the initiative. First, the administration made an alliance with the PAN that included recognition of PAN's electoral victories (when they occurred), the continuation of the economic program, and a new reform of the electoral law. Second, the administration tried to dismantle the catchall anti-neoliberal front and particularly to cut the links between popular organizations and the FDN-Democratic Revolution Party (PRD). Third, it reformed the PRI.

The Salinas administration called for a "dialogue" with the parties and met with PAN leaders the day after Salinas took office. In 1989 the PAN won the election for governor in Baja California and the PRI acknowledged its loss – for the first time in postrevolutionary history. The PAN supported a free-market orientation and the privatization of state-owned firms was accelerated, including telecommunications and banks.[16]

After the 1988 election the Federal Electoral Commission, which was in charge of organizing and overseeing the electoral processes, lost public and party confidence. With PRI and PAN support, the Chamber of Deputies passed in 1990 a new electoral law, the Federal Code of Institutions and Electoral Procedures, that replaced the discredited Federal Electoral Commission with the Federal Electoral Institute (IFE). Its main feature was the addition of six independent voting magistrate councilors to IFE's General Council, its top decision-making board. These magistrate councilors were elected by the two-thirds vote of the Chamber of Deputies from a list sent by the president. The magistrate councilors were seen as guarantors of the fairness of the electoral process.

The Salinas administration moved quickly to break apart the coalition of movements and parties that had developed during Cárdenas's campaign. In its first formal act, the administration created the National Solidarity Program (PRONASOL). The program was designed to distribute benefits to the urban and rural poor directly from the office of the president. It was targeted to areas of opposition strength where the administration wanted to recover popular support or create tension between the popular organizations and the FDN–PRD. Since Cárdenas believed that the government had stolen the election for the PRI, he declared illegitimate and illegal the Salinas administration and considered "traitors" those parties, groups, or individuals dealing with the administration. This proved to be a political miscalculation. It was impossible not to deal with an acting government, and the FDN could not survive the contradictory demands of loyalty from the party leaders and the offer of governmental resources through PRONASOL. During 1989, dozens of popular organizations signed "concerted agreements" with the administration to receive PRONASOL money to meet people's demands, such as for roads, schools, drinking water, and sewage disposal (Presidencia 1994). When the broad and diverse coalition embodied in the FDN turned into a party, the PRD, several parties such as the PFCRN, the PPS, and the PARM, refused to join. Later on, several popular

---

[16] In 1988 there remained 379 state-owned enterprises out of a public sector of 1,155 in 1982. By the end of the Salinas administration there remained 213 state-owned enterprises, at least 40% of which were in the process of being privatized (Rogozinski 1993).

organizations that had signed concerted agreements with the government, particularly those with a Maoist lineage, founded the Labor Party (PT). The PRD thus failed to establish itself as the main interlocutor of a pacted transition and left the PAN as the main beneficiary of the 1988 electoral outcome.

Given their poor electoral results, many PRI sectors, particularly labor, were reduced to inefficient pressure groups, unable to deliver the vote to the party. Many labor candidates lost in single-member district contests (Molinar 1990). Since the free-market program inflicted hardship on wage earners, labor did not support the restructuring program. In the PRI's Fourteenth National Assembly, the party's territorial structure, representing local forces, received more weight and influence in the selection of candidates, reducing the leverage of the labor and peasant sectors (Loyola and León 1992; Marván 1990). Through PRONASOL the administration reached groups that did not belong to the PRI, establishing direct links with other constituencies.

Encouraged by the recommendations of the Inter-American Human Rights Commission to the government and motivated by frustration with the 1988 official results, organizations interested in observing elections mushroomed, with the purpose of overseeing electoral processes and reporting their findings. Initially, most members of these organizations were close to opposition parties that believed that having fair and clean elections would suffice to remove the PRI from office. Later on, hundreds of citizens without party links participated in electoral observation, not to favor one candidate or party in particular, but to ensure free, impartial, and fair elections regardless of their results.

The administration's policies (notably PRONASOL) and bold actions against union bosses reversed the 1988 electoral results: The 1991 midterm election for Congress produced a landslide victory for the PRI. Nonetheless, electoral processes tainted with fraud raised massive protests in Guanajuato and San Luis Potosí. In Guanajuato the PRI governor-elect resigned before taking office, and the State Congress appointed a PANista interim governor (Valencia 1994, 1998). In San Luis Potosí, the candidate run by an opposition coalition denounced the election and claimed that it had been stolen. Protests ensued, and the governor resigned two weeks after having taken office. In 1992 the PAN won the governorship of Chihuahua. That same year the PRI, after tallied elections, called itself the winner in Cárdenas's home state, Michoacán. There was a series of protests similar to those staged in Guanajuato and San Luis Potosí. The governor resigned after three weeks in office, and a PRI interim governor was appointed by the state legislature. Recognizing PAN victories and denying PRD triumphs was called "selective democracy" by the media. The resignation of these three PRIista governors shows the power acquired by the coalitions between popular movements and political parties demanding fair and clean elections.

To contribute to a smooth transmission of power in 1994, the administration engaged in the second electoral reform of its term. The governability clause was dropped. The size of the majority party in the Chamber of Deputies was limited to 315 seats (which meant that no single party would have the two-thirds vote required to amend the Constitution), and the size of the Senate doubled (from 64 to 128 seats), raising to 25% of the Senate the minimum percentage of seats available to the opposition. The reform also ensured the indirect election of the chief of the Federal District.

In 1993–4 several events shattered the government's political calculations and provoked a crisis in the governmental elite. Salinas picked Luis Donaldo Colosio, secretary of social development (created to run PRONASOL), as the PRI's presidential candidate. The regent of the Federal District, who had jockeyed for the nomination, felt let down and resigned. The Zapatista uprising in Chiapas (January 1, 1994) was countered by a military mobilization and swift changes by the secretary of the interior. The former regent of the Federal District was appointed as peace negotiator, and the governor of Chiapas took a leave of absence. Under still unclear circumstances, Colosio was murdered (March 23, 1994) and Salinas handpicked a new presidential candidate.

The Salinas administration's poor record on electoral processes (sixteen interim governors were appointed during his term, a number of them to appease protestors), political violence at the highest level, and an Indian armed movement in the resource-rich state of Chiapas created an atmosphere of distrust and insecurity that made urgent the organization of credible electoral processes. The alternative was a controversial election (as were most elections under Salinas) followed by protests, repression, loss of governability, and eventually an interim president appointed by the Chamber of Deputies. Obviously, the costs of having a controversial election were far too high. Thus, the administration embarked on its *third* electoral reform. The main concern with the upcoming election was the impartiality of the IFE. Thus, the 1994 reform of the electoral law introduced to IFE's General Council six citizen councilors, elected by a two-thirds vote of the Chamber of Deputies from a list sent by the parliamentary groups. IFE's General Council was chaired by the secretary of the interior and had four representatives from Congress (two deputies, two senators, one from the majority, and one from the second party in each chamber). Only these eleven members had the right to vote. Each registered party had one representative in the General Council who could speak but not vote. Thus, the majority vote in the institution in charge of organizing and overseeing the federal election relied on six honorable citizens without party links. They were seen as guarantors of the fairness and impartiality of the 1994 election in the middle of the worst political turmoil in Mexico in recent times. A PRI–PAN majority had passed the 1990 and 1993 reforms; the 1994 reform also had the support of the PRD.

The mobilization of citizens in the 1994 election showed the presence of an array of varied nongovernmental organizations (NGOs) with significant mobilization capacities. Hundreds of civil organizations took responsibility for the security of the Zapatista representatives during the peace negotiations in Chiapas. A National Democratic Convention organized by the Zapatistas was held in the Chiapas rain forest, with thousands of participants (Presidencia 1994). The 1994 election was closely monitored by thousands of national and foreign observers, some of whom received advice and funds from the United Nations (Pozas Horcasitas 1997), and Ernesto Zedillo was elected president. The Zedillo administration called for "definitive" electoral reform, which was passed in 1996.

Discussion and Conclusion

The postrevolutionary Mexican state had not only failed to promote equal treatment under the law but, conversely, segmented the population into different categories receiving special treatment. The first and major cleavage introduced was between the "revolutionary family" and the "counter-revolutionaries." Successive governments presented themselves as popular governments that would reward the classes and groups that made the revolution. But not every peasant and worker would be entitled to the same rewards. The state had the last say about which social organizations and political parties would be recognized as legal representatives of legitimate interests. Labor, peasant, and business organizations as well as political parties required official recognition and validation to represent their particular sector. Unions had to be registered before the secretary of labor, peasant organizations before the secretary of agriculture, business organizations before the secretary of industry and commerce, and political parties before the secretary of the interior. This meant that the government, *despite the*

Constitution, could decide which groups would have their right to association protected and which would not. Officially sanctioned organizations were committed to support the government and, in return, expected special consideration of their demands. Any action by nonregistered organizations or parties could be declared illegal and persecuted. Thus, corporatist arrangements based on privilege and political reciprocity transformed the constitutional rights of freedom of association and participation into privileges granted by the state to loyal organizations. Political loyalty (that is, unqualified support for government policies) was considered the chief desideratum. Denials of registration, threats of losing it, and registration of third parties were serious constraints to the formation and survival of independent organizations. Within certain limits, corporatism made bearable the government's control of the electoral system. But since elected officials in Mexico lacked constituent responsibilities, atavistic authoritarianism and corruption bloomed.

The formation of autonomous social movement organizations whose identity was cemented by an anticooption ideology, and that were independent of corporatist and patron–client networks, started slowly in the 1940s with peasant organizations and spread afterward to labor. The knitting together of autonomous organizations into independent and informal networks of leaders, organizations, and aggrieved populations started in the 1960s and became robust in the 1970s. I have referred to this knitting together of uncooptable leaders and groups the social movement for democracy. Currently, corporatist networks of trust have not disappeared but are in decline or disintegration since they have become unable to secure rewards for loyal organizations. Increased electoral competition and the privatization of the state-owned sector have contributed to the weakening of corporatist and clientist structures.

The formation of autonomous networks that demanded that the government honor its constitutional obligations and act impartially broke with the taken-for-granted practices of privilege and mutually profitable relationships between the government and loyal groups, of bending or overlooking the law at the incumbent's convenience, and of the primacy of personalized familial and group interests that had characterized Mexico's political evolution since colonial times. These networks included both grassroots and elite organizations. The economic elites built alternative and independent networks of trust through the Business Coordinating Council and other entrepreneurial organizations and through their support of the PAN and a number of private universities.

In 1970 there were only four registered parties: the PAN, PRI, PARM, and PPS. All of them had proved unable to deal with challengers' demands. After the 1977 Political Reform, the party system opened to independent parties. The current party system has three main competitors: the PAN, PRI, and PRD. Although there are many jurisdictions in which either the PRD or the PAN is weak, leaving the other in more of a two-party competition with the PRI, in only a couple of states is the PRI still completely dominant.

The current legal-institutional framework, resulting from eight major electoral reforms that started in 1972, has opened the arena of party competition. The 1996 electoral reform included safeguards against most causes of complaint and guarantees the integrity of the elections.[17] Postelectoral protests and mobilizations have almost disappeared. The electoral system is more credible and reliable, creating real possibilities of partisan alternation in office to the higher level. The possibility of reversible policy changes was reduced after Mexico signed the GATT (1986) and joined the North American Free Trade Agreement (NAFTA) (1994), declared the central bank autonomous (1993), and signed a free trade agreement with the European Union (2000). Together these measures institutionalize market-oriented policies and remove this area of policymaking from discretionary decision making, thus assuring the business community policy continuity despite party alternation in the executive branch of the government.

In 1996, the IFE was granted autonomy from the executive and legislative branches. All decisions are made by independent electoral councilors elected by a two-thirds vote of the Chamber of Deputies from a list sent by the parliamentary groups. Party and Congress representatives have the right to participate in General Council deliberations but cannot vote. In 1994, a series of independent audits found the voters' list clean and reliable. A new tamperproof voter card was issued. The rules for access to the media tend to correct media bias. Parties must file reports on revenues and expenditures, making funding more transparent. Campaign limits remain too high, giving an advantage to the PRI, since it has greater access to resources, but the PAN and PRD together receive more funding than the PRI. Polling

---

[17] In April 1999, with the PAN, PRD, PT, and PVEM majority vote, the Chamber of Deputies passed a bill reforming the electoral law to ease the requirements for the formation of coalitions, oversee campaign spending, and eliminate overrepresentation in the Chamber of Deputies. The PRI-dominated Senate killed the bill. *Reforma*, August 13, 1999, p. 8A.

station officials for election day are chosen by two successive lotteries. Both national and foreign individuals and organizations may observe all phases of the electoral process and report their findings. The vote count is more reliable and verifiable. Representation in the Chamber of Deputies is fairer since 60% of its seats are filled by single-member districts and 40% by proportional representation. Overrepresentation in the Chamber of Deputies is limited to 8%, and the maximum number of seats one party can have is fixed at 300, below the two-thirds required by law to amend the Constitution. The Senate has opened seats for the second party in each federal entity and for proportional representation from a single national list. A Legislative Assembly of the Federal District was created. The mayor of the Federal District was elected by direct popular vote and delegates by indirect vote in 1997 (delegates were elected by direct popular vote until the year 2000). Approval of the elections now depends on authorities different from those elected and independent of the parties and the government. The Electoral Court of the Judiciary Branch is the top authority in electoral disputes. The law established stiff criminal penalties for violation of the electoral law.

In 1970, the PRI had 178 out of 213 seats in the Chamber of Deputies, had all the seats in the Senate, controlled all state legislatures, and ruled in all states, in the Federal District, and in almost every municipality in the country. By 1988 things had changed significantly. Many believed that the presidential election was stolen from Cárdenas, the PRI barely kept its majority vote in the Chamber of Deputies, and the opposition gained access to the Senate for the first time and had the majority vote in two state legislatures. The PRI ruled in the Federal District, in thirty states (all but Baja California), and in 89% of the municipalities. As a result of the gradual leveling of the playing field, by the end of 1999 the PRI had lost the majority vote in the Chamber of Deputies and had to negotiate with other parties to pass bills and the annual budget. The PRI still had a majority vote in the Senate and in seventeen state legislatures, and ruled in twenty-one states (out of thirty-one) and in 69% of the municipalities (Berrueto 2000). Out of twenty-nine elections for governor between 1995 and 1999, the PRI won eighteen governorships, the PAN seven, and the PRD four. Federalism and checks and balances have expanded by having different parties in federal, state, and municipal executive offices and legislatures. Increased lobbying and negotiation among government branches and parties has become far more common. However, despite the democratization that has occurred, the party that has ruled Mexico for seven decades still holds considerable

139

occupancy in all elective offices. But perhaps more significantly, electoral processes are no longer questioned and postelection protests have almost disappeared, which makes the outcomes of the elections legitimate even if the PRI wins.

One of the dilemmas of the Mexican transition to democracy has been that there are important differences among the three major parties and little common ground for compromise. As Collier (1992) notes, the PRD has had the strongest commitment to democratization since it opposes market-oriented reforms and has been excluded from decision making. The PAN supports market-oriented policies and has been more willing to compromise with the government in a gradual transition out of fear that the PRD would be the greatest beneficiary of a more competitive polity. The PRI wants to continue the market-oriented reforms and to rule the country. Thus, the PAN and the PRI have more in common than the PRD and the PAN.

Once market-oriented policies had been institutionalized and multiparty electoral and legislative coalitions were becoming usual, there was the possibility of a PAN–PRD alliance to oust the PRI from power and push for a quick consolidation of uniform sets of rights and obligations binding governmental agents and citizens at large. But negotiations to form a broad electoral coalition were unsuccessful because the PAN and the PRD disagreed on the method for selecting the coalition's presidential candidate. When the negotiations started, both parties had already nominated their candidates and neither candidate was willing to jeopardize his nomination. The failure to form an electoral coalition revealed that both parties are suspicious of each other's commitment to democracy and policy agenda (the PAN has been closer to the PRI on crucial legislative matters). The PAN and the PRD considered granting concessions to each other to consolidate an electoral coalition, a worse outcome than having the PRI hold executive power for six more years. Thus, pressure for alternation in power was not so great as to force them into a settlement.

Once the threat of an electoral alliance vanished, the PRI was faced with the possible loss of those who might have felt passed over in the nomination of its presidential candidate. But the PRI nominated its candidate in an open primary in which reportedly 10 million people voted, dissuading possible splinters. In the 2000 presidential and congressional elections, eleven parties competed, running six presidential candidates. The PRI's candidate was Francisco Labastida. Five parties (the PRD, PT, PAS, Convergence for Democracy [CD], and PSN) formed the "Alliance for Mexico" to support Cuauhtémoc Cárdenas for president (who ran for the third consecutive time). Two parties (the PAN and Ecological Green Party of Mexico [PVEM]) formed the "Alliance for Change" to run Vicente Fox.

After a world record of seventy-one uninterrupted years of government tenure, the PRI acknowledged the loss of the 2000 presidential election and stepped down peacefully from the federal executive branch: The PAN candidate, Vicente Fox, was declared the winner. Besides the presidency, the PRI lost, for the second consecutive time, the majority vote in the Chamber of Deputies, although it still holds 42% of the seats, closely followed by the PAN (41%) and by a recoiling PRD (10%). The PRI also lost, for the first time ever, the majority vote in the Senate, although it still holds 47% of the seats, followed by the PAN (36%) and a distant PRD (12%). If any bills are going to pass, given this congressional makeup, it will require much more lobbying, negotiating, and accommodating than ever before between the executive and Congress. Fox won the presidency but did not inherit *presidencialismo*, one of its features being a Congress subservient to the executive branch. In the states, the PRI still keeps the lion's share of power. It rules in nineteen states, the PAN in nine, and the PRD in three and the Federal District. Additionally, the PRI has majority vote in twenty-two out of thirty-two state legislatures. Alternation in power has provided enormous relief to the Mexican polity. From now on, for the first time in decades, political debates will not be centered on what else is needed to have fair, clean, and impartial elections. Instead, they will focus on the policy agenda and on how to solve Mexico's problems.

The transition to democracy in Mexico resulted from a long, complex process of contestation between and within elites, popular movements, and political parties. This essay calls for closer attention to the interweaving between contentious and routine politics, particularly the role of popular movements in the transition to democracy. In the Mexican transition, social movements were politics by other means, the only means available to popular groups when routine, legal, and institutional means were ineffective or closed. It has been demonstrated that since the 1940s, the ineffectiveness or closure of institutional channels to bring benefits to the popular groups that made the revolution and the lack of protection of their legal activities from arbitrary governmental action pushed leaders and movements out of legal (but not tolerated) protests into radical, clandestine, and illegal ones. In the 1980s, political reform opened the electoral arena of competition, but the manipulation of electoral processes was confronted by coalitions between movements and parties demanding the enforcement of the rules of institutional politics by noninstitutional means. Nonetheless, even at the turn of the twenty-first century, pressure for alternation was not great enough to force the opposition into a settlement to oust the PRI from the executive branch, which also indicates that a split opposition is an important variable that deserves as much attention as a split governing elite in democratization processes. The transition to democracy in Mexico required the formation of social movement organizations with nonnegotiable autonomy; the knitting together of these organizations into networks of organizations, leaders, aggrieved populations, and political parties; and the design and enforcement of a legal and institutional framework that leveled the playing field of electoral competition, protected citizens' rights from arbitrary governmental action and limited governmental unresponsiveness and unaccountability.

There have been important gains on protected consultation in Mexico even though a new Constitution has not been drafted and alternation in the highest office occurred only in December 2000. Compared to the 1970s, the 1980s, and the early 1990s, the proportion of persons who belong to the polity has increased, as well as the number of independent parties representing them. The degree to which polity members exercise binding control over governmental agents, resources, and activities has increased through elections, institutional protection, and civil organizations.

Peaceful alternation of ruling parties has taken place, but clearly, democratization is far from complete. Despite the creation of the National Human Rights Commission, Mexico's record of human rights abuse is monstrous, particularly among political opponents[18] and the indigenous population.[19] In terms of social equality, the record is dismaying: Mexico's income distribution is among the worst in the world, and about one-half of its 95 million inhabitants live below the poverty line. Categorical inequality persists in the form of racism, injustice, and discrimination. This is the rationale behind guerrilla groups (like the Zapatistas in Chiapas and other armed movements in Guerrero, Oaxaca, and elsewhere) who, despite the

---

[18] From 1988 to 1992, the PRD registered 136 of its members murdered (PRD 1992). The number increased to 639 up to 1999. *La Jornada*, May 5, 1999, p. 7.

[19] In June 1995, state policemen murdered seventeen peasants in Aguas Blancas, Guerrero. In December 1997, a paramilitary group tolerated by the government murdered fourty-five men, women, and children in Acteal, Chiapas.

progress achieved in the formation of alternative networks of trust, in the formation of independent parties, and in the legal-institutional framework, still are trying to start all over again and constitute a new polity to reduce categorical inequality (by race and class). Until significant improvements to reduce categorical inequality are accomplished, nobody can be assured that Mexico's democracy is fully consolidated.

PART II

Parties and Social Movements

5

Parties out of Movements

PARTY EMERGENCE IN POSTCOMMUNIST EASTERN EUROPE

John K. Glenn

The essays in this volume challenge the distinction between social movements and institutional politics by arguing that movements are deeply entwined with normal politics. This essay extends this argument to the new democracies of Eastern Europe. It analyzes the transformation of the social movements that assumed power in new governments after the fall of communism, and shows how social movements may give rise to institutions of political consultation and accountability between states and their citizens. Yet, in the wake of rapid regime change and the absence of long-standing domestic models for democratic institutions, the antiregime social movements did not smoothly evolve into democratic parties. Rather, both international actors and domestic constituencies influenced divisions and conflicts, and produced different outcomes in each case.

The cases presented in this essay suggest that movements are transformed by governing and, moreover, that the parties that emerge from movements do not necessarily conform to standard notions of political parties. Initially, movements may form parties around political cleavages rather than the socioeconomic interests traditionally emphasized by the scholarly literature. Further, international actors may influence this development by encouraging movements to adopt new organizational forms and issues – areas lacking historical precedent. These forms and issues are not simply imitated, however, but are subsequently adapted to mobilize domestic public support. The results thus do not necessarily conform to Western parliamentary models of parties and politics.

To develop these claims, I compare the transformation of social movements into political parties in two countries, the Czech Republic and Slovakia. These countries had previously been united in the federal

147

state of Czechoslovakia, although with distinct Czech and Slovak provinces. Similar revolutionary movements emerged in the Czech and Slovak regions during the fall of communism in 1989–91. Yet party development soon diverged, with a Western market-oriented party winning elections in the Czech Republic and a populist semiauthoritarian party winning elections in Slovakia, both in 1992. The emergence of new parties in these cases was affected by both domestic struggles among opposition groups and external models and assistance, producing results that could not be foretold from either factor alone.

Before turning to the scholarly literature, I discuss the emergence of new political parties in the Czech Republic and Slovakia to highlight the puzzles involved.

The Puzzle

The emergence of new parties in Eastern Europe in the 1990s offers a valuable opportunity to develop the claims in this essay because of the perception that, with the fall of communism, the Western model of parliamentary democracy had triumphed across the world (Fukuyama 1992). Others have gone further to argue that there is an emerging "world culture" in which all countries will adopt the common forms of Western parliamentary systems (Meyer et al. 1997). Close observers have argued that the revolutions in Eastern Europe in 1989 did not introduce new models of political authority, as in earlier revolutions in France, the United States, and Russia. Rather, the democratic movements sought "a restatement of the value of what we already have, of old truths and tested models, of the . . . essentials of liberal democracy and the European Community as the one and only real existing Common European Home" (Ash 1991, p. 122).

Yet analysts of postcommunist politics frequently found themselves puzzled by developments in the 1990s, unable to map Western models of "right versus left" onto the emerging political spectrum in Eastern Europe (Ekiert 1992). Collier and Levitsky observed that "although the new national political regimes in Latin America, Africa, Asia and the former communist world share important attributes of democracy, many of them differ profoundly both from each other and from the democracies in advanced industrialized countries" (1997, p. 430). These observations highlight the need to analyze how international models were appropriated by emerging political parties after the fall of communism, and also how they were adapted to mobilize domestic support in dynamic times.

The fall of communism in Czechoslovakia in late 1989 was especially dramatic because of the hard line taken by the communist regime until its demise. Repression and relative economic security prevented the emergence of democratic challengers until the regime became isolated internationally and provoked mass protest by its violent repression of a student demonstration in November 1989. Rather than representing parties with defined constituencies, the revolutionary civic movements in Czechoslovakia proclaimed that they represented a united "society" against the state. Once in power, however, this revolutionary unity came under strain, with internal disagreements about the appropriate policies for the new government. The movements faced enormous challenges in rebuilding a state that had been ruled for over forty years by the Communist Party, including the drafting of a new constitution and a legal code, review of the state administration, establishment of free markets, and creation of an independent judiciary (see Elster et al. 1998).

The forms that the successors to these civic movements would take were initially unclear. In the immediate postcommunist environment, political parties were associated in most people's minds with communism, and the movements maintained their identities as broad coalitions in the first free and fair elections in 1990 (in which they secured popular support for a two-year mandate for economic and political liberalization). As the Czech prime minister argued in 1990:

[T]he dominant feature of public political opinion is distrust and even unwillingness to participate in political parties. This is true even among people who are politically active. This is the reflection of an instinctive distaste for political parties in general, and for everything that is associated with party apparatuses, discipline, leaders' privileges, perks and so on. These are vague, over-generalized dislikes, and spring from the experience of Communist rule. (Whipple 1991, p. 173)

In the first postcommunist elections of 1990, the antiregime movements Civic Forum (in the Czech Republic) and Public Against Violence (in Slovakia) ran candidates. While Civic Forum won a majority of the vote, Public Against Violence had already splintered and won only a plurality (Krejčí 1995, pp. 340–1).

The subsequent emergence of new political parties in Czechoslovakia would not happen automatically. Rather, the evolution of parties out of movements was profoundly affected by still unsettled debates about the postcommunist economic transformation and about the constitution, which specified the relationships between the two republics. Indeed, parties themselves continued to be viewed with ambivalence. President Václav Havel declared in the summer of 1991 that political parties in Czechoslovakia were not well developed, with only a tenuous link to the people they claimed to represent:

Loyalty to the party leadership and even the party apparatus becomes more important in deciding political careers than the will of the electorate and the abilities of politicians. Party structures can create something of a shadow state within the real state. Electoral optimism and pre-election maneuvers become more important than the actual interest of society.... It could hence easily happen that the electorate is governed by people who were not really voted in by them at all. (Wheaton and Kavan 1992, pp. 176–7)

The number of parties and party identification of deputies changed with dizzying speed between 1990 and 1992. For example, in the 1990 elections, eight parties and coalitions won seats in the Czechoslovak Federal Assembly; by the next elections, the breakup of the civic movements had created more than twenty parties and factions and a core of independent deputies who abandoned their initial party identifications without acquiring new ones. In the Slovak National Council, seven parties grew to eleven in the same period. In 1994, there was only one party in the Czech National Council that had the same delegation it started with after the 1992 elections. As Leff observes, at the beginning, "the voter had no guarantee that the party supported in one election would even exist by the next and that candidates pledged to the program in one party would have retained the same partisan affiliation between elections" (1997, pp. 103–4). Two months before the June 1992 elections, nearly one-third of the Czech electorate declared itself undecided about which, if any, political party to support (Wolchik 1995, p. 227).

In this dynamic period, transnational party organizations from established democracies sought to assist movements in establishing democratic political parties and institutions. The National Democratic Institute (NDI) reports that it sought to provide immediate assistance in Czechoslovakia:

In a December 1989 survey mission to then-Czechoslovakia, an NDI delegation met with recently-elected President Václav Havel who said to the group, "We need advice, here, now, immediately. Not from government but from professionals who know election laws. If you can bring somebody to Prague by Monday, that would be wonderful." ... NDI was able to respond quickly to President Havel's request. The following week, NDI sent a four-person international team of election law experts to consult with the Czechs and Slovaks who were writing the rules for the first free election in 44 years. (National Democratic Institute for International Affairs 1996, p. 12)

Assistance to new or emerging democratic political parties is often seen as a fundamental part of international democracy assistance since political parties are understood to be necessary components of stable democracies, providing the mechanism by which diverse voices and interests are articulated and claims are made within the polity.

For example, two satellite organizations of the National Endowment for Democracy, the NDI and the International Republican Institute (IRI), define their mandates in terms of promoting party development. NDI's 1996 Mission Statement declares its aim to be "democratic development that focuses on the roles and functions of political parties and other institutions fundamental to democracy" (NDI 1996). More specifically, NDI identifies three areas of political party assistance: (1) operational assistance addressing the institutional structures of a political party that make it an effective organization that can consolidate citizens' interests; (2) election assistance, namely, the planning, researching, campaigning, and monitoring of elections; and (3) governance or assisting in orienting new members, educating constituencies, building coalitions, and seeking public input.

Yet despite this assistance, the transformation of civic movements into political parties was neither smooth nor uniform. The civic movements broke up into competing political parties in 1991, and subsequent elections in 1992 demonstrated the success of those new political parties that had broken away from the dissident base of the original revolutionary movements. The Civic Democratic Party, led by Finance Minister Vaclav Klaus in the Czech provinces, and the Movement for Democratic Slovakia, led by Vladimir Mečiar, each won approximately 33% of the vote for the Czechoslovak Federal Parliament (Olson 1993, p. 310). Despite public opinion polls suggesting that there was no popular support for the division of the country, the leaders of the two strongest parties declared their inability to work together and proceeded to divide the country into two new countries that took strikingly divergent paths. While Klaus's government in the Czech Republic increased its integration into Western political institutions by becoming a member of the North Atlantic Treaty Organization (NATO) and a first-round candidate for membership in the European Union, government consolidation in Slovakia took another turn. Mečiar's government instituted a semiauthoritarian regime characterized by harassment of the political opposition, independent media, and minorities. Subsequently, Slovakia was refused membership in both NATO and the first wave of candidates for membership in the European Union.

The Emergence of Political Parties

The classic explanation for the transformation of movements into parties is Robert Michels's (1962) organizational argument that mass movements are inevitably channeled into formal organizations that favor an oligarchic elite rather than the masses. Because "democracy is inconceivable without organization," the initial democratic aspirations that give rise to movements, he argued, will inevitably be subverted by a political class possessing organizational skills that enable them to impose their will upon the party (Michels 1962, p. 61). Similarly, the literature on political parties and revolutions predicts that revolutionary movements will break up in a process of political struggle whereby an initial "honeymoon" period of artificial unity is succeeded by the forging of a "dominant coalition" to address the concerns that initiated state breakdown (Goldstone 1991, p. 422). The logic of these explanations includes cynical interpretations of Jacobin ruthlessness in eliminating enemies, as well as pragmatic ones that argue that different skills are needed to rule a government (such as the securing of revenues and resources, including popular support, money, and technical expertise). Because parties must maintain at least periodic social support, the literature in political science and sociology argues that new parties represent social cleavages within nation-states (Bartolini and Mair 1990; Lipset and Rokkan 1967). Scholars have sought to apply this approach to postcommunist Eastern Europe, distinguishing parties by their presumed social bases (Kitschelt 1996) or by a combination of social bases, issue dimensions, and the stability of party competition (Evans and Whitefield 1993).

Efforts to apply the literature on societal cleavages within nation-states to new democracies in Eastern Europe have come under two main criticisms: (1) They assume that new political parties will take the same path as parties in earlier parliamentary democracies, and (2) they ignore the increasing influence of international actors upon postcommunist polities. First, it is problematic to assume that new parties in emerging democracies will follow the same path of development as earlier parties in Western parliamentary democracies. Scholars have argued that a simple application of parliamentary models to the new parties in Eastern Europe either "ignores the very substantial changes that have taken place in the nature and role of parties in well-established Western democracies or it anachronistically presumes that parties in today's neodemocracies will have to go through all the stages and perform all the functions of their predecessors" (Schmitter 1992, p. 426). Others have observed that in postcommunist Eastern Europe, "clearly articulated links between new parties, on the one hand, and social groups, on the other, are generally lacking and processes of representation are subject to considerable confusion" (Pridham and Lewis 1996, p. 19).

Challenging the view that "there are interests out there – real, particular, independent, societal interests, waiting for the chance to politically articulate their views and to use the state to implement these views," Ost (1991, p. 4) argued that the historical legacy of state socialism obstructed the articulation of societal interests on which political parties can be based. In these conditions, scholars have emphasized the process by which parties emerged around political discourses and identities (Ekiert 1991, 1992; Kubik 1992). Similarly, others have argued that the Solidarity government in Poland could only claim to represent "theoretical" rather than "real" economic interests that would benefit from its economic program, illustrated by the declaration of a candidate for minister of industry in September 1989: "I represent subjects that do not yet exist" (Staniszkis 1991, p. 184).

Second, the focus on domestic societal cleavages is unable to explain the impact of international actors upon state building. It is, I emphasize, beyond the scope of this essay to test the impact of international factors upon democratization in general. As Schmitter notes, "the international sphere is almost by definition omnipresent since very few polities in the contemporary world are isolated from its effects; however its causal effects are often indirect, working through national agents" (Schmitter 1996, p. 501). Many scholars, however, argue that parties are increasingly bound by global politics: "Britain's membership in the European Community is the most obvious symbol of constraint upon a British government's powers of decision" (Rose 1984, p. 151). Others go further to argue that the Westphalian system of nation-states no longer exists, that national governments are "not simply losing autonomy in a globalizing economy. They are sharing powers – including political, social, and security roles at the core of sovereignty – with businesses, with international organizations, and with a multitude of citizens groups, known as nongovernmental organizations" (Mathews 1997, p. 50).

Although the current attention to transnational organizations is not without precedent (Huntington 1973; Keohane and Nye 1972), some have argued that international factors played a more influential role in the democratic transformations in Eastern Europe than in the preceding southern European and Latin American transformations (Pridham 1995). Others have observed that the mechanism of influence has changed, that "the international context surrounding democratization has shifted from a primary reliance on public, inter-governmental channels of influence towards an increased involvement of private, non-governmental organizations" (Schmitter 1996, p. 39; see also Boli and Thomas 1997; Clark, Freidman, and Hochstetler 1998; Pridham 1996).

In Eastern Europe, new party systems were shaped by the interaction between domestic political competition and international models of party organization promoted by nongovernmental organizations (NGOs), whereby new organizational forms and issue areas were adopted that lacked historical precedent but were adapted to mobilize public support.[1] This entails the creation of interfaces between new parties and international organizations offering resources, as well as local adaptation of international models for domestic audiences.

This approach highlights the potential for conflict between international models and domestic conditions, unlike the emphasis on imitation in the literature on "global culture" (Meyer et al. 1997) and the consensual knowledge in "epistemic communities" (Haas 1992) and "international issue-networks" (Sikkink 1993). This essay does not assume that international assistance will necessarily have positive effects or succeed in its aim of promoting democracy (Carothers 1996; Robinson 1996); rather, it analyzes the variable impact of international actors in light of national political and historical contexts. These cases highlight the ambiguity of the concept of "democracy" in the post–Cold War world. To international organizations, parties may speak of one vision of democracy (a formal one in which institutions are replicated in different contexts) while simultaneously deploying a different vision for their domestic audiences (a substantive one in which the challenges of the communist legacy figure prominently). These different visions do not necessarily undercut each other. Indeed, ambiguity may be a virtue, enabling domestic actors to appear to respond to both international and local concerns while avoiding policy commitments to either.

---

[1] This argument draws on insights in the international relations literature concerning international bargaining and domestic political constituencies (see Knopf 1993; Moravcsik 1993; Putnam 1993).

The Emergence of New Political Parties in the Czech Republic and Slovakia

To develop the claims made in this essay, I contrast the process by which new political parties emerged out of revolutionary movements in the Czech Republic and Slovakia in light of international assistance by NGOs.[2] I focus on the U.S. National Endowment for Democracy (NED) and two of its beneficiaries that specifically target political parties, the National Democratic Institute and the International Republic Institute. Although these were hardly the only international actors active in this period, assistance from the NED targeted for democratic institutions and elections in Czechoslovakia, the Czech Republic, and Slovakia between 1989 and 1994 can be calculated to be approximately 40% of all similarly targeted foundation assistance.[3] In the following sections, I contrast the emergence of new parties in each country.

The Czech Republic

After the fall of communism in Czechoslovakia in 1989, a "government of national understanding" (composed of all political forces) was formed, not by new political parties but by broad-based civic movements claiming to speak for society. In the Czech Republic (which made up two-thirds of the population of the federation), this movement called itself Civic Forum and was embodied in the former dissident Václav Havel, who served as president of the federation. The NED provided nine grants intended to assist Civic Forum in the 1990 elections, totaling $842,485 (although some of the grants were broadly intended for the federation as a whole). NED's assistance can be categorized as general election assistance (advising the drafting of a new election law and sending an international observation team), equipment provision (such as fax machines and computers), and party training (including seminars on party organization, civic education, and voter participation).

In the June 1990 elections, twenty-three parties and movements competed (all but five of which were new organizations). Civic Forum won 53% of the vote, with the Communist Party coming in a surprising second,

---

[2] Here I present only a summary of party development and the breakup of Czechoslovakia. For more detailed accounts, see Blahoz (1994), Butorova (1993), Draper (1993), Innes (1997), and Wightman (1991).

[3] According to Quigley (1997, pp. 142–5, 150–1), $1,088,000 out of $2,717,000.

winning 13%. Attention to international assistance to Civic Forum in the 1990 elections reveals a broadly positive portrait, although not one in which international actors may claim to have "caused" democracy. Rather, at best, they might claim to have supported the "democrats." The project to assist the writing of the election law led to a threshold whereby parties had to receive at least 5% of the popular vote to enter parliament. This threshold enabled Czechoslovakia to avoid the parliamentary fragmentation that developed in Poland, which had a 3% threshold. Since Civic Forum received seats proportional to the votes received only by parties or movements that reached the threshold, they were able to consolidate a firm majority in both houses of parliament.

We also should not underestimate the importance of infrastructural assistance provided by various NGOs. The Institute for Democracy in Eastern Europe (IDEE) sought to meet immediate needs for administrative assistance in governing and running election campaigns at a time when the new civic movements had virtually no preexisting resources, financial or organizational. At this time, the Czech currency remained unconvertible, limiting the ability to purchase modern equipment from abroad. Thus, assistance from Freedom House that provided newsprint to the Civic Forum publication *Lidove Noviny* must be placed in historical context; this assistance helped transform an underground dissident newspaper into the sole alternative to the Communist and satellite party-controlled newspapers after the revolution, initially serving as Civic Forum's voice in the media. Both the civic movements and *Lidove Noviny* operated in this early period largely as they had in the revolutionary periods, overwhelmed by the tasks facing them in light of the resources they had at their disposal. It is not possible to quantify the impact of such infrastructural assistance at a time when stable budgets were still being created, but the ability of international NGOs to act quickly and provide resources to meet short-term needs was extremely valuable. One cannot be sure of the counterfactual consequences of the absence of such provisions (whether the movements would have faltered or whether other actors may have met these same needs), but it is clear that such needs existed and that international NGOs sought to provide assistance unlikely to have been provided efficiently otherwise.

In this period, NDI and IRI conducted "skills-based" training workshops, which typically presented the model on which political parties operate in the United States, emphasizing the creation of new political organizations (including ties to local media, the office of a political organization, and voting districts), the tasks of a political party during an election campaign (such as door-to-door or mail-order campaigning), and fund-raising. Initially few, if any, of the members of Civic Forum were experienced in running elections, and careful organization was necessary. In addition to the assistance to the civic movements, IRI reported that its workshops were attended by 150 individuals representing twenty-four political parties, including some who were not part of the umbrella coalitions.

Civic Forum, however, did not simply adopt a Western-style campaign, but rather adapted it to reinvoke the spirit of the 1989 revolution. Despite Havel's declaration that it was a temporary organization, Civic Forum maintained its identity as a civic movement representing society in the 1990 elections. Civic Forum's election slogan was explicitly antiparty, declaring: "Parties Belong to Party Members: Civic Forum Belongs to All." de Candole argued that this primarily reflected the beliefs of the dissident-turned-politicians, drawing on "the rejection of partisanship [that] formed the philosophical core of Charter 77" (de Candole 1991, p. 20). The consequences of the maintenance of this identity included the refusal by Civic Forum to create membership procedures or a hierarchical organization during the 1990 elections. Its membership principles declared that

Civic Forum is a movement of all citizens who agree with its programmatic principles from 11.26.1989 and actively support their fulfillment, and of those citizens who are not and do not want to be members of any political party.... Membership of united citizens in Civic Forum is informal. They are not joined by individual membership, membership cards or by paying membership contributions.[4]

Civic Forum sought to demonstrate its ability to run as a credible opposition to the Communist Party and a proponent of economic reform. Its platform was represented by the broad slogan "Return to Europe," with the democratic system, market economy, and cultural values that this implied. At the same time, Civic Forum sought to avoid a traditional appeal for votes. As Miriam Horn observed, "For too long politics had been paternalistic and pedantic, wagging its finger at the children of the state. Now the imperative voice would be jettisoned. It would not be 'Vote for Us,' but only, 'Civic Forum, a chance for the future' " (Horn 1990, p. 12). The "merriness" that characterized Civic Forum in the fall of communism was evident in its electoral style, marked by irony and deliberate antipolitics. On May 1, traditionally a socialist holiday, "campaign workers donned huge essay mâché heads, with scowling, puffy faces marking them as members

---

[4] Koordinační Centrum OF Praha [Coordination Center of Civic Forum Prague] (1990, p. 72).

of the old regime, and mugged and pranced on the backs of trucks winding through the streets" (Horn 1990, p. 11).

After the 1990 elections, the successor parties to Civic Forum adopted, as well as adapted, Western forms of party organization in different ways, taking different positions on key electoral issues. The debate over the future of Civic Forum crystallized around competition for chairmanship of Civic Forum between the former dissidents led by Martin Palouš and new political figures led by Václav Klaus, culminating with Klaus's election as chairman in October 1990. On the one hand, Palous argued that Civic Forum should continue to be governed during the transition period by the "consensus-oriented politics" that were the legacy of the dissident opposition under communism, especially the petition movement, Charter 77.[5] Similarly, Jiří Dienstbier, the foreign minister and former spokesman for Charter 77, argued that Klaus's attempts to introduce hierarchical qualities into Civic Forum were unnecessary and "inhumane."[6] On the other hand, Finance Minister Klaus argued that the nonhierarchical nature of Civic Forum had begun to hamper its ability to implement political and economic reform. Contrary to Civic Forum's electoral program in the 1990 elections, Klaus declared the need to create formal membership structures that would enable the building of an effective party and link the regions in hierarchical party structures for effective coordination. Over differences between these two groupings on the appropriate form of the movement, Civic Forum dissolved in February 1991 into the Civic Democratic Party (*Občanská Demokratická Strana*, or ODS), led by Finance Minister Klaus, and Civic Movement (*Občanské Hnuti*, or OH), led by Foreign Minister Dienstbier.

In its founding program, ODS argued that many of the most serious problems facing Czechoslovakia had "arisen due to the hesitant policies pursued by Civic Forum throughout 1990. Little action was taken against many surviving totalitarian structures. The Civic Democratic Party finds it intolerable that many important posts are still held by communists."[7] In December 1990, as chairman of Civic Forum, Klaus had declared his constituency to be young people, Christians, and entrepreneurs, and not artists and intellectuals, among whom "trends toward leftism originate."[8] Strikingly, such a constituency did not reflect preexisting social cleavages

---

[5] Interview with the author, April 19, 1994.
[6] Quoted in de Candole (1991), p. 21.
[7] In *East European Reporter* (1991), Vol. 4, p. 48.
[8] Quoted in de Candole (1991), p. 22.

or even a clearly defined social group. At that time, entrepreneurs, when privatization of formerly state-owned companies had not yet taken place, can hardly have been said to exist as a social group with concrete interests. Rather, ODS's constituency was defined in political terms by those who sought to marginalize the former dissidents who had created and led Civic Forum during the revolution.

Consistent with its claims that the greatest problems facing the country concerned its relationship to the past, ODS supported the screening (or "lustration") law that banned former communist functionaries and secret police collaborators from elected or appointed public or professional positions in the state and joint-stock companies in which the state held a majority interest (Welsh 1996). Although the law was condemned by the European Union as unconstitutional, the ODS incorporated the same principles into its founding statutes, which declared, "I am not a member of any political party and I have never been a member of the People's Militia, StB [secret police], nor a collaborator for them." The eventual law on lustration, passed in October 1991, was led and publicly supported by parliamentarians from ODS. Antileft discourse was repeated by Klaus throughout the 1992 election campaign, when he described OH as a "left wing party, using the term 'liberal' in the American sense, not in the European sense, to my regret" (1992, p. 22). In a claim that would be repeated in the 1992 elections, ODS linked support for its market reforms with support for democracy and the federal state. Rather than provide unequivocal support for Czechoslovakia, ODS's program declared that the party "wishes to retain the existing Czechoslovak Federation, if the federal state proves to be viable and does not hinder further social change. However, there must be unified defence and foreign policies and financial and tax policies throughout the whole country."[9] This program was accompanied by the creation of institutional party structures across the country that would provide it with a network with which to conduct the 1992 electoral campaign. With this network, it also raised more money (43 million Czech crowns in 1991) than OH (18 million Czech crowns) (Mlynar 1992).

By contrast, OH declared its alliance with the principles of Civic Forum, as set out in its original 1989 founding document, and its intention to fulfill the 1990 election program, "which has not as yet been implemented."[10]

---

[9] In *East European Reporter* (1991), Vol. 4, p. 49.
[10] Ibid., p. 50.

Consistent with its origins, it sought to maintain the unity of society. In contrast to ODS's identification of its supporters as a specific set of potential voters, the OH program called for "dialogue and cooperation with the democratic right and the democratic left." It argued for a "radical but not ruthless" reform of the economy and held the lustration law to be unacceptable from an ethical and legal standpoint. OH's most prominent leader, Foreign Minister Jiří Dienstbier, repeatedly criticized the law and, in an ironic twist of fate, voted with the Communist Party to oppose it in parliament. In contrast to ODS's conditional support for the federation as long as it could be "viable," OH argued that there should be even greater autonomy for ethnic groups: "We believe that the Czechoslovak Federation should be retained. But the new constitution must make it possible for the [provinces of] Moravia and Silesia to also enjoy autonomy; whether as self-contained lands within the Czech republic, or as member of a tripartitite federation of Bohemia, Moravia, and Slovakia."[11]

After the 1990 elections, international assistance to Civic Forum's successors dropped off dramatically. The NED provided several grants in this period broadly targeted to the federation as a whole. It granted NDI $74,000 to organize party-building workshops on improving party organizations and on the mechanisms of grassroots organization and communications, and it awarded IRI $57,000 to sponsor a series of four training seminars in Czechoslovakia and Hungary to encourage the informed participation of women and youth in the political process. It granted the Association for Independent Social Analysis $19,300 to enable this Prague-based association to conduct a survey in advance of the June 1992 elections on Czech and Slovak attitudes toward political parties, participation in the electoral process, democratically elected government, and economic and social reform. Further, with funding from the U.S. Agency for International Development (AID), NDI provided assistance aimed at longer-term political party development to six parties in each of the Czech and Slovak republics in 1991 and 1992.

As noted, in the 1992 elections ODS garnered the largest percentage of the vote, while the OH failed even to reach the electoral threshold to enter parliament. After Klaus's victory in the elections, President Havel called upon him and Vladimír Mečiar, as the leaders of the majority parties, to form a government, but both party leaders quickly decided that this was impossible without agreement on the nature of the Czechoslovak state.

[11] Ibid., p. 51.

Klaus declared that "today's maimed federation was not capable of guaranteeing a continuation of economic reform" (Zak 1995, p. 262). With this, both leaders prepared to divide the state, even as preelection public opinion polls in 1992 showed that the division of the country was supported by less than one-third of the population in Slovakia and even less in the Czech Republic (Butora and Butorová 1993, p. 721).

Slovakia

In Slovakia, the emergence of political parties took a different direction from the Czech Republic and proved to have negative consequences for democracy. After 1989, current and former Communists retained greater influence than in the Czech provinces. The Slovak Communists were not seen as compromised by the repression of the student demonstrations in Prague in 1989 at the hands of the Czech Communist leaders, nor were they as repressive in general as their Czech counterparts. The Slovak opposition that formed Public against Violence (*Verenost' Proti Nasiliu*, or VPN) was also not as large, nor as prepared to create a new government, as Civic Forum. Indeed, VPN's highest representatives in the federal government were recent or former Communists (Prime Minister Marian Čálfa and Speaker of Parliament Alexander Dubček), as were those in the Slovak government (Prime Minister Milan Čič). Unlike Civic Forum, which maintained its broad identity until the elections, VPN divided almost immediately when its vice prime minister in the federal government broke off to form the Christian Democratic Movement (*Krest'ansko – Democraticke Hnutie*, or KDH). In the June 1990 elections, when faced with its weakness in public opinion polls, the movement's leaders deliberately chose to include the better-known former Communist politicians on their slate of candidates and saw a corresponding rise in the movement's popularity (Antalova 1998).

Again by contrast to the Czech Republic, international assistance to Slovakia was a fraction of the sum provided to the federation as a whole, although VPN can be said to have benefited from the grants by NED to draft a new election law and to monitor the elections. This suggests the need for international assistance to pay greater attention to ethnic differences within federal states, although it should be emphasized that these were national elections and that the capital of the country at that time was Prague. The only grant targeted to assist VPN was an $180,000 grant from IDEE which provided equipment and operational assistance that enabled VPN to equip four regional offices, partly fund its newspaper, *Verejnost'*, and support the

Center for Research for Social Problems which conducted public opinion surveys and sociological studies.

Like Civic Forum in the Czech Republic, VPN did not simply adopt Western models of election campaigns in the 1990 elections but rather sought to re-create the "merry" spirit of the revolution. Rather than run as a political party, VPN's program, titled "A Chance for Slovakia," declared that this was "a chance for all," and that it sought "to guarantee that the democratic changes which have begun will continue and not be turned, back."[12] The VPN headquarters in Bratislava prepared a show of caricature and parody of the symbols of communist rule, including "shrouded busts of Lenin and torn Communist Party flags spread across the floor for the visitors to walk on." As Horn observed, "Having long endured politics imposed from above, full of insufferably wooden rhetoric, elaborate ceremony, and self-important men in cheap suits and slicked-back hair, they decided the only antidote was to make this campaign into a carnival" (Horn 1990, p. 11). Notably, however, while Civic Forum won the majority of the vote in the Czech Republic, VPN won only roughly 35% of the vote in Slovakia (averaging its support in both houses), with the newly formed Christian Democratic Movement winning roughly 17% and the ex-Communists winning 13%.

After the 1990 elections, VPN splintered again. The split surrounded a leadership struggle for the movement, although the formation of new parties took a less democratic route than in the Czech Republic. After Slovak Prime Minister Vladimír Mečiar failed to win the chairmanship of VPN in February 1991, his close associate, the Slovak foreign minister, appeared on television and declared that the leadership of VPN had attempted to censor Mečiar's weekly television speech (a claim later disavowed). Based on the popular perception that he was a victim of communist-style politics, Mečiar's popularity soared. Subsequently the Presidium of the Slovak National Council (controlled by the VPN leadership) called for Mečiar's resignation, leading him to form the Movement for a Democratic Slovakia (*Hnutie za Demokraticke Slovensko*, or HZDS), while the remainder of VPN merged itself into the Civic Democratic Union (*Obcianska Demokraticka Unia*, or ODU). In April 1991, Mečiar was officially replaced as prime minister not by a representative of the weakened ODU but by the leader of the Christian Democratic Party, Ján Čarnogurský. Opinion polls at that

---

[12] "*Šanca pre Slovensko* (program *hnutie Verenost' Proti Nasiliu*) [A chance for Slovakia (the program of the movement Public against Violence)]," copy.

time indicate that although ODU and KDH continued to control the cabinet, HZDS polled support from about 27% of the electorate. With the support of the parties on the left (such as the former Slovak Communist Party), Mečiar's party could count on over 50% of the electorate, while ODU and KDH together could only count on about 30% (Wheaton and Kavan 1992, p. 233f).

Just as Václav Klaus in the Czech Republic sought to link the issue of the federation to acceptance of his economic reforms, new political parties in Slovakia also tied the relations between the republics to claims about the proper speed or direction of economic reform. Because heavy industry dating from the Communist period was located primarily in Slovakia, many argued that market reform had to take a different path than in the Czech Republic. Further, the emphasis in the Czech Republic on the lustration of all officials who had been Communist Party members was perceived as a threat in Slovakia, where many prominent ex-Communists (including Mečiar and the speaker of the federal parliament, Alexander Dubček) remained active in politics.

The question of the proper relationship between the republics was unclear during the election campaign of most Slovak parties, creating uncertainty as to the consequences of electoral victory for one party or another. Mečiar's HZDS took an ambiguous stand, emphasizing Slovak "sovereignty" and "autonomy" but without specifying his intentions for the future of the republic. This enabled him to "take sovereignty onto his agenda but in such a way that left Slovakia's potential legal status completely ambiguous" (Innes 1997, p. 420). Draper refers to Mečiar's advocacy of "confederation" as "a code word for loosening the bonds without breaking them" (1993, p. 22). While Slovak Prime Minister Ján Čarnogurský from the KDH declared his support for the federation, he at the same time identified his goal as "a star for Slovakia in the European flag" (Čarnogursky 1992). That is, Slovakia would remain part of the Czech and Slovak federation until entry into the European Union, when each republic would enter as a sovereign nation. Only the marginal Slovak National Party, which received little support in public opinion polls, called outright for an independent state, while the successor to VPN, ODU, declared in its founding program, "We favour the maintenance of a stable, democratic Czech and Slovak Federative Republic based on equal rights for all citizens and nationalities."[13] Although positive toward the federation, this statement

---

[13] In *East European Reporter* (1992), Vol. 5, p. 66.

avoided answering the constitutional question of how relations would be institutionalized.

International assistance to new political parties in Slovakia after the 1990 elections was nearly nonexistent. According to Quigley (1997), none of the international actors studied in this essay had offices in Slovakia until after the breakup in 1993. As noted, the NED provided several grants in this period broadly targeted to the federation as a whole, including assistance aimed at longer-term political party development in 1991 and 1992 to six parties in each of the Czech and Slovak republics (although the available data do not indicate precisely which six parties in each republic participated).

In the 1992 elections, Mečiar's HZDS received the largest percentage of the vote, followed by the ex-Communists and Slovak Nationalists (with the KDH fourth and the Civic Democratic Union failing to reach the electoral threshold). Mečiar quickly announced that he had a mandate that included the independence of Slovakia, a Slovak constitution, and international recognition of a sovereign Slovakia, agreeing with Václav Klaus to divide the country. While the absence of international assistance cannot be said to have caused Mečiar's success, the contrast with the victory of the democratic market reformers in the Czech Republic is striking. The failure of the VPN's heir, ODU, suggests that Western models of party organization do not take hold automatically across political and historical contexts, nor does initial success in founding elections guarantee the continued success of democratic parties. It highlights the danger of splintering the democratic opposition, rendering it vulnerable to populist challengers.

Further, Mečiar's electoral success cannot be explained in terms of the resonance of Slovak nationalist claims or the values of the electorate. After the election, public opinion polls indicated that the largest percentage of surveyed Slovak voters, 36.6%, indicated only negative feelings about the split of the country; this compared to 26.7% who felt only positive and 21.8% who felt ambivalent (Butorova 1993, p. 70). Research on HZDS voters reveals a range of opinions about the proper role of the federation: 14% believed that Slovakia should be part of a unitary Czechoslovak state, 29% favored federation, 22% favored confederation, and 19% preferred an independent Slovak state (Frič 1992, p. 79). As Martin Butora and Zora Butorová observed, "what proved to be crucial was not the public opinion but the lack of sufficiently strong political groupings on both sides that could have shared their basic ideas and concepts about the form of the common state and could have cooperated in a systematic and efficient way in the preservation and development of this shared vision" (Butora and Butorová 1993, p. 721).

Analysis and Conclusions

In this essay I argued that new parties in postcommunist Eastern Europe will not necessarily follow the paths of parties in previous Western parliamentary democracies and that the literature on party formation ignores the impact of international actors. Let me return to both claims. First, contrary to the traditional focus on socioeconomic cleavages, this essay argues that the legacy of the Leninist regime prevented the development of preexisting interests that parties could simply reflect; rather, new parties emerged out of revolutionary movements through competition and mobilization for electoral support. Although Czechoslovakia was the only country in East Central Europe that could claim a democratic legacy predating communism, the new parties did not reflect prior historical cleavages and the previously dominant social democratic parties of the First Czechoslovak Republic did not reemerge as powerful political forces; rather, a new Western market-oriented ODS led by Finance Minister Klaus emerged in the Czech Republic to govern successfully.[14]

This is not to minimize the very real economic differences in each country due to different experiences of industrialization under communism. Rather, it is to argue that the polarization of the new political parties was not the result of ancient ethnic differences or inexorable economic forces but instead the political result of leaders of new parties competing for electoral support in uncertain conditions. As I have argued, in the dynamic conditions of postcommunist reform, political identities and economic interests are in greater flux than in stable periods. Under such conditions, as the literature on contentious politics suggests, leaders of new political parties are likely to act like social movement entrepreneurs seeking to mobilize potential supporters in light of varying opportunities, resources, and ways of framing their claims (McAdam, McCarthy, and Zald 1996). Notably, rather than reflecting public sentiments to divide the country, the dominant successor parties in the Czech Republic and Slovakia sought to mobilize votes in the absence of public support for separation by linking their claims for economic reform with the appropriate relationship between republics. The electoral success of ODS and HZDS suggests that both

[14] See Rothschild (1974) for electoral data on interwar parties in Czechoslovakia.

parties successfully linked their views on economic reform, the lustration law, and the relationship between republics, as well as benefited from their organizational advantages in the election campaign.

Second, attention to the interaction between international and domestic factors draws together previously disparate insights on party emergence. The divergent paths taken by the two countries suggest the limits of applying Western models of party organization across contexts and the need for democratic actors to be strengthened beyond founding elections. All claims of influence must be measured in light of complex, dynamic developments, especially when the amounts of funding are relatively small and their activities or efforts rarely create binding arrangements (in contrast to international monetary institutions that can implement economic sanctions or governmental organizations that can enforce political sanctions). This essay highlights the interactive processes whereby international models of party organization are adopted in some cases but adapted to mobilize popular support.

Any assessment of transnational assistance to political parties in the 1990 elections must begin with the observation that Civic Forum and VPN, while prodemocratic, were not political parties in the traditional sense of the word. Initially, revolutionary movements are unlikely to have a strong party identification and may seek assistance from all sources, given their perceived need for help, while international pressures may lead other parties or movements to reject assistance from seemingly appropriate partners. For example, Václav Klaus's ODS, despite his Thatcherite rhetoric, chose to establish links with the German Christian Democrats rather than British conservatives, whose stance against European integration might have hindered entry to the European Union (Pridham 1996, p. 209).

Such international efforts, the cases suggest, play a more significant role when revolutionary movements face the initial problems of governing, than in the subsequent period of competition among new parties. NED's observation that it could prepare an election advising team for President Havel within a week suggests that international nongovernmental organizations can provide assistance more quickly than most government bureaucracies (Quigley 1997). Pridham observes, "external support may be an important moral or material resource for party strategies, particularly at this time when new party systems are being constructed" (1995, pp. 27–8). Nonetheless, these cases make it clear that despite such support, party formation and development can take unforeseen directions as a result of internal struggles.

The development of new political parties in the Czech Republic and Slovakia reveals the limitations of democracy assistance targeted solely to free elections. International assistance after the 1990 elections declined dramatically, and the nature of funding for political parties changed as well, with the state itself becoming a major source of funds, reimbursing parties for election expenses, and providing salaries for elected members (Lewis 1998). According to Nadia Diuk, senior program officer at NED at the time, NED's assistance to political parties was limited by two primary factors: the domestic politics of financing assistance to Eastern Europe and the evolving understanding of assistance to promote democracy.[15]

First, the dramatic decline in funding between 1990 and 1992 was the result of changes in U.S. policy concerning assistance to Eastern Europe. NED was asked to administer the first year of funding for Eastern Europe (the Support for East European Democracy [SEED] program) in 1990 because of AID's inexperience with democracy assistance and with the region. However, it subsequently lost this funding when congressional policy reallocated control to AID. After 1990, NED had to rely upon its own appropriation and its partners, NDI and IRI, upon their regular allocations of funds, which were significantly smaller. Although NDI and IRI began to apply for funding directly from AID, the process was lengthier and slower than for NED funding, which may explain the time gap between the diverse projects underway in 1990 and the comparatively little funding for the elections in 1992.

Further, many policymakers in Washington had little experience with assistance to new political parties, having worked previously only with development aid. They therefore initially believed that democracy assistance was largely complete once founding elections had been held and the "democrats" were in power. While NED had a history of work in the region, the 1990–2 period was one in which funders and policymakers were also learning about the need for ongoing assistance to prevent reversals in democratization. Mečiar's rise to prominence in Slovakia in 1991 highlights the vulnerability of new democratic parties to more authoritarian populist challengers and the lack of stable electorates for new parties. It is striking that nearly one-quarter of the vote in each republic in 1992 was for parties that failed to reach the electoral threshold and enter parliament.

By stressing how new party leaders adapted Western models to mobilize electoral support, I have sought to avoid making leaders of the new parties

---

[15] Interview with the author, March 23, 1999.

seem either overly cynical or dupes (summed up in Václav Klaus's rejection of international assistance as "soft advice for hard currency"). Transnational links between parties with similar ideological tendencies have a long postwar history, beginning with the German *stiftungen* (Pinto-Duschinsky 1991, 1997; Pridham 1996). The failure of the dissident-led successors to the revolutionary movements is notable in light of their failure to adopt Western models of party organization. Consistent with Michels's arguments about the need for organizational hierarchy in modern political parties, Václav Klaus declared that the success of his ODS in the Czech Republic

was the final blow to those who advocated the ideas of "unpolitical politics," to those who saw the future as a world full of civic movements and temporary initiatives without party structures or clearly defined organizational rules, to those who wanted a world based on brave and innovative ideas implemented directly by enlightened intellectuals who tried to stay above the complicated world of politics. (Klaus 1997, p. 110)

If the Czech Republic and Slovakia are suggestive, the "antipolitics" of dissidents and revolutionary movements is virtually powerless against the imperatives of contemporary political competition. This essay suggests that as social movements gain political power, even in the context of emerging democracy, they must confront the issue of transforming themselves into parties, despite inexperience or even reluctance to engage in party politics. To survive, they need to compete for electoral support. As Paul Hirst argues: "'Civil society' as a homogeneous political force is an idea at variance with modern pluralist democracy, which relies on the divisions of civil society expressed in political competition contained within the party system to ensure social and political order" (Hirst 1991, p. 234).

Further comparative research would demonstrate even greater variations in the nature of party emergence after the collapse of communist states. Such research should compare Czechoslovakia with other postcommunist countries, such as Poland (where party fragmentation hobbled postcommunist governments) or Hungary (where parties had emerged prior to the round-table negotiations). Comparison with political parties in the former Soviet Union or with new parties in South Africa might provide contrasting paths of democratization (Klandermans, Roefs, and Olivier 1998). Analysis of assistance to the former Yugoslavia might highlight the risks of assistance in conditions of war.

In conclusion, it is evident that the triumph of democratic *movements* does not lead to any simple model of triumphant democratic *parties*.

Parties out of Movements

Nor – at least in these cases – did international assistance and guidance produce determinate outcomes. Rather, the development of parties out of movements involves complex and contingent interactions among movements, new parties seeking electoral support, the public they seek to mobilize, and the international agencies that provide both assistance and guidance for party formation.

6

From Movement to Party to Government

WHY SOCIAL POLICIES IN KERALA AND WEST BENGAL ARE SO DIFFERENT

Manali Desai

Can the relationship between parties and movements explain variations in the social policy agenda of governments? This essay attempts to answer this question by addressing a heretofore neglected puzzle in Indian politics. Why has the same leftist political party, which has dominated the political scene in the two Indian states of Kerala and West Bengal since Independence in 1947, implemented far-reaching social policies in one of these states but not in the other? I will argue that the differences in policies reflect historical differences in social movement–party dynamics during the later stages of the Indian nationalist independence movement, from roughly 1920 until 1947. These dynamics created different relationships between the party and civil society in the two states. In Kerala, leftists undertook grassroots organizing and captured political power considerably earlier than in West Bengal, and became deeply engaged in an agenda for antipoverty reforms that was not easily set aside for electoral concerns. In West Bengal, the left party came to power later, with leaders who were far more isolated from popular movements; these leaders focused first on securing political power and less on social reform. By taking a historical perspective on these outcomes, I open up the black box of party decision making to show how policy evolution depended not only on party ideology or on structural constraints, but also on the historically specific contexts of social movement dynamics in Kerala and West Bengal during the late nationalist period.

What do the concepts "parties" and "movements" mean here, and what is the relationship between them? Parties are organizations that exist to place and keep political groups or individuals in political power. I borrow from Panebianco (1988, p. 53) in emphasizing that parties in their formative phase are shaped in large part by the leadership's ideological aims and political goals. These and, most important, the strategies and tactics that leaders derive from their theory of the situation, are crucial in shaping not only the party's identity, but what it actually does.[1] However, not every aspect of the party's eventual institutionalization can be traced back to this "founding moment." Instead, I will show how the early choices made by parties created a situation of path dependency; these paths or trajectories depended on the interaction of party goals with specific conditions in their political environment and social structure. Parties are relatively autonomous in that they represent strategies and tactics that are meant to be applied to a specific historical situation,[2] but their success or failure is also conditioned by circumstances that are not entirely within their control.

Movements are broad mobilizations of ordinary people to seek a particular goal or goals. In some cases, such as the Indian nationalist movement, parties are born in the contexts of movements and out of schisms within movements. All the left parties in India were born in this context, and the dynamics of the nationalist, anticolonial movement, as well as the left parties' analysis and understanding of it, determined to a large extent what the parties did and what choices they made. Thus the nationalist movement, and crucially the regional dynamics of the anticolonial movement, structured the pathways of party formation and growth in each of the two regions.

An historical perspective on party evolution thus has two important general implications. The theoretical literature on political parties often elides those instances in which parties are simply social movements by another name. If the boundary between institutionalized and noninstitutionalized politics in modern societies is "fuzzy and permeable," as Goldstone suggests in the introduction to this volume, then this claim must be advanced even more forcefully in the case of societies where parties have only recently emerged from social movements. In these instances, focusing on the organizational character of parties, and separating them from the study of their genesis in social movements, can lead to blind spots. The exclusive focus

---

[1] The parties examined here were formed during or just before the 1930s and 1940s, the period of direct concern in this essay. The Communist Party of India (CPI) was founded in 1920, while the Congress Socialist Party (CSP) was formed in 1934. I thus focus less on the eventual organizational characteristics of both parties than on their early defining aims, strategies of political struggle, philosophies of revolution and the tactics by which to bring it about, and, most important, their different (and shifting) orientations toward the nationalist, anticolonial movement under the leadership of the Indian National Congress.

[2] Przeworski (1985, p. 101) makes the crucial point that "[p]olitical parties are not simply reflections of class structure or expressions of class interests . . . [but] are relatively autonomous from both the social structure and state institutions."

on parties as organizations might reflect a bias toward the more established democracies of the West whose parties have indeed strayed from their insurgent origins. Yet, as Panebianco (1988, p. xiii) states: "The way in which the cards are dealt out and the outcomes of the different rounds played out in the formative phase of an organization, continue in many ways to condition the life of the organization even decades afterwards . . . the crucial political choices made by its founding fathers, the first struggles for organizational control, and the way in which the organization was formed, will leave an indelible mark." Indeed, a second, and related, point that emerges from this study is that political struggles waged at one time under party leadership can for decades afterward impact the extent of their political power. Thus there can be significant (and unintended) "lag effects" through which political struggles affect future generations. These claims also point, methodologically, to the usefulness of case studies, which through diachronic analysis can open up the black box of parties with ostensibly similar characteristics. A cross-sectional approach would miss this inherently historical process (Rueschemeyer, Stephens, and Stephens 1992).

This essay analyzes the historical trajectory from movement to party formation, and then to institutionalization in power, of the Communist Party of India (CPI) in Kerala and West Bengal (the party later split in West Bengal, the dominant wing becoming known as the Communist Party–Marxist, or CPM). It shows why the same party has pursued different social policies, resulting in sharp differences in poverty alleviation, in the two states since Independence.

Social Policies and Social Development: Kerala and West Bengal Compared

Kerala's welfarist state has been widely celebrated as a model of how social policies can considerably reduce poverty and inequality without high rates of economic growth (Franke and Chasin 1989; Dreze and Sen 1995). One of the first measures of the Communist government in Kerala (formed in 1957) was to implement the most radical land reform legislation (Agrarian Relations Bill) in all of India: The law granted tenurial rights to all cultivators and imposed ceilings on the size of landholdings. The CPI also passed the Education Bill, which doubled expenditures on primary schools. Since then successive governments, both Communist and noncommunist, have extended the public food distribution system to cover 97% of the population, set up Fair Price Shops, provided comprehensive free meal programs in schools, and distributed food supplements through health centers to expectant and nursing mothers. The Communist-led governments also established special nutritional and educational programs for tribal and slum children. In 1974, the Kerala government passed the Agricultural Laborers Bill, with the aim of reducing underemployment and insecurity of employment and increasing wage levels. Kerala has since achieved the highest agricultural wage rates of any Indian state (Jose 1984; Kumar 1982). In the fifty years since Independence. Kerala is reported to have reduced poverty on average by 2.4% a year – roughly 120 times the improvement in Bihar, one of the poorest states in India (World Bank 1998).

In West Bengal, the most radical antipoverty measure the Communist Party undertook since it began to win election to continuous terms in 1977 was to record the land titles of sharecroppers in a program titled Operation Barga. The result of this program was to grant sharecroppers, who had been left out of all prior land legislation, title to their land. The impetus for taking the reforms off paper (they had been written as early as 1950 during the Congress regime in Bengal), and actually implementing them came from the Communists. During the united front government in 1969–70, peasants were asked to identify land held above the ceiling, and more than 500,000 acres were distributed among the landless (Dasgupta 1984, p. A-86). When the CPM returned to power in 1977, they ensured that the legislation was properly implemented. This provides direct evidence that left parties are more likely to push for redistributive reforms. However, the Bengal case also provides evidence that all left parties do not succeed in alleviating poverty to the same extent. The literacy rate among women in Kerala is 86% compared with 47% in Bengal. The male literacy rate in Kerala is 94%, while it is 68% in Bengal. These figures put Bengal slightly above the Indian average (Dreze and Sen 1995, p. 47). The average life expectancy of Kerala's population is on average ten years more than Bengal's. The CPM in Bengal has not taken much of a lead in providing health, education, or housing; currently, these do not differ too much from those provided by other state governments in India (Mallick 1993; Dreze and Sen 1995, p. 56).

The comparative logic in this analysis uses West Bengal (Bengal during the colonial period) as a contrasting case to highlight the turning points in Kerala's historical trajectory toward the development of a welfarist state. The historical sequence leading toward the endpoint in Kerala is probed by asking what crucial variables or turning points were absent in Bengal that might have allowed for an outcome similar to that of Kerala.

I shall analyze the comparative sequences in Kerala and Bengal by focusing on the relationship between structure and agency in the determination of the historical trajectories in Kerala and Bengal. First, I examine the differences in social structure, particularly the shifts that occurred as a result of colonial land tenure and commercial policies during the nineteenth century. Here, I am interested in the manner in which colonial policies gave rise to the potential for – as well as barriers to – radicalism among peasants and workers, and opportunities for leftist parties to build a base. I then consider different dimensions of agency: (1) What were the differences in left formations that emerged in the two regions, that is, how did these parties emerge and how were the organized? (2) Who constituted the dominant leadership of these parties, what were their prior political experiences, and what strategies and tactics did they adopt? (3) What was their analysis of the specific situation in each of these regions, and how did they utilize the nationalist movement to build their own influence? I then ask, what was the relative importance of each of these factors in determining the different outcomes?

Colonial Rule, Agrarian Structure, and the Potential for Agrarian Radicalism

In colonial India, with its overwhelmingly agrarian population, the possibilities for the growth of left parties depended fundamentally on peasant radicalism (or the potential for it). I first begin by asking how British policies concerning land tenure, revenue extraction, and commercialization affected the agrarian structures and shaped the potential for agrarian radicalism.

During the colonial era, Kerala was made up of three separate provinces – Malabar, Travancore, and Cochin. Malabar, the northernmost province, came under direct British rule in 1792; Travancore and Cochin were princely states, ruled indirectly by the British through a series of treaties over the course of the nineteenth century. In Kerala, the different forms of colonial rule – direct versus indirect – had sharply contrasting effects on the respective agrarian structures. In Malabar, the British identified the landholding castes (*jenmis*) as the "landlord they knew at home," granting them private proprietorship rights to land and reducing all other tenants – *kanomdars* and *verumpattomdars* – to the level of insecure tenants-at-will. As population grew, in the absence of corresponding industrial growth the person/land ratio also increased, landlords found their position considerably strengthened. During the late nineteenth century they began evicting tenants on a large scale in order to extract higher rents (Panikkar 1989). Because most landlords were upper caste (Namboodiripads and Nairs), and the tenant-cultivators and agricultural laborers below them were lower caste (Tiyyas, Pulayas, Cherumas), the reinforcement of landlord power left the caste hierarchy – perhaps the most iniquitous in India – untouched.

In sharp contrast to the policy followed in Malabar, the British pushed for a policy of granting proprietorship rights to tenants on state-owned lands in Travancore and Cochin (this policy was also known as the *ryotwari* policy. Implemented by the princely states "from above," the land reforms were intended to promote commercialization and the growth of cash crops.[3] The land reforms in Cochin did not challenge landlord domination to the extent that they did in Travancore, because the princely state was weaker and landlords constituted a larger proportion of the agrarian population (40% compared with less than 20% in Travancore).

In Bengal, the British land policy was enacted through the Permanent Settlement of 1793, which, as in Malabar, granted revenue collectors from the Mughal period the title of "landlord" with full proprietorship rights. However, the predominant unit of agricultural production was the small peasant family farm, cultivated by family labor. The British were anxious to preserve the peasants' rights to the land as far as possible, in part out of fear of peasant insurgency and in part to encourage the growth of commercial crops. Legally, then, two sets of rights came to be recognized: the right of proprietorship and the right of occupancy.

The growth of trade in rice and jute had the effect of encouraging extensive rent exploitation and sub-infeudation based on rights of occupancy. Jute was a popular crop because peasants could get cash advances when their food stocks from previous rice harvests were low, but the market in jute fluctuated tremendously and peasants could never rise above the subsistence level (Chatterjee 1984, pp. 7–9). The major proprietors or *zamindars*, forced by the state's high revenue demands, farmed out jungle lands and other cultivable wastelands on tenurial leases to a class of "enterprising men" who then cleared the land and settled it with tenant-cultivators. As cultivated area and rent increased over the mid-nineteenth century, a gap arose – in favor of the landlords – between the fixed land revenue demanded by the British

[3] See Varghese (1970). As early as 1829, the Travancore state took measures to prevent the eviction of tenants by landlords if they had been paying their dues regularly. The Royal Proclamation of 1867 formalized this reform. The Travancore Janmie and Kudiyan Regulation of 1896 gave full ownership rights to peasant proprietors on state-owned lands, and higher tenants on private lands were given full security of tenancy (Tharakan 1984).

and the higher rent that could be extracted from the actual cultivators. In turn, this gap in revenues spawned a huge increase in rentier interests. It was estimated in 1918–19 that proprietors and intermediate tenure holders in Bengal took as much as 76.7% of the gross rental, paying the rest as land revenue (ibid.). The resulting structure of interests at the top consisted of a few wealthy landlords, followed by numerous estates below that were held by "petty proprietors-tenureholders-cum-professionals," also known as *bhadralok*.

A similar process of fragmentation and differentiation of rights took place at the level of land occupation. Increasing population growth in the late nineteenth and early twentieth centuries and rising demand for land led to this process of sub-infeudation, which featured the rise of numerous intermediaries who sought a larger share of the rent. The pressure on land was exacerbated by the absence of rural industries or industrial growth. As a result of the codification of different rights – legal rights against eviction, against enhancement of rents, and so on – the subletting and mortgaging of occupational interests became common practice. By the nineteenth century, the land tenure relations in Bengal had congealed along a few different lines: In north Bengal the dominant divide was between tenant-farmers or rich farmers (known as *jotedars*) and laborers, drawn primarily from semitribal groups (known as *adhiars*). The rich tenant-farmers dominated the produce market, made decisions about production, and extracted a large proportion of the produce as share rent and loan interest (Bose 1986, p. 15). In many parts of North Bengal, agricultural laborers were completely landless and serflike. In West and Central Bengal, the land tenure relations consisted of a "small-holding demesne labor" complex in which "gentlemen" absentee farmers (*bhadralok*) held villages surrounded by peasant sharecroppers. In East Bengal, the dominant form of landholding was smallholding, where the typical unit was the small peasant family farm. Table 6.1 shows the comparative agrarian structures that had developed in the regional zones of Kerala and Bengal in 1931.

The figures in this table reveal several interesting comparative differences in land tenure structures within Kerala and Bengal as well as between them. First, the proportion of owner-cultivators was clearly far more sizable in Bengal than in Kerala (barring the province of Travancore). Indeed, the majority of agricultural land in Bengal was in the direct possession of owner-cultivators or *raiyat*.

Yet these figures can only reveal broad categories of agricultural occupation; they do not tell us much about the different categories of gradations

Table 6.1. *Land Tenure Patterns in the Regions of Kerala and Bengal*

Region	Noncultivating Owners	Owner-Cultivators	Tenants	Agricultural Laborers
Kerala				
Malabar	2.18	6	23	68
Travancore	–	61	6	31
Cochin	–	19	21	56
Bengal				
South and Southwest Bengal	9.4	41.5	8.4	40
North Bengal	7.7	48	14	29.4
East Bengal	7.9	65	6.1	20

Note: Figures for Kerala taken from Kannan (1988) and Jeffrey (1978, p. 135). Figures for Bengal calculated from Chatterjee (1984, p. 39).

The numbers are percentages of the total agricultured population.

of *raiyati* (occupational) rights that existed in the land. The flip side of British enforcement of clear land rights in Bengal was peasant households' loss of land (depeasantization). Depeasantization was particularly exacerbated by two conditions: the Depression of the early 1930s and rising population. When crop prices dropped sharply during the Depression, the flow of money credit stopped and numerous peasant smallholders found themselves heavily indebted. Landlords and rich peasants purchased their land, and numerous peasants were proletarianized in the process. This trend was particularly acute in West and Central Bengal, where the landholding structure "tended to sag in the middle, and was reinforced at the extremities by the extension of the landlords (*khamar*) and a land poor, if not wholly landless, rural work force" (Bose 1986, p. 167). Often peasants were not evicted outright, as they were in Malabar; they continued to cultivate the land, but with inferior rights and higher rents (Bose 1986). When peasants lost their land outright and became laborers, as in South and Southwest Bengal, sharecropping became the preferred mode of cultivation for landowners, as they became interested in securing a share of the produce with the spread of the market in jute and rice (Dhanagare 1983).

In Malabar and Cochin, occupancy rights were weaker, and in Malabar in particular, tenancies had become increasingly insecure during the turn of the century. Landlords began to favor the year-to-year lease (also known as *verumpattom*) over longer leases (known as *kanom*). The Depression exacerbated these trends. In Malabar, cultivators who had managed to attain some degree of independence from landlords during the price boom of the 1920s found themselves flung back into dependence on them after prices crashed in the 1930s (Menon 1994). Smallholders had to turn increasingly to agricultural labor to supplement their incomes. Between 1921 and 1931 the percentage of cultivating tenants within the total agricultural population fell from 34% to 21% and the proportion of agricultural laborers rose from 58% to 68% (Kannan 1988, p. 46). Table 6.1 reveals that the proportions of agricultural labor were higher overall in Kerala than in Bengal; although the western and central regions of Bengal had the largest number of agricultural laborers within Bengal, their numbers were far higher in Malabar.

Let us turn now to the second question: In which areas did British land tenure policies have the effect of increasing the potential for agrarian radicalism, and in which regions was this potential muted? Moore (1966, pp. 459, 469–70) argues that the weakening of landlord repression and the failure of landlords to take to commercial activity increases the potential for peasant radicalism. Among peasants "the types of solidary arrangements ... are important ... as they constitute focal points for the creation of a distinct peasant society in opposition to the dominant class." Weak solidarity results in part from certain types of residential patterns; for example, isolated farmsteads instead of integrated villages weaken the possibilities of peasant rebellions. Paige (1975, pp. 37, 60–2) similarly argues that sharecroppers in decentralized systems have strong incentives for collective action because they are interdependent and work cooperatively. In addition, because they have "weak ties to the land, working-class occupational homogeneity and work group interdependence," they exhibit forms of radicalism much like an industrial wage force. For Wolf (1969) the most revolutionary peasants are middle peasants because they are most vulnerable to market shocks, and, more important, because of their independent base, they possess tactical resources to challenge landlords. Scott (1976) and Moore (1966) are perhaps most directly concerned with the nature of the link between landlord and peasant. Scott focuses on the manner in which the market erodes the paternalistic ties between landlords and peasants, where the demands of the landlord cross the "consensual" line of exploitation and snap the earlier bond between them. For Moore, where the link between landlord and peasant is strong, rebellions are likely to be weak. This link, he argues, is weakened where there is strong competition for land or population growth. Apart from these general propositions, Moore also discusses a critical aspect of agrarian relations in India that is surprisingly neglected by Paige and Wolf – namely, caste. For Moore, caste has had the general effect of muting peasant radicalism. According to Moore (1966, pp. 334–41), the caste system has encouraged (1) the tendency for opposition to take the form of another caste segment and (2) submissive behavior on the part of peasants.

These theories, useful as they are in delineating the potential for radicalism, cannot explain a number of peculiarities. In Malabar, prior to the 1930s, out of the same set of tenancy relations in the northern and southern districts, there arose two very different reactions on the part of peasants to landlordism. During the late nineteenth and early twentieth centuries, Muslim tenants in south Malabar led a series of fierce rebellions against Hindu landlords, refracting their understanding of class exploitation through a religious lens. In north Malabar, Hindu peasants exhibited no such tendency toward radicalism. This paradox simply cannot be accounted for unless we take into account the differences in the two peasant communities. The particularly rigid and hierarchical caste system in Malabar precluded the independent occurrence of collective action among Hindu tenant-cultivators. In Malabar, not simply untouchability but unseeability and distance pollution were enforced by the upper-caste Nairs and Namboodiripads. It was a system that finely tuned an upper caste "conception of disgust." Upper castes maintained this imbalance of power through symbolic violence[4] as well as physical force.[5] The daily reinforcement of submissive behavior and its underlying material basis – landlord–tenant relations – would not have easily allowed for collective action. Horizontal intracaste relations were also weak, largely because settlement patterns tended to cluster in and around the landlord's estate (*tarvad*). Thus unlike their Muslim counterparts in South Malabar, for whom the mosque was a crucial site of mobilization during the Moplah Rebellions, Hindu peasants did not have corresponding sites of mobilization (Wood 1987). Apart from occasional meetings in marketplaces, poor tenants and cultivators were separated and dispersed by the residential pattern of isolated homesteads and

---

[4] Lower-caste tenants were forced to use "repugnant forms of address" about themselves and to prostrate themselves before their upper-caste landlords.

[5] Portions of lower castes were kept as slaves, and their masters were authorized "to punish them for refractory conduct, a power which it may be imagined, was frequently abused in no small degree. Even those that were not avowed slaves used to be treated almost as such" (Extracts from Dewan's letter quoted by Resident in his letter to Acting Chief Secretary, Government of Madras, March 9, 1870, Regional Records, Vol. I, p. 280).

the segmented and hierarchical nature of the caste system. Here, the conditions that Moore (1966) outlines for weak peasant solidarity appear to be met.

The structural barriers to the growth of peasant radicalism, however, were not insurmountable. The same peasants joined a militant movement during the mid-1930s under the aegis of the Congress Socialist Party. Why and how this occurred will be discussed in the second half of this essay.

Turning now to Bengal, in the northernmost regions, the potential for radicalism among agricultural laborers was acute because they constituted a nearly landless force in opposition to the landholding rich tenant-farmers (see Paige 1975, pp. 60–2, for an elaboration of the theory). In the western and southwestern regions of Bengal, the increase in sharecropping, depeasantization, and proletarianization (that was in addition caste-homogeneous) created some potential for rebellion. However, landlords continued to maintain a strong position through the Depression years, particularly as the competition for land was intense. In the eastern regions of Bengal, the smallholding peasant communities were cemented by religious homogeneity, as most of them were Muslims. The potential for antilandlord consciousness was high among the peasantry, but their actions could potentially also take overtly religious expression, as political maneuvering by Hindu and Muslim communalists eventually proved more powerful than class-based actions.

In sum, one cannot read off the potential for peasant radicalism from a simple structural breakdown of land relations. Regions with similar land relations differed in radicalism; regions with different patterns of land tenure produced similar leftist movements. To explain the development of left parties and mobilization, we need to explore the specific choices and strategies adopted by left leaders and organizations in the various regions of Kerala and West Bengal.

Political Cleaveages and Leftist Mobilization

The remainder of this essay will address the crucial issue of the "relative autonomy of politics" in the specific historical conjunctures of late nationalist Kerala and Bengal. I focus particularly on the political struggles that gave rise to the left parties – the Congress Socialist Party (CSP) in Kerala and the Communist Party of India (CPI) in Bengal – and the effect of party strategies and tactics in determining (1) the differences in their social bases and (2) the extent to which they became political forces in the two regions.

I focus on three dimensions of these parties: the social origins of party leadership, party strategies and tactics, and the relationship of parties to movements. I argue that in Kerala the origins of CSP leadership in anticaste social reform movements mattered because they propelled the leadership toward tactics that linked class-based organizing with wider social change. Thus, while the CSP's nominal goals differed very little from those of the CPI after 1936, when the CPI adopted the line of a "united front from below," its actual practices and implementation of political struggles drew on years of experience prior to its formation as a left political party. These shared experiences of working together also gave the leadership a cohesion that the CPI in Bengal lacked because of its own fragmented and internally fractious origins. The CSP in Kerala furthered its cohesive functioning by working within the Congress Party throughout the 1930s. These tactics also gave them the advantage of being able to utilize the political opportunity that opened up in the nationalist movement during the early 1930s, a time when the Congress Party was weak and internally divided. Cooperation with Congress lent the CSP the character of a broad social movement, that is, the party was identified synonymously with a multifaceted movement that was aimed at gaining independence from the British and ending monarchical rule in the princely states of Travancore and Cochin, with winning the adult franchise and greater economic rights for poor peasants and workers, and with a series of radical antilandlord campaigns. The CPI in Bengal was much weaker, both as a party and as a movement. Its primary gains in establishing a social base were made in the 1940s, tapping the potential for agrarian and working-class radicalism to some extent between 1939 and 1945. Consequently, the Bengal CPI emerged with a much more restricted base than did the CSP in Kerala.

Comparative Social Origins of Radicalism in Kerala and Bengal in the Early Twentieth Century

In Kerala, most of the leaders who eventually joined the CSP in 1934 began their political careers as anticaste activists. Drawn primarily from the upper-caste Namboodiris and Nairs, they began contesting what they perceived as outmoded and oppressive intracommunity practices such as the joint family system of inheritance, insularity from the outside world, and wasteful customs.[6] Their critique was conditioned by the spread of colonial

[6] The Namboodiri Yogakshema Sabha (founded in 1908) pressed for four main objectives: (1) to allow all young Namboodiri men to marry within the community; (2) to study English;

rule, wherein land reforms, commercialization, and bureaucratization had allowed a degree of upward mobility for lower castes. More importantly, radical anticaste activity was simultaneously being initiated by the lower castes themselves – such as the Ezhavas in Travancore, the Tiyyas in Malabar, and the Pulayas – who led a series of campaigns aimed at ending untouchability, caste pollution rituals, and prohibition from using temples and public roads, as well as promoting access to education and the general extension of civil rights.

Although the early phase of lower-caste activity (at the turn of the nineteenth century and the first two decades of the twentieth century) was somewhat moderate, and aimed at securing middle-class Ezhavas and Tiyyas access to education and entry into administrative bodies, in its later phase a number of radical critiques of caste began to develop. For example, in 1933, a split in the Ezhava movement became apparent, with younger, more radical members seeking to replace the old slogan "one caste, one religion, one God" with the atheistic and radical "no caste, no religion, no God." In 1933 a number of such radicals formed the All-Travancore Youth League. They argued that Ezhavas belonged to a community separate from the larger Hindu community, and many sought conversion to Buddhism. Militant struggle was also espoused by the Ezhava leader K. Aiyyappan, who stated at a meeting of 2,000 Ezhava coir workers : "Just as the Russians managed to obtain freedom by putting an end to their Royal family, so the Ezhavas also must fight to the very end without caring [for] the guns of the sepoys, batons of the Police or even the Maharaja" (cited in Jeffrey 1978, pp. 156).

Caste reform fervor had begun to sweep through a section of the upper castes simultaneously. E. M. S. Namboodiripad, a CSP leader and later a Communist leader, was actively involved in a social reform organization during the 1920s known as the Yogakshema Namboodiri Sabha. The objective of the young Namboodiris was to contest what they perceived as the feudal practices of their caste community, as well as the superstition and customs that they saw as redundant in the new era of Western education and upward mobility. A number of younger, disillusioned, and often (not always) deracinated Namboodiris and Nairs (who had formed their own caste association, known as the Nair Service Society) sought to extend

---

(3) to abolish the practice of purdah (veiling) among women; and (4) widow remarriage. Similarly, the Nairs formed the Nair Service Society in part to abolish subdivisions within the Nairs that prevented them from marrying within their own community. Wasteful ceremonies often compelled poor Nairs to go into debt or sell their possessions (Gopalan 1959).

their critique of caste even further. By the late 1920s, marriage reform laws and family partition acts were in place, and most of the objectives of the caste associations had been realized. A number of them began looking for a broader forum for social change.

In Bengal, as in Kerala, there was a large sphere of anticolonial political activity whose ideology, modes, and techniques of struggle lay outside the sphere of Gandhian nationalism. But unlike in Kerala, this radical opposition did not emerge from an indigenous critique of caste, one that began with the self-activity of lower castes; instead the dominant leitmotif of radical non-Congress nationalism in Bengal was armed struggle and secret society conspiracies. By 1900, a number of revolutionary terrorist groups had come into existence. Inspired by the European Enlightenment, urban middle-class youth took to revolutionary politics as early as 1870. They planted bombs and seized arms in daring raids. By 1908–10, two groups in particular dominated the terrorist movement – Jugantar and Anushilan Samiti. They advocated revolution through armed struggle and strict discipline. The basic unit of these organizations was the *dal*. It consisted of a group of followers who owed complete loyalty and devotion to the leader. One important effect of the "cult of authority" that drove the entire movement was that when the leader of the *dal* died, the entire faction disintegrated (Gordon 1974). Jugantar was a loose federation of revolutionary groups and lacked the centralized coordination of Anushilan Samiti. Most important, the multiple terrorist groups (the Dacca Anushilan Samiti had "hundreds of branches under its control [Gordon 1974, p. 241]) were exceedingly fragmented, and the movement itself was decentralized.[7] The two groups were also bitter rivals. In the postterrorist phase of Bengali nationalism, this rivalry persisted within the Congress leadership.

The types of radicalism, nationalist as well as social, that emerged in Kerala and Bengal during the early decades of the twentieth century cannot be traced solely to differences in the social formations between the regions. Historians of modern Bengal often claim that the upper-caste makeup of the radical leadership was responsible for the great social distance that existed between activists and those being mobilized (Chatterjee 1984; Sarkar 1983). But the comparison between Kerala and Bengal shows that while it

---

[7] "The aim and object or method and technique were almost similar, but the counsels and loyalties of each were its own. For secret societies have to work in narrow grooves and cannot risk their very existence in the name of a revolutionary united front" (Gordon 1976, p. 242).

was the upper castes that primarily constituted the radical leadership during the nationalist period in both regions, there were critical differences in the type of leadership they represented. In Kerala, upper-caste social reform leaders were beginning to question the entire concept of caste and were engaged in a project to dissolve the caste hierarchy. Moreover, the absence of the rural–urban split that characterized Bengal meant that the CSP and anticaste leaders were drawn from the very districts in which they were organizing, and were thus in a sense less outsiders than were the urban activists in Bengal. On the one hand, the Nair and Namboodiri leaders came from the same families that would meet tenant resistance by "ex-communicating them, forcing extra-legal levies upon them, eviction and ultimately ruin" (Logan 1887/1951, pp. 231–2). But on the other hand, they could invoke the trust of poor peasants precisely because of this very factor. The painstaking work of organizing and unionizing the peasantry was possible only by first breaking caste barriers. The high-caste Congress socialists showed unprecedented willingness to make physical contact with lower castes and defy old norms regarding appropriate caste behavior.

In Bengal, both terrorists and those who did not choose their methods were drawn from the *bhadralok* – the "respectable" people. The *bhadralok* were drawn from the landed gentry or employed in professional and clerical occupations. They were high caste – drawn from the three upper castes of Brahmins, Kayasthas, and Vaidyas – and maintained caste-based rituals religiously, among other means by avoiding manual labor. In the twentieth century the *bhadralok* found themselves dislocated for a number of reasons: (1) removal by the British government from their positions in administrative, local, and self-government bodies, courts, and legislative councils; (2) reduction in their incomes from land; and (3) the rise in influence of Muslims in Bengal's institutional life. For a while, the challenge from Muslims led the *bhadralok* toward Hindu revivalism, which inflected much of the activity of the terrorist groups. But as they found their influence waning further, they turned away from Hindu revivalism toward communism (Franda 1971). It would certainly appear that, when compared with the activists in Kerala, the *bhadralok* leaders did not gain their political experience in mass political activity.

While it is true to some extent that the upper-caste *bhadralok* were elitist outsiders attempting to organize an illiterate peasantry, this observation has given rise to the somewhat ad hoc view that the elite origins and attitudes of party members explain the elitism of the Communist Party in Bengal (Chatterjee 1986, pp. 177–81). But there is vast evidence that Communists were successful in organizing poor peasants and tribals in the northern and central areas of Bengal, and in leading mass strikes in Bengal's jute mills and railway industry during the late 1930s and 1940s.

Instead of an emphasis on the social origins of radical leaders, I draw attention to what consequences the *forms* of radicalism had for the party–movement relationship in the two regions. The predominance of the specific organizational form of terrorism in Bengal meant (1) fragmentation of the movement and (2) political training in violence and secret, underground political work. The use of violent tactics, in turn, had another effect – massive state repression of terrorist groups, which continually threatened to destroy them (Gordon 1974).[8] The remaining terrorists who survived repression scattered even further into various left parties. In Kerala, in contrast, a well-developed network of activists engaged in antiuntouchability and anticaste campaigns that had developed over the 1920s eventually formed a coherent leadership bloc. They, in turn, constituted the central leadership of the CSP. Their tactics of political struggle among tenant-cultivators and workers – highly visible and inclusive demonstrations, marches, and public meetings – were an extension of their earlier tactics of protest against the system of caste-based disabilities and exploitation.

Left Party Strategies within the Late Nationalist Movement, 1934–1939

The process of party formation in democracies has not received much attention in the literature on political parties. Instead, much more has been written about the activities of parties once they are already full-fledged organizations (Michels 1958; Panebianco 1988; Przeworski 1985). I propose that party formation occurs at particular historical conjunctures when leaders and activists with certain political and ideological orientations adopt formalized strategies of intervention, connecting in specific ways with specific social groups but not simply reflecting the interests of these groups. Those strategies and tactics for achieving their goals have effects independent of the kind of social base they can form and the kinds of changes they can bring about. This way of understanding party formation allows us to

---

[8] In the fall of 1923 and early 1924, the British government arrested large numbers of revolutionaries, citing immediate threats to law and order. Between 1932 and 1934, the British successfully brought the terrorist movement to an end (Sarkar 1987).

pay attention to the relative autonomy of parties from social structures. In the specific context of late nationalist India, left party formation was further complicated by the larger context of an ongoing movement for independence, which was dominated by another party – the Indian National Congress (Congress Party).

The CSP was formed in 1934 among imprisoned Congress Party members disillusioned with what they perceived as Gandhi's compromises with the British and the elitism of Congress's tactics, which kept most poor peasants and workers outside the fold of the anticolonial movement. "[M]ere political freedom is of little use to the masses of mankind," they declared (Chaudhuri 1980, p. 31). Their task, they decided, was to wean "the anti-imperialist elements in the Congress away from its present bourgeois leadership and to bring them under the leadership of revolutionary socialism." In December 1935, at the Annual Conference of the CSP held at Faizpur, it was agreed that the CSP would attempt "a gradual and, as far as possible, amicable change in the composition of its [Congress's] leadership and its programme . . . [to bring about] a complete reorganization of the Congress from the bottom upwards" (Rusch 1973, p. 251). They would set up parallel offices to those of the Congress in every district, work on enlarging Congress membership, particularly by drawing in mass membership from peasants and workers' unions, and forcing the Congress to attend to their demands. In addition, it was decided that the CSP would form independent peasants' and workers' organizations and link their programs with that of the Congress. The CSP would exist as a party parallel to the Congress, gaining strength independently within the Congress Party while functioning independently of it. The CSP believed that in course of time this strategy would effect a wholesale transformation of the Congress Party.

This strategy offered significant advantages to the CSP. Their alliance with the Congress Party attached them to the cause of nationalism, and the label "congressman" gave them legitimacy. At the same time, they were able to pursue their programs of mass mobilization and greater social justice. In fact, their program did not manage to divert the Congress Party from its strictly nationalist agenda, and as noted later, in 1939 leading elements of the CSP realigned themselves with the CPI. However, throughout the 1930s, the strategy of working within Congress as the CSP was extremely beneficial.

In Malabar, most of the released detainees from the civil disobedience campaigns of 1931–2, who were members of the Kerala unit of the Congress Party, joined the CSP. While in prison, they had been rapidly radicalized by contact with revolutionaries from Punjab and Madras. The decision to join the CSP was a conscious one. As Namboodiripad explained: "[T]here was no doubt that if such a monolithic political organization like the Congress would be honest to its own resolution, that could go a long way in strengthening the relation between the Congress and the vast body of the labor and peasant populations" (Namboodiripad 1976, p. 158). This decision meant explicitly rejecting alternatives such as the Communist League in Trivandrum, southern Travancore. Although they "had a better understanding of the basic tenets of socialism than us . . . they had not yet made any beginning to organize workers' unions or peasants' unions even in their rudimentary forms. They also did not have any plan to strengthen the Congress and utilize it as a tool to consolidate the worker-peasant movement. That way they were not even successful in building up a *broad-based* communist *movement* even in the vicinity of Trivandrum, the centre of their activities" (ibid., p. 159; my emphasis).

In comparison, when the detainees were released in Bengal in 1932, they found a political field on the left that consisted of a number of different parties – the CPI, the Communist League, and the Labour Party. Although a CSP unit was formed in Bengal in 1934, the ex-terrorists were not keen to join it because of its closer adherence to Gandhian methods, particularly its policy of nonviolence (Laushey 1975, p. 112). They therefore determined to make the CPI their vehicle for political organizing.

The CPI was formed in 1920, over a decade before the CSP. Until 1935 the CPI branded the Indian National Congress as a "reactionary organization and an ally of British imperialism" and argued, moreover, that "the most harmful and dangerous obstacle to the victory of the Indian revolution is the agitation carried on by Left elements of the National Congress" (Draft Platform of Action 1930 in Democratic Research Service 1957). In 1935, at the urging of the Comintern, the CPI's position shifted abruptly to a Popular Front policy. According to this new policy, the CPI was to penetrate and capture the nationalist movement by working through the CSP. Citing reasons for entry into the Congress Party, the CPI argued that it "must take advantage of the present situation in the National Congress in order to actively and persistently mobilize the masses for the struggle against the imperialist offensive" (extract from "The Communist Review" for October 1935 in Roy 1976). But there was to be "no question of the workers entering the Congress en masse" or "strengthening the Congress" (ibid.) Notably, the CPI argued that Bengal constituted a "special case," where by joining the Congress Party would "revive the bankrupt semi-feudal strongholds.... There being no other alternative than secret work in Bengal, it would be best to concentrate under the legal cover of the Congress upon the secret work of the Party" (ibid.).

By 1937–8, the CPI in Bengal had positioned itself with the nationalist movement in a manner not too different from that of the CSP. However, they were committed to a significantly different extent to building and transforming the Congress Party. This strategy marked the efforts of the CSP in Kerala. By contrast, in Bengal, beyond penetrating the Congress Party, the CPI made little attempt to work within the nationalist movement. What were the consequences of these strategic choices for their ability to build a base and acquire political influence?

Structure and Agency in Determining the Historical Trajectories of Kerala and Bengal

In 1937 the colonial authorities in Madras observed that in Malabar "[S]ocialists...have been very active in organizing unions among all sorts and conditions of workers, barbers, boatmen, motor employees and municipal scavengers, as well as industrial workers" (*Fortnightly Report*, September 1937, L/P&J/5/197, IOL). Under the aegis of the CSP, a militant peasant movement arose in north Malabar, protesting illegal levies, high rents, and insecure tenurial rights of poor tenants. Unions sprouted rapidly in Travancore and Cochin among coir workers, agricultural laborers, and plantation workers. The CSP also fully exploited its unique position in the princely states. Because the Congress Party had a policy of abstaining from involvement in the princely states, the CSP was the only party to involve itself in class-based mobilization, as well as taking the lead in the political demand for the removal of the monarchies. In contrast to the high levels of popular mobilization in Kerala, in 1937 the political commentator for the *Statesman* observed that in Bengal "the masses waited, unorganized, outside party politics" (cited in Gordon 1974, p. 298).

In Kerala the CSP formed its base during the 1930s among small cultivators, poor tenants, and agricultural laborers through the mobilizing activities of the Malabar Karshaka Sangham (MKS) (affiliated with the All India Kisan Sabha, or Peasants Union). The local units of the MKS were mainly confined to northern Malabar (the CSP could not interest the Muslim tenants of southern Malabar in the aftermath of the brutal suppression of the Moplah Rebellion in 1921). Tenants were rapidly unionized in the densely populated districts of northern Malabar. For example, by 1939 there were eighty-nine local units in Chirakkal *taluk*, or district, with 9,901 members. In Tellicherry, in Kottayam *taluk*, there were sixty-eight local units with 5,900 members. In Kasargod *taluk* there were 10,000 members (*The National Front*, May 14, 1939, cited in Kunhi Krishnan 1993). Trade union membership also grew during these years in virtually every sector of the economy. In particular, the CSP was able to base itself firmly among coir[9] workers in the villages that dotted the coast of Travancore. Of the 30,000 wage laborers in the coir industry in the district of Alleppey alone, union membership was estimated at 7,400 in 1939, reaching 17,000 by June 1942 (Jeffrey 1984). But the real significance of CSP activity in this period did not simply rest on its leadership of class-based mobilization. It also became synonymous with a number of different social movements.

In the three regions of colonial Kerala – Malabar, Travancore, and Cochin – the years 1935 to 1939 were a period of rapid mobilization of larger and larger numbers of people drawn from all social strata, who became increasingly involved in a range of protest actions including demonstrating against landlordism (such as illegal levies imposed by landlords, evictions, and casteist oppression), temple entry, unemployment, poor working conditions, and low wages, as well as against the princely states in Travancore and Cochin and anticolonial demonstrations. The CSP brought a number of unique mobilizing tools to the process of movement building. Of these, the procession (*jatha*) was particularly significant. Processions were also important in the context of the dispersed nature of rural settlement in Kerala because they could reach people in remote villages. The peasant leader from Andhra Pradesh, N. G. Ranga, remarked on the "special contribution" of the MKS activists, of the "bugle call" used at the end of the workday to draw peasants from the "thousands of homesteads removed from the other almost by furlongs and miles."[10] The CSP thus facilitated, for the first time, the forging of geographical links that were vital in constructing a movement out of disparate campaigns.

The use of reading rooms became a central means of connecting groups of workers and peasants. Reading rooms had a tradition dating back to the caste associations of the 1920s, which were set up with a view to building membership in these associations. The use of reading rooms as a mobilizing and organizing tool reflects the manner in which prior political experience

---

[9] Coir is a fiber made from coconut husk.

[10] N. G. Ranga, "Jenmi System Doomed Malabar," *Congress Socialist*, January 22, 1939, vol. 4, no. 4.

with caste politics informed the tactics of the CSP leaders in the post-1934 period. CSP members set up reading rooms in villages and organized them by union – for example, the Beedi Workers' Union in Cannanore, north Malabar, and the peasant unions in the forest regions of northeast Malabar. The party newspaper, the *Prabhatham*, was circulated in this fashion, as was a range of radical literature.

During this period the CSP was the dominant party, apart from smaller parties such as the Communist League, involved in organizing the growing ranks of workers in cottage industries, coffee and rubber plantations, and agriculture. They succeeded in forming unions of workers in a range of industries but, most important, in the devastated coir industry, where workers in Travancore were concentrated. On October 21, 1938, for example, the CSP organized a general strike in the two coir towns of Alleppey and Shertallai. Among the twenty-six demands raised by the workers were the demand for adult franchise and responsible government, annulment of the Emergency Act, ending of control over presses, a freeze on wage cuts, prompt payment of wages in cash, recognition of minimum wages, medical aid and maternity benefits, and free education (NAI, 20/9/40). The demand for responsible government – that is, for the removal of monarchical rule and its replacement by parliamentary democracy – had been raised earlier by the Travancore State Congress, made up of professionals and civil servants from the Ezhava, Syrian Christian, and Nair communities. However, the CSP raised the same demand more consistently and in a more militant fashion. By doing so, the CSP successfully represented itself as a party that penetrated a number of ongoing social movements.

Why did the CPI in Bengal fail to achieve the movement character that was so clearly a part of the Kerala CSP's identity by 1937? I argue that in order to understand why both parties achieved different degrees of "hegemony" in the two regions, we need to pay attention not simply to larger party strategies, but also to how these strategies were put into effect in the specific contexts of Kerala and Bengal at particular historical moments. The contexts were defined by the agrarian and social (caste) structures that defined each region; but the possibilities for building movements of transformation were circumscribed not only by these structures, but also by the historical time at which their respective strategies were implemented. While in Kerala the CSP constituted itself as a cohesive party whose members possessed tremendous experience in building mass movements, in Bengal the CPI's experience involved secret underground terrorism. By isolating themselves further from the possibility of growing, that is, by adopting a position of working outside the nationalist movement until 1936–7, they missed the crucial historical opportunity seized by the CSP in Kerala between 1934 and 1937.

The CPI's agrarian campaigns in Bengal began only in 1939–40. Three factors are critical to understanding their limitations: (1) the role of *jotedars*, or middle/rich peasants, in muting class conflict in West Bengal, (2) the inability (despite certain adversities) of the CPI to utilize the post-Depression conditions to create a base for itself in any region other than North Bengal, and (3) Hindu–Muslim conflict in East Bengal.

In his important work on agrarian Bengal in the late colonial period, Bose (1986) argues that the sharp class dichotomy between village landlords and sharecroppers, as found in North Bengal, explains the strong wave of Communist-led anti-*jotedars* campaigns that developed in 1939–40. In contrast, in West Bengal, "the ties of dependency in the peasant small-holding demesne labor complex . . . showed a strong tendency towards muting any expression of protest by the diverse dependent social groups" (p. 278). It is instructive to compare West Bengal with Malabar to see what differences between them might explain the very different outcomes. In West Bengal, conflict between the rich tenant-farmers and poor peasants/sharecroppers was notable primarily for its absence. Instead, *jotedars* succeeded in temporarily uniting peasants in anticolonial campaigns such as protesting the implementation of village taxes in 1920–1. In 1930–1, as the Congress sought to extend the civil disobedience movement to the countryside, poor peasants and sharecroppers began to protest the *jotedars* themselves. But the Congress quickly intervened and attempted to strike a bargain between the *jotedars* and sharecroppers (Sanyal 1979). The contrast with Malabar highlights two points of importance: First, the *jotedars* were of the same caste as the lower peasants – known as Mahisyas – and Congress's success in uniting them temporarily depended to a large extent on utilizing the caste movement for self-upliftment among the Mahisyas. In Malabar no equivalent section to the *jotedars* was to be found: The organized upper tenantry (*kanomdars*) had succeeded in winning reforms through the Malabar Tenancy Act of 1930 and consequently had withdrawn from the Congress Party. Second, in comparison with the CSP in Kerala, the "right" Congress in Bengal dominated the rural campaigns and succeeded in creating a base well before the Communists began to enter the rural scene. It is difficult to accept Bose's argument that the ties of dependency between landlords and peasant smallholders negated the possibility of class conflict in West Bengal. In Malabar, such ties of dependency, although critical to the quiescence of peasants before 1934–5, were challenged by the presence of the CSP in the countryside. The relative absence of the CPI (or an equivalent organization) from the rural scene in Bengal during the 1930s is at least part of the explanation for why these ties of dependency persisted.

In comparison to the relative quiescence in the western districts of Bengal, the northern districts, primarily Dinajpur and Jalpaiguri, were the site of militant sharecropper revolts against *jotedars* during 1939–40. Share-croppers removed the entire harvest to their own houses, and there was a general spread of a "no-rent" movement (Bhattacharyya 1978). The CPI played a crucial role in negotiating with *jotedars* on behalf of the share-croppers to reduce the former's arbitrary and excessive demands, and were viewed by both actors and the colonial state as an important force in the countryside. However, there appears to have been a readiness among share-croppers to engage in militant struggles against *jotedars* that needed little outside impetus (ibid.).

However, the CPI was unable to sustain these struggles and build a move-ment in the countryside that might have substantially challenged *jotedar* dominance. In late 1939, at the outbreak of World War II, the CPI opted for a new policy of prioritizing the revolutionary possibilities opened up by the war, at the cost of the earlier policy of unity with left forces within the Congress Party. The task at hand was the "revolutionary utilization of the war crisis for the achievement of National Freedom." A resolution adopted in October 1939 by the CPI Politbureau argued that "the capture of power is an immediately realizable goal" (Overstreet and Windmiller 1959, p. 177). The result of this pronouncement was "the most effective repression yet undertaken against the Communist movement in India." In North Bengal, the newly launched peasant movement was immediately suppressed and forced to retreat. As one of the peasant leaders, Sunil Sen recalls, the peasant movement "was virtually driven underground . . . [and] there was considerable demoralisation after the collapse of the *adhiar* move-ment" (Sen 1972, p. 28).

It would appear paradoxical, then, that by 1939 the CPI dominated the All India Kisan Sabha (Peasants Union) all across India, as well as in Bengal; and its membership in Bengal rose from 34,000 in 1938 to 83,160 in 1943, doubling to 177,629 in 1944 (AIKS Organizational Reportage; Rasul 1969, p. 22). Most of the gains in membership were made after July 1942, when the CPI was legalized for its adoption of the People's War line, in which they essentially traded with the colonial state a policy of quiescence for legality. Even though they could not engage in mass peasants' struggles, they could consolidate organizationally during this period (Dhanagare 1983). The Communist activists of the Bengal Kisan Sabha (Peasants Union) engaged in famine relief work during 1943–4, setting up relief committees and grain cooperatives. In the process, they began to build support among the poor peasants and sharecroppers, which found expression in the sharecroppers' revolts in the famous *tebhaga* (two-thirds) movement of 1946–7. Sharecoppers demanded from the *jotedars*, the right to retain two-thirds of the produce for themselves. Hence the movement was known as the *tebhaga* movement. It was a powerful movement in which many peasants were killed by police forces. In the ensuing struggle with the state, the peasants lost; by March 1947 the *tebhaga* movement was in decline.

The CPI also made some inroads into organizing sharecroppers in East Bengal; however, Hindu–Muslim conflict in this region quickly overcame any possibilities that may have existed for building a mass base there. The Muslim peasants in East Bengal, many of whom participated in the *tebhaga* movement, were gradually won over to the Muslim League.

The comparison with Kerala highlights another structural feature, which oddly enough in Bengal became a barrier to radicalization and movement building. In comparison to Kerala, the caste system in Bengal was less hierarchical. Historically, Brahminical Hinduism was never as deeply entrenched in Bengal as in other regions of India. As early as the twelfth and thirteenth centuries, Bengali Brahmins interdined with lower castes and ate meat and fish. As in Kerala, lower castes in Bengal attacked Brahminincal customs and succeeded in weakening the ruling class ideology further during the eighteenth and nineteenth centuries.

The relative weakness of caste as a social schism in comparison with Kerala meant that caste did not necessarily become the mechanism for class-based exploitation. Although *zamindars* (large landlords) were primarily Brahmins or upper-caste Kayasthas, the *jotedars* came from a variety of castes that included both the upper castes as well as low-caste cultivators known as *sadgops, namasudras, aguris,* and so on (Kohli 1989). The extraction of agrarian surplus from low-caste cultivators and tenants in the form of rent or produce by the *zamindars* or *jotedars* in Bengal was not accompanied by the high degree of social exclusion and degradation that applied to low-caste cultivators and laborers in Kerala.

Because *jotedars* often belonged to the same caste as poor tenants and sharecroppers, caste could not become an important mobilizing factor for the latter, as it did in Malabar after the 1930s. Instead, *jotedars* in West Bengal were able to develop unity among various sections of the peasantry and direct their collective political activity against the colonial state. However, where a clear class division existed between *jotedars* and laborers or *adhiars*, as in North Bengal, the latter mobilized against the former in successive waves during the 1940s. In contrast, in Kerala, the perception of a clear division between classes was made possible, ironically, by the very factor that inhibited conflict: the hierarchy of the caste system. Here the CSP played a crucial role, because its upper-caste leaders and activists politicized caste and class as the same issue, lending both issues a double potency. But furthermore, while in Kerala the upper-caste Nairs and Naboodiripads joined the lower castes in their struggle for expanding civil rights and against caste discrimination, in Bengal there was no such move to destroy the caste hierarchy from the top. In other words, in Bengal there was not to be found the radical potential inherent in the political and social flux surrounding caste movements that occurred in Kerala.

Thus in Kerala, analytically speaking, the CSP was able to convert the caste system into an advantage over Bengal. The conversion of a vertical hierarchy into an advantage was facilitated by the relative homogeneity of the agricultural and nonagricultural proletariat, which made possible a clear class confrontation, as happened in Malabar.

I have argued here, then, that two critical aspects of agency made it possible to successfully utilize possibilities for leftist mobilization inherent in structures in late nationalist Kerala and Bengal. First, I considered the prior field of political activity in which the agents were involved, the forms of radicalism with which they were experienced, and the tactics they adopted. The focus on elite terrorist tactics in Bengal meant that while the CSP in Kerala could constitute itself as a coherent party or party faction, the CPI and other left parties in Bengal were highly fragmented and dissipated as they entered the period 1934–40. Second, the political choice of strategy, of participation in or opposition to the dominant nationalist movement and the Indian National Congress, determined the ability of each party to take advantage of historical opportunities, that is, of political openings in the nationalist movement that existed in 1934. The CPI's willingness to enter Congress only as late as 1936–7 allowed it little time to build its influence in Bengal before it was once again subject to state repression in 1940. As a consequence, the two parties emerged with varying degrees of hegemony in their respective regions by the 1940s.

Emergent Communist Party Electoral Bases and Areas of Strength in Post-Independence Kerala and Bengal

After 1940, both the CSP and the CPI underwent further changes. In Kerala, core members of the CSP had secretly decided to join the CPI, and in 1939, after a heated struggle with the "right" faction of the Kerala Pradesh Congress Committee, they were dismissed from the Kerala Congress Party. The majority of the CSP members in Kerala joined the new CPI unit in 1940. In West Bengal in 1964, the CPI split into a Marxist faction (CPM) and a "right" faction (CPI). Thus, after the 1940s, the dominant left parties in both Kerala and West Bengal had changed their formal identities. In Kerala, the dominant party was the CPI, and in West Bengal it was the CPM.

However, in personnel and policies, these were the direct descendants of Kerala's CSP and West Bengal's CPI. Indeed, after 1940, when the CSP in Kerala had already converted to the CPI, there was little need to distinguish their platforms, as both parties identified themselves as Communist. To understand the differences between the two parties, why the CPI in Kerala enacted wider-ranging welfare legislation than the CPM in Bengal, we need to trace their development back to the 1930s. The differences in their origins would have a critical effect on the policies that these parties pursued, despite having similar announced goals, from the 1940s on.

In 1948, after a short wave of violent insurrectionary activity, the CPI renounced these tactics and adopted the path of parliamentary struggle. From then on, winning electoral victories became a central concern. However, while the CPI was strong enough to win elections in Kerala in 1957, the Communists in Bengal (at that time the undivided CPI) began to build their electoral strength only after 1969. As one observer noted, "[p]erhaps the most striking feature of the Communist electoral effort in West Bengal is how limited it has been" (Weiner and Field 1974, p. 9). When the CPM finally won elections in 1971 (after the CPI broke into two factions in 1964 – the left CPM and right CPI), it was engaged in stiff electoral competition with the Congress Party, and its concern had shifted further to rapidly securing an electoral base. In contrast, the CPI that won elections in 1957 in Kerala was more deeply enmeshed in civil society, with less distance from social movements than its counterpart in Bengal, and its radical policy agenda was driven by its identity as a popular party. Decades of involvement with mass social movements had put an indelible stamp on the Kerala CSP/CPI, giving it far greater abilities to implement wide-ranging social welfare programs than its Bengali counterpart.

7

Parties, Movements, and Constituencies in Categorizing Race

STATE-LEVEL OUTCOMES OF MULTIRACIAL CATEGORY LEGISLATION

Kim M. Williams

This essay tries to explain why so many state legislatures in the 1990s considered and in some cases adopted state laws that required the addition of a multiracial category on state documents such as school forms, employment applications, and birth and death certificates. Between 1992 and 1997, six states passed multiracial category laws, similar legislation was introduced in five other states, and two states added a multiracial classification by administrative mandate. This sudden explosion of state legislative activity is remarkable given that, as recently as 1967, sixteen U.S. states actively enforced anti-miscegenation laws. Less than thirty years later, almost as many states had considered some form of multiracial category legislation.

Grassroots activists provided the spark that initially ignited debates concerning the multiracial category. These activists challenged the logic of racial categories, arguing that the only pure thing about race is its social salience. The multiracial movement, which can be formally dated from 1988, is led by people who consider themselves to be multiracial or are in interracial relationships, often with young children. Its leaders have argued that it is both inaccurate and an affront to their identity to force them and/or their children into a "monoracial" box. Emphasizing the fact that the multiracial population is growing exponentially and that, in increasing numbers, millions of Americans are not identifying within the officially mandated categories, the multiracialists have argued a case that has increasingly gained attention and response from a wide array of elected officials.

Multiracial movement activists and organizations are best known for their attempts to get a "multiracial" category added to the 2000 census. Although the movement did not exactly accomplish that, it did spur the Office of Management and Budget (OMB) to make the unprecedented and controversial decision to allow respondents to "mark all that apply" (MATA)

197

on the 2000 census. But when we ask how it is that a relatively small and disorganized social movement could draw such attention to itself and, in effect, bring the issue of multiracial status to national attention, it is my contention that we must look at prior, and until now largely unexplored, developments at the state level.

This essay is one of only a handful in the political science literature to examine the multiracial movement, and it is perhaps the only published work on the politics of the multiracial category issue in state legislatures. In the literature addressing the political implications of the multiracial category issue, attention has been devoted overwhelmingly to developments at the federal level. Yet it should come as no surprise to students of American social movements that the multiracial movement first made inroads at the state level; there is an abundant literature documenting the merits of federal systems for relatively weak and/or disorganized challengers.

Looking at the campaign for state-level multiracial designations reveals some surprising results. My research shows that the diffusion of these policy initiatives is not explained by cleavages between Democrats and Republicans or blacks and whites. Rather, a more unconventional set of factors emerge as salient at the state level, including minority suburbanization trends, new-generation versus old-generation black leadership divisions, and the role of minority (not just black) demographics statewide.

The argument I develop unfolds in several steps. First, I explain how the politics of creating a multiracial category are different in state legislatures than in the federal government. Then I turn to the task of relating these stakes to a broader discussion of the multiracial movement: who is in it, what does it do, and where is it active? Next, I draw upon several strands of social movement theory, as well as complementary aspects of the American state politics literature, to evaluate the lines of reasoning generated by dominant theoretical frameworks to explain the outcomes in question. After considering and rejecting a number of competing explanations, I demonstrate that the best line of explanation for understanding these state-level outcomes involves attention to a newly emerging configuration of class, race, and suburbanization in the post–civil rights era.

The Stakes

Federal-Level Issues

While racial categorization has always been problematic, it is only in recent years that we have seen the rise of a widespread and protracted grassroots struggle surrounding its *problematization* in this country. In other words, it is not a new disclosure that race is not a biologically tenable concept. What is new is that the "social construction of race" is not ordinarily, for example, the subject of congressional hearings. The multiracial category initiative emerged as a highly contentious matter at the federal level, largely due to the fact that racial statistics in the United States are linked to the enforcement of a wide array of civil rights and voting rights laws. Since the 1960s, data on race and ethnicity have been used extensively by federal agencies to monitor civil rights enforcement in areas such as employment, housing and mortgage lending, and educational opportunities. Not only do racial statistics impact the allocation of material resources, they also affect the distribution of political power: The Voting Rights Act of 1965 mandated the creation of political boundaries that would allow minority groups to concentrate their votes, and racial statistics provide the basis on which the Voting Rights Act is enforced.

Hence the alignment of allies/opponents of the multiracialists' efforts: The most ardent opponents of the multiracial category effort at the federal level were civil rights organizations such as the National Association for the Advancement of Colored People (NAACP) and the National Council of La Raza (NCLR). Their objection centered on the belief that the addition of a multiracial category on the census would diminish the traditional minority count, in that substantial numbers of people previously counted as black, for example, would choose "multiracial" if given the option. Not only could this adversely impact the efficacy of the Voting Rights Act, they argued, it would also undermine various state and federal programs aimed at minorities. In contrast, a number of prominent congressional Republicans registered support for the multiracial category initiative. Elsewhere, I argue that these legislators viewed the multiracial category issue as a way to undermine civil rights gains, yet seem progressive in the process of doing so.[1]

At least in regard to the 2000 census, the federal debate over the addition of a multiracial category has largely been resolved. In 1997, as noted earlier, the OMB made the controversial decision to allow respondents to mark all that apply on the 2000 census. While this was not exactly what the multiracialists wanted, many multiracial social movement organizations (SMOs)[2] regarded it as a step in the right direction. Civil rights groups also saw this

---

[1] For a more thorough discussion, see Williams (2001).

[2] There are approximately forty multiracial SMOs across the country (deduced from my efforts to identify, research, and survey these organizations from 1997 to 1999).

as a reasonable compromise, given that the OMB assured the civil rights lobby that the tabulation procedures would not jeopardize existing legislation intended to protect minorities. Nevertheless, MATA is a stopgap measure that does not adequately address the logical flaws in racial categorization and the rapidly changing demographic profile of the United States. It is difficult to avoid the conclusion that the MATA decision is more aptly regarded as a beginning than an end; further examination of racial categorization, and the material and political resources connected to it, is imminent (Williams 2001).[3]

State-Level Issues

Although the lion's share of analysts' attention to the multiracial movement has focused on federal-level developments, between 1992 and 1997 Ohio, Illinois, Indiana, Michigan, Maryland, and Georgia passed multiracial category legislation. In the same time period, Florida and North Carolina added a multiracial designation by administrative mandate, and multiracial category bills were introduced in Minnesota, Texas, Oregon, and Massachusetts.[4] Finally, a multiracial category initiative was introduced (but failed) in California. The states' legislation requires the addition of a multiracial category on state documents such as school forms, employment applications, and birth and death certificates. But in light of the fact that the OMB dictates the official racial categories used in nationwide data collection, these developments have been all but ignored in media coverage and in the literature emerging on the multiracial movement.[5] Why? *For the purposes of federal reporting, those identifying as multiracial on state forms are necessarily "recollapsed" into the standard racial and ethnic categories mandated by the OMB.* In this sense, adding a multiracial category at the state level does not carry substantive material or political stakes: Federal monies and/or the composition of legislative districts are not at risk.

This fact has facilitated the successful packaging of the multiracial category issue at the state level as a "feel-good" measure related to personal identity and expression. In other words, at the state level, the multiracial category issue can be regarded as a matter of symbolic representation.

[3] See, for example, National Research Council Committee on National Statistics (1996).

[4] Further state-level action is unlikely, however, given the 1997 MATA decision by the OMB.

[5] However, a cursory overview of state-level developments can be found in Spencer (1999).

Projecting into the future, analyzing the relevant legislative activity at the state level gives us traction on a bigger question: which elected officials are most receptive to this country's inexorable shift away from a monotypic definition of race.

Movement Characteristics

In spite of the fact that fully one-fourth of U.S. states ($n = 13$) have introduced and/or passed multiracial category legislation over the past decade, a thorough profile of the multiracial movement is, for the most part, lacking in the literature. I do not have the space here to chronicle the movement's history and characteristics in detail. For our purposes, I recount only the most basic elements of its organizational structure and philosophy. The origins of the current multiracial movement are found in the handful of local multiracial organizations that formed on the West Coast in the late 1970s and early 1980s. In 1977, Interracial-Intercultural Pride (I-Pride), based in Berkeley, California, was the first of these contemporary multiracial groups to form. Since 1977, approximately eighty multiracial organizations have been established across the country, although a number of these groups have since disbanded. Currently, there are approximately forty active multiracial groups across the United States and roughly an additional fifty student groups on college campuses. While the student organizations (clustered for the most part in California and on the East Coast) and some of the larger local organizations are politically engaged, most of the multiracial groups across the country are more oriented toward socializing than political advocacy per se.[6]

However, in 1988, a number of local organizations joined forces to create the Association for Multi-Ethnic Americans (AMEA) as an umbrella advocacy organization, primarily for the purpose of pushing the Census Bureau to add a multiracial category on the 1990 census. Soon after the establishment of AMEA, two other national umbrella organizations formed: Project RACE (Reclassify All Children Equally) and A Place for Us (APFU). I have personally interviewed all of the multiracial movement's national leaders as well as the majority of local leaders. My research in this regard reveals that only SMOs affiliated with one of the three multiracial umbrella organizations have ever undertaken any political activity. In other

[6] See Williams (2001).

words, if the questions revolve around the multiracialists' political endeavors, the answers are to be found in the activities of the umbrella-affiliated organizations.

In the series of interviews I conducted with the national multiracial leadership from 1997 to 1999, a recurring theme centered on their view of the multiracial movement (and/or their personal involvement in it) as *related to but somehow a step beyond* the civil rights movement. Ramona Douglass, recent past president of AMEA, said that she has "been a part of the civil rights movement since the early 1970s and marched in the South with the Ku Klux Klan dancing in my face. We [multiracial activists] are changing race as we know it."[7] Susan Graham, president of Project RACE said, "our objective is civil rights and equality for all."[8] Carlos Fernandez, another movement leader, has argued that it is the "biological aspect of race and racial mixture that is essential to racist thinking[;] this attitude finds expression in the failure of our society and its institutions to officially acknowledge racial mixture, potentially the basis for breaking down traditional lines of social separation" (Fernandez 1992, p. 133). Note how the multiracialists have shrewdly drawn on the symbolism of the civil rights movement, yet in the process cast themselves as more progressive than the so-called progressives (i.e., the civil rights lobby).

But is the multiracial movement actually challenging race, as we know it, as its leaders passionately aver? Are multiracial movement activists well positioned to, and seriously concerned about, waging an assault against institutional and other forms of racism? The evidence on this matter is ambiguous. In the interviews I conducted from 1997 to 1999 with all of the organizational leaders of multiracial groups across the country ($n = 40$, response rate: 75%) in addition to four case studies of groups in the Bay Area, Washington, D.C., Atlanta, and Chicago (resulting in fifty case study interviews), a serendipitous string of interesting facts converged:

- Ironically, and in spite of the fact that multiracial leaders *say* that multiracial identity is constitutive of "people across all racial mixes,"[9] not many multiracially identified adults are involved in the multiracial movement. This is largely an effort of monoracially identified parents *on behalf of their children*

[7] Ramona Douglass, personal interview, June 14, 1998.
[8] Susan Graham, personal interview, April 6, 1998.
[9] See, for example, Root (1996).

- Although there are far more documented Asian–white than black–white marriages in the United States, multiracial SMOs consist *almost exclusively of black–white couples*
- In accord with Census Bureau data suggesting that the vast majority of black–white marriages in the United States are between black men and white women,[10] multiracial SMOs mirror this gender/race dynamic
- In accord with most organizations of this sort (i.e., local groups concentrated on family issues), there is a gender gap; women tend to become the leaders of these groups more often than men
- Across the board, most local organizational leaders are middle-class and live in suburbs.

And so, we end up with the compelling fact that most multiracial organizations are in fact run by white middle-class women living in suburbs. Furthermore, 47.5% of all respondents[11] reported that their family income is above $60,000 per year; 20% said it is between $45,000 and $60,000. Only 10% of all respondents reported annual family incomes below $30,000. In terms of educational attainment, 50% of all respondents reported having earned at least a college degree; within that group, 30% have earned a master's degree. Only 6.3% of all respondents reported that their formal education ended with a high school diploma.

Regarding individual measures of political attitudes, most respondents identified as either strong (26.3%) or moderate (41.3%) Democrats and declared themselves either strongly (32.5%) or moderately (37.5%) in favor of affirmative action. However, in part because only 30% of organizational leaders reported that combating racism in their local communities was a priority in their groups, it is difficult to link these broad measures of liberalism on the part of multiracial activists to any evidence of support for a wider progressive platform and/or to sustained consideration of racial or class issues within or beyond local multiracial SMOs. Furthermore, 53.6% of all respondents said that the multiracial movement should welcome the

---

[10] Black–white marriages by gender in the United States from 1960 to 1997 were as follows (data available for 1960, 1970, 1980, 1990, 1991, 1992, 1993, 1994, 1995, 1996, and 1997): Black male–white female marriages were 67% of all such marriages; white male–black female marriages were 33%. Source: U.S. Bureau of the Census (1998).

[11] I conducted a leadership survey of all adult-based organizations ($n = 40$; response rate = 75%), plus four case studies, resulting in fifty additional interviews. Many of the questions asked in the leadership survey and case study questionnaire intentionally overlap. Thus, when I refer to "all respondents," I am referring to data compiled from both sources ($n = 80$).

support of Republicans, while 40% said that the multiracial community should be "wary of support" from Republicans.

These findings seem to fly in the face of the national leaders' claims about the sociopolitical aspirations of the multiracial movement. Yet all of the national leaders have repeatedly asserted that the multiracial movement has the potential to bridge the racial divide and diminish racial tension. Although many local leaders lament the fact, local multiracial SMOs have not been able to attract a particularly diverse following, even within their own organizations. Looking at data from all respondents, when asked an open-ended question as to how they identify racially, 56.3% said "white," 22.5% said "black," and 17.5% said "multiracial." The remaining 3.7% include those identifying as Asian American, Latino, Native American, or of the "human" race.

Summing up, a rather unexpected picture emerges when we explore the sociopolitical positioning of local-level multiracial organizations. Overwhelmingly, adult participants do not themselves identify as multiracial, and they have not been able to attract a particularly diverse membership base (either racially or on measures of socioeconomic status). They are also divided as to what a political articulation of "multiracialness" should entail and whom they should welcome and/or eschew as allies. Furthermore, they are hazy on the matter of whether or not multiracial people can or should be at the forefront of efforts to lessen racial tension. How, then, have the multiracialists been able to achieve so many political victories in a relatively short time?

Existing Theories and the Explanations They Generate

A number of theories have been advanced to account for the development of social movements, but far less attention has been devoted to explaining the impact of such movements on public policy. Although linking social movement pressure to policy outcomes is not a new concept, it is an endeavor that, surprisingly, students of social movements have often avoided undertaking until relatively recently. The reasons behind this avoidance are well documented in the introduction to this volume and need not be recounted here. However, the basic coordinates are as follows: It was only with the U.S. protest movements of the 1960s that the concept of social movements as amorphous and irrational was finally shattered. Until that time, many analysts regarded social movements as fundamentally opposed to and separate from organized, purposeful behavior. This orientation left little conceptual room to seriously consider and explore the ways in which social movements might significantly impact public policy. For this and other reasons (including the fact that most analysts continue to demonstrate much more sustained interest in the emergence of movements than in their longer-term institutional impact), outcomes have often been neglected in the study of social movements.

Unfortunately, at the other end of the spectrum, the American state politics literature generally remains much less developed than research on federal-level politics. Although analysts do occasionally examine the impact of social movements on the formulation of state legislative policy, the literature on U.S. state politics does not devote much attention to such matters due to (a) the difficulty in obtaining comparable data from state to state (some state legislatures are much more professionalized than others, which can result in wide discrepancies in the availability of detailed information about legislative processes) and (b) the overwhelming tendency of American state politics analysts to emphasize endogenous factors (e.g., partisan breakdown of the legislature, competitiveness between the parties) over exogenous ones (social movements, interest groups) in explaining state policy outcomes. Although my particular theoretical concern – the intersection of a social movement and state legislative outcomes – is not expressly emphasized in either body of work, the respective literatures nevertheless provide us with strong theoretical cues. To follow, I consider the most promising of these cues/approaches in turn and evaluate the effectiveness of each with appropriate data.

Resource Mobilization

The resource mobilization (RM) approach to the study of social movements reached its apex in the late 1970s. Emphasizing the preexisting organizational and material resources available to social movements and movement entrepreneurs, RM predicts that SMOs with a preponderance of resources (namely, money, large memberships, and relatively high levels of internal professionalization) will enjoy the most success. Although RM has steadily fallen out of favor among students of social movements, it is worth considering for our purposes, as there is certainly *some* relationship between multiracial movement advocacy and these state legislative outcomes. Before the multiracial movement began to assert itself politically in the late 1980s and early 1990s, there was no momentum whatsoever on the part of state legislatures to formally recognize multiracial people. Therefore, we

Table 7.1. *The Multiracial Trend in the United States*

Year	Interracial Marriages (in millions)	Year	People Choosing "Other" as Their Racial Category (in millions)
1960	0.2	1960	0.2
1970	0.3	1970	0.7
1980	1	1980	6.8
1990	1	1990	9.8
1993	1.2	–	–
2000	1.4	2000[a]	15.3

[a] *Note:* For the 2000 Census, the terminology was changed from "other" to "some other race."

Source: Susan MacManus and Lawrence Morehouse, "Redistricting in the Multiracial Twenty First Century," in Georgia Persons, ed. *Race and Representation* (New Brunswick, N.J.: Transaction Publishers, 1997, p. 122); U.S. Bureau of the Census, 1960, 1970, 1980, 1993, and 2000.

must seriously consider the possibility that the multiracialists' efforts, as a function of their organizational and material resources, might best explain the relevant outcomes.

As RM stresses both activated and potential resources, the first step in applying the RM framework to the case at hand involves underscoring the fact that there has been an exponential rise in the number of self-identified multiracial people and families in the United States over the past forty years. As Table 7.1 indicates, the number of people to whom a multiracial movement would most likely appeal has risen dramatically over the past few decades. Although the number of interracial marriages in the United States still represents only a small fraction of the total marriages, this should not detract from our understanding of the epochal shift that is currently taking place. Currently, between one-fourth and one-third of all marriages involving Japanese Americans are now outgroup marriages, more indigenous people marry outside the indigenous population than marry within it, and marriages between blacks and whites have increased by 300% since 1970 (Hollinger 1995, p. 42). By the Census Bureau's own admission, the "growing racial and ethnic diversity of the American population, as well as changing attitudes about race and ethnicity," have converged to render the current categorical schema "in danger of becoming obsolete" (Edmonston and Schultze 1995, p. 140).

Even closer to the matter at hand, another set of figures lends further support to an RM line of reasoning: the increase in the number of multiracial SMOs over the past twenty years. In 1977, there was one active multiracial organization: I-Pride, based in Berkeley, California. By 1984, approximately twelve multiracial SMOs existed across the country; by 1994, there were twenty; and by 1999, forty.[12] Although many of these groups have formed and since disbanded, the overall trend demonstrates that the number of multiracial organizations has continued to grow and that the biggest increase occurred between 1994 and 1999, precisely when many states began to consider the addition of a multiracial category on state forms. Similarly important for an RM rationale is the fact that the resources of most multiracial organizations have grown (albeit modestly) over the past two decades in terms of membership, professionalization, and financial reserves.[13]

Yet as far as state-level policy outcomes are concerned, there is no evidence to suggest that multiracial movement activists have been able to convert the aforementioned potential resources into actual ones. For if this were the case, we should expect to find evidence supporting at least one of two trends: (a) that successful outcomes are more prevalent in what can be considered the most multiracial states (relating to potential resources) and/or (b) that successful outcomes are more likely to occur in states with the strongest multiracial groups (relating to actual resources).

However, Table 7.2 demonstrates no identifiable pattern of relationships between policy outcomes and either the potential or tangible resources of multiracial SMOs. In short, the RM approach ultimately gives us little leverage in explaining state-level outcomes. Consider these facts:

- In only two out of the eight successful cases has multiracial category legislation passed in what can be identified as the states with the strongest and most politically active multiracial organizations (Illinois and Georgia)
- In one of these two cases (Illinois), the main activists were not affiliated with a multiracial organization
- The most extensive advocacy campaign launched at the state level to add a multiracial category occurred in Georgia, but a rally on the steps of the Georgia capitol building, which drew approximately twenty supporters, was the extent of the "popular pressure" that the multiracialists in that state were able to muster

[12] Deduced from my efforts to identify, research, and survey these organizations from 1997 to 1999.
[13] Deduced from my efforts to identify, research, and survey these organizations from 1997 to 1999.

Table 7.2. *Multiracial Category Outcomes, Multiracial States, and Multiracial SMO Strength (by State)*

State	Multiracial State[a]	Strong Multiracial Group(s)	Policy Outcome[b]
Ohio	No	No	S
Illinois	Yes	Yes	S
Georgia	No	Yes	S
Indiana	No	No	S
Michigan	No	No	S
Maryland	No	Semi	F then S (governor vetoed bill the first time)
North Carolina	No	No	S
Florida	Yes	No	S
Minnesota	No	No	P
Oregon	No	No	P
Massachusetts	No	No	P
Texas	Yes	Semi	P
California	Yes	Yes	F

[a] I define a multiracial state as one in which at least two or more minority groups each makes up at least 10% of the population. Source: U.S. Census Bureau (2000).
[b] S, success; P, pending; F, failure.

- In five of the thirteen cases in which we see the introduction and/or passage of multiracial category legislation, local multiracial groups played absolutely no role in introducing this legislation in their states (Indiana, North Carolina, Florida, Oregon, and Massachusetts).

While the multiracial population in the United States is growing rapidly, and though the membership of active multiracial organizations has grown over time, we cannot explain these state-level outcomes as a function of these developments. The evidence overwhelmingly indicates that the multiracialists' resources cannot account for the implementation of multiracial category legislation in any of the states in question. We move then to another possibility, the political process approach.

Political Process Explanations

Like RM, the political process approach registers the importance of grievances and existing organizational resources, but it emphasizes the relevance of political opportunities that permit the movement some prospect

of success. In other words, the crucial difference between the RM and political process approaches is that in the latter, the institutional structure in
which a movement operates is viewed as a crucial determinant of the timing and fate of that movement, while the former places more emphasis on
the group's internal resources. Unfortunately, in the recent literature, the
concept of political opportunities has been stretched to encompass such a
wide range of "opportunities" that the original idea is in danger of losing
its analytical bite. Thus, I regard political opportunities here as they were
originally conceived, that is, in terms of structural changes and power shifts.
This requires paying attention to the role of elites, in particular to (a) the
stability or instability of electoral alignments and (b) the presence or absence
of other elite allies (McAdam 1996).

First, addressing the issue of electoral alignments, the most striking development to consider in this regard is the dramatic shift in power that took
place in state legislatures in 1994. At first blush, the Republican ascendance
in state legislatures in that year would seem to explain the outcomes of concern. This is so because Republicans in Congress have shown much more
support for the multiracial category effort than Democrats (Williams 2001),
which would reasonably lead us to think that we might find a similar pattern
of partisanship at the state level. Yet Table 7.3 shows that it is difficult to
interpret these state-level outcomes as a function of the partisan power shift
that took place in state legislatures in 1994.

Table 7.3 brings two important facts to light: First, far more Democrats
(nine) have sponsored multiracial category legislation at the state level than
Republicans (two). Second, the roll-call votes on multiracial category legislation have, in most cases, been unanimous or close to unanimous. I
will return to both of these issues shortly, but the point to emphasize at
present is this: It is impossible to view the success of state-level multiracial category legislation as a result of the Republicans' strong showing in
the 1994 elections, given that decidedly more Democrats have initiated
such legislation than Republicans. Moreover (with the exceptions of the
Michigan house and the Ohio senate), the roll-call votes make it difficult
to view this issue as having a partisan dimension at the state level.

Turning to the presence/absence of other elite allies or opponents, the
multiracial movement received endorsements from two nationally recognized advocacy and political groups: the Libertarian Party and the Japanese
American Citizens League (JACL). A number of lesser-known organizations also endorsed the multiracial movement, including the International Institute for Interracial Interaction in Minneapolis, Minnesota; the

Table 7.3. *Multiracial Category Legislation: Party Sponsorship and State Roll-Call Votes*

State	Party/Leg. Sponsor	Party of Governor	Roll-Call Vote
Ohio (passed in 1992)	Democrat (Czarcinski)	Republican	90 to 7 (House) 19 to 12 (Senate)
Georgia (passed in 1994)	Democrat (Abernathy)	Democrat	175 to 5 (House) 52 to 0 (Senate)
Indiana (passed in 1995)	Republican (Server)	Democrat	99 to 0 (House) 47 to 0 (Senate)
Michigan (passed in 1995)	Republican (Voorhees)	Republican	62 to 41 (House) 34 to 2 (Senate)
Illinois (passed in 1996)	Democrat (Carroll)	Republican	115 to 0 (House) 53 to 0 (Senate)
California (introduced in 1996)	Democrat (Campbell)	N/A	N/A (did not make ballot)
Minnesota (introduced in 1997)	Democrat (Betzold)	N/A	N/A (did not come up for a vote)
Oregon (introduced in 1997)	Democrat (Beyer)	N/A	N/A (did not come up for a vote)
Massachusetts (introduced in 1997)	Democrat (Keating)	N/A	N/A (did not come up for a vote)
Texas (introduced in 1997)	Democrat (Ellis)	N/A	N/A (did not come up for a vote)
Maryland (passed in 1998)	Democrat (Healy)	Democrat	124 to 10 (House) 46 to 0 (Senate)

Note: North Carolina and Florida: administrative mandate; no vote or legislative sponsor.

National Coalition to End Racism in Taylor, Michigan; and Healing Racism in St. Louis, Missouri. Most of these external elite allies, as well as the external elite opponents (including most prominently the NAACP the National Urban League, NCLR, and the National Coalition of American Indian Tribes) focused their energies on federal-level developments, by and large ignoring state-level multiracial category legislation.

While both external allies and opponents have demonstrated concern with the federal-level developments, it would be reasonable to assume that their efforts might have also had some impact, indirect or otherwise, on the state-level developments under consideration here. However, upon consideration of the timing of these endorsements, the allies with the highest profile – the Libertarian Party and the JACL – did not express support for the multiracialists until 1997, well after most of the successful state-level legislative activity had taken place. Moreover, neither of these organizations favored a multiracial category per se. The Libertarian Party wanted to eliminate racial classifications from all government forms but was not in favor of instituting a multiracial category. "If millions of Americans withheld their racial data from the government," Steve Dasbash, the Libertarian Party's national chairman, wrote in a press release in July 1997, "the politicians' framework for American Apartheid would crash to the ground."[14] In short, the Libertarian Party viewed the multiracialists' cause as a step toward ending the "handing out of favors"[15] based on racial preferences.

The JACL also did not explicitly endorse the addition of a multiracial category on the 2000 census, but for different reasons than the Libertarian Party. The JACL supported the OMB's ultimate MATA decision as a way to "acknowledge the rights of multiracial people to identify truthfully and accurately, *without* hurting minority groups that need accurate reporting of race and ethnic data for civil rights purposes."[16] In other words, JACL support must be viewed as an endorsement for the MATA decision, not for the addition of a multiracial category on the census. And again, both of these endorsements came after much of the state-level legislation had already been passed.

Party Control

At this juncture, there is no compelling evidence to suggest that either the strength of multiracial SMOs or electoral alignments and external elite allies provide us with promising lines of explanation to account for the outcomes in question. I also looked into party control, a mainstay explanatory factor in the American politics literature; however, this line of reasoning also came up short. Table 7.4 demonstrates a slight trend toward Democratic Party control in the states in question during the legislative sessions in which multiracial category bills were introduced and/or voted upon. However, comparing these states in these years with party control averaged across all

---

[14] Libertarian Party press release, July 10, 1997 (unpublished).
[15] Ibid.
[16] JACL "Policy Position on the Multiracial Category," July 9, 1997 (unpublished; emphasis in the original).

Table 7.4. *Party Control in State Legislatures*

Year of Legislation	State	House D	House R	Senate D	Senate R	Governorship
1996	California	54%	46%	63%	38%	Republican
1994	Georgia	64%	36%	64%	36%	Democrat
1996	Illinois	51%	49%	47%	53%	Republican
1995	Indiana	44%	56%	40%	60%	Republican
1997	Massachusetts	84%	16%	85%	15%	Republican
1998	Maryland	71%	29%	68%	32%	Democrat
1995	Michigan	49%	51%	42%	58%	Republican
1997	Minnesota	52%	48%	64%	36%	Republican
1992	Ohio	54%	46%	39%	61%	Republican
1997	Oregon	48%	52%	33%	67%	Democrat
1997	Texas	55%	45%	47%	53%	Republican
	U.S. Average (1990–8)	55%	45%	55%	45%	

Note: This table identifies party control in each state during the legislative session in which multiracial category legislation was introduced or passed. North Carolina and Florida: administrative mandate; no vote or legislative sponsor.

Source: Statistical Abstract of the United States (1998, 2001).

states from 1990 to 1998,[17] we see the same pattern: Democrats controlled a majority of seats in the states with multiracial category legislative activity, and they controlled a majority of seats in all state legislatures. In summary, the dynamics of multiracial category legislation cannot be explained through party control.

New Coalition, New Cleavage: Suburbanization and the Multiracial Trend

None of the explanations just discussed can be systematically applied toward an understanding of the dynamics involved in the introduction and/or subsequent fate of multiracial category legislation at the state level. To develop a better explanation, first I focus attention on a factor that the previously discussed alternative explanations would not have us readily

---

[17] I use party control averages from 1990 to 1998 because this is the most relevant time span for state-level multiracial category initiatives. Source: The Council of State Governments, biennial (copyright).

Table 7.5. *Class/Racial Composition of Multiracial Category Bill Sponsor's Districts versus Class/Racial Composition of the Nearest City*

State	Legislative Sponsor Race/Party	Median Family Income and Percentage Black in Bill Sponsor's District[a]	Median Family Income and Percentage Black in Closest Metropolitan City[b]	
Georgia	Abernathy Black/D	$39,221 80% black	$22,275 67.1% black	Atlanta
Illinois	Carroll White/D	$41,141 3%	$26,301 39.1%	Chicago
Maryland	Healey Black/D	$45,407 41%	$24,045 59.2%	Baltimore
Indiana	Server White/R	$41,497 3%	$29,006 22.6%	Indianapolis
Michigan	Voorhees White/R	$33,453 11%	$18,742 75.7%	Detroit
Ohio	Czarcinski White/D	$45,790 2%	$21,006 46.5%	Cleveland
Calif.	Campbell White/D	$65,914 2%	$30,925 14.0%	Los Angeles
Minn.	Betzold White/D	$45,627 1%	$25,324 13.02%	Minneapolis
Mass.	Keating White/D	$57,799 1%	$29,180 25.6%	Boston
Oregon	Beyer White/D	$27,093 1%	$25,369 1.25%	Eugene
Texas	Ellis Black/D	$29,872 14%	$26,261 28.1%	Houston

Note: All districts are suburban districts. Florida and North Carolina are not noted in the table because multiracial category initiatives were instituted by administrative mandate in these states.

[a] *Source:* Barone (1998).
[b] *Source:* U.S. Bureau of the Census (1994).

consider: shifting trends in, and emerging cleavages related to, minority suburbanization. *The one constant that we find across all of the states involved is that multiracial category legislation has been initiated only in cases where the legislative sponsors of multiracial category bills represent middle-class suburban constituencies.*

Table 7.5 raises a number of interesting questions. Why are legislators representing wealthy suburban districts apparently the ones most inclined to sponsor multiracial category legislation? Why does such support transcend racial and party lines? How do we move from bill sponsorship to an understanding of the legislative outcomes in question? The answer starts with the attributes of contemporary American suburbs.

Although U.S. suburbs are generally thought of as essentially white and largely conservative, demographic data undermine these assumptions. In recent decades, there has been an increasingly rapid departure from urban areas by middle- and working-class minorities. "From 1980 to 1990, the black population in U.S. suburbs grew on average in the United States by 34.4 percent, while the Hispanic population grew by 69.3 percent and the Asian population by 125.9 percent (the comparable figure for whites was 9.2 percent)" (McManus and Morehouse 1997, p. 119). By 2000, in metropolitan areas with populations above 500,000, over half (54.6%) of all Asian Americans, almost half (49.6%) of all Latinos, and nearly 40% of blacks (38.8%) lived in suburbs (Frey, 2001).

What does the suburbanization trend have to do with the outcomes in question? The preceding data on the class and racial composition of the bill sponsor's district in each state, vis-à-vis comparable data for the closest metropolitan city, demonstrate a strong pattern: Multiracial category legislation has been introduced only by legislators representing one of two types of state legislative districts:

- *District Type 1*: Wealthy suburban districts with a large- or medium-sized black middle class (Georgia, Maryland, Michigan, and Texas) or
- *District Type 2*: Wealthy suburban districts with very few blacks at all (Illinois, Indiana, California, Minnesota, Massachusetts, Ohio, and Oregon).

Recall that state-level multiracial category legislation is largely a symbolic gesture, which explains the generally low levels of partisanship and political conflict surrounding this issue at the state level. But why does this symbolic gesture take root in some contexts as opposed to others, and what can we learn on a broader scale from the patterns of support/opposition therein?

District Type 1

These suburban districts with a large/medium-sized black middle class (Atlanta, Baltimore, and Houston) are, not surprisingly, adjacent to cities

214

Table 7.6. *Minority Suburbanization Trends*

Closest City Center	Latino Suburban Population Growth (1990–2000) **Average U.S. Growth: 72%**[a]	Black Suburban Population Growth (1990–2000) **Average U.S. Growth: 38%**	Asian Suburban Population Growth (1990–2000) **Average U.S. Growth: 84%**
Atlanta	403.8%	97.8%	169.7%
Baltimore	78.5%	55.9%	72.1%
Boston	75.4%	39.2%	91.1%
Chicago	250.8%	101.8%	105.1%
Cleveland	247.2%	44.0%	59.5%
Detroit	42.6%	46.3%	91.9%
Eugene	111.3%	11.5%	11.9%
Houston	101.4%	53.9%	94.3%
Indianapolis	263.2%	263.6%	172.7%
Los Angeles	28.7%	2.1%	28.8%
Minneapolis–St. Paul	161.3%	156.0%	113.3%

Note: Suburb = primary metropolitan statistical area (PMSA) (or metropolitan statistical area when no PMSA exists) minus central city. Populations of Minneapolis and St. Paul were added together to derive a central city total.

[a] *Sources:* John Lewis Mumford Center for Comparative Urban and Regional Research, "The New Ethnic Enclaves in America's Suburbs" (July 9, 2001).
http://mumford1.dyndns.org/cen2000/suburban/SuburbanReport/page1.html; Frey (2001) and author's analysis of 1990 Census (STF-1) and 2000 Census (SF-1) data.

consisting of a large or medium-sized black population. Blacks in these cities are moving to the suburbs at a higher rate than those in Detroit and, including Detroit, at a higher rate than average in the United States. Furthermore, Table 7.6 shows that blacks are not the only minority group outpacing nationwide suburbanization trends in Type 1 cases. In the suburbs of Atlanta, Baltimore, and Houston, the growth of the Latino and Asian populations is also increasing at a faster rate than that of suburbs as a whole. Finally, these cases (Detroit excluded) represent all of the instances in which we see black legislative sponsors of multiracial category legislation.

Multiracial category bills are likely to be initiated by legislators representing a large/medium-sized black middle class: This is the baseline definition of Type 1 cases. But the evidence suggests that in addition to a critical mass of middle-class blacks, multiracial category legislation (for Type 1 cases) is most likely to emerge from districts governed by young

Table 7.7. *Proponent/Opponent District Characteristics*

State	Proponent's District		Opponent's District	
Maryland	Healey	$45,407	Boston	$29,345
	22th (House)	41% black	41st (House)	84% black
Michigan	Voorhees	$33,453	Vaughn	$18,602
	77th (House)	11% black	4th (House)	88% black
Ohio	Czarcinski	$45,790	Mallory	$20,230
	46th (House)	2% black	31st (House)	60% black
Texas	Ellis	$29,872	Jefferson	$21,223
	13th (House)	14% black	143rd (House)	45% black

Source: Barone (1998). Income is reported as average household income for all residents in the respective legislative districts.

"new-generation"[18] black legislators who represent fast-growing, racially diverse suburbs that are adjacent to high-growth metropolitan areas. This is the profile of the black legislator and/or legislative district that is most conducive to the emergence of multiracial category legislation at the state level in district Type 1. Furthermore, Table 7.7 provides evidence to support this pattern from the reverse angle: Where there has been opposition to the legislation, it has come exclusively from older black legislators representing urban (city center) districts with a large proportion of poor blacks.

Because the *n* is small, it is impossible to generalize beyond the data. However, the opponents are all older black legislators, who, in general, tend to be motivated by traditional civil rights issues.[19] What I think we are seeing in Table 7.7 is preliminary evidence of a cleavage that is beginning to surface in state and local elections around the country and is likely to transform minority politics over time (as older black legislators retire or otherwise vacate their posts). The cleavage relates to the increasingly contested issue, among minority elites, regarding what is in the minority's interest. In other words, I suspect that in general, new-generation black legislators are more inclined to support multiracial category legislation because they do not view civil rights issues in the traditional sense that older black legislators

---

[18] "New generation" is a term used to distinguish between the first cadre of blacks elected to office just after the implementation of the Voting Rights Act and those elected more recently, i.e., over the past ten to fifteen years. Evidence suggests that the latter have been less driven by traditional civil rights issues and are more inclined to adopt biracial, entrepreneurial modes of operation. See, for example, Canon (1999) and Bositis (2001).

[19] See for example Cohen (1999) and Walton (1995).

do and because they are more apt to embrace biracial coalition formation strategies.

I will return to the issues of minority interests and new cleavages in the next, and final, section of the essay. First, however, I take a closer look at the case of Detroit, which is the exception to all of the factors that I have identified as salient for Type 1 cases: Detroit exhibits lower levels of black suburbanization than other Type 1 cases, lower than average levels of minority suburbanization in at least one other minority group (Latinos or Asians), and the legislative sponsor is a white Republican. While my Type 1 typology fails to explain why we see multiracial category legislation emerging from suburban Detroit, it is not surprising that subsequently, the most conflict surrounding the multiracial category issue in all states centers on this case, as is clearly reflected in the Michigan roll-call votes. Black state Representative Ed Vaughn led the opposition to the multiracial category bill in that state. In a telephone interview with this author, Representative Vaughn said the following about multiracial category legislation at the state level:

On the surface it seems harmless, but there are mean-spirited people who want to scuttle black power. I fought the bill very hard. I argued that it was strictly an effort to destroy black economic power. The black representatives [in Michigan] were jumping on board until I came along. So many blacks don't want to be black. Why would [Ralph] Abernathy [the black legislative sponsor of the Georgia multiracial category bill] support it? Abernathy is confused. These Negroes are totally confused. If I could have talked to Abernathy, I'd have changed his mind. The issue did not become controversial in other states because they didn't have me in other states.[20]

Although Detroit does not fit my typology for Type 1 cases, it does lend support to my broader argument about a potential cleavage emerging between old-generation and new-generation black legislators. For Vaughn, the new generation is confused; for Abernathy, the old generation is "living in the past."[21]

District Type 2

Type 2 districts typify the common public perception of suburbs as being significantly wealthier and whiter than the closest city center. Although

[20] Michigan State Rep. Ed Vaughn, telephone interview, December 3, 1998.
[21] Georgia State Sen. Ralph Abernathy III, telephone interview, December 15, 1998.

Type 2 districts resemble those of Type 1 in terms of income disparity vis-à-vis city centers, the resemblance stops there. Contrary to Type 1 cases, there is no thematic characteristic that binds Type 2 bill sponsors to each other. The only potential pattern involves the fact that many of these bill sponsors are white Democrats from liberal/progressive states. California, Oregon, Massachusetts, and Minnesota fit this characterization; Indiana, Ohio, and Illinois do not.[22] I will bracket this discussion momentarily, as patterns of racial diversity and liberalism in these states are discussed more extensively in the conclusion.

From Bill Sponsorship to Legislative Outcomes

While legislators representing middle-class suburban districts *introduced* multiracial category legislation, the success or failure of these initiatives ultimately depended on the votes of all legislators in those states. In moving from bill sponsorship to legislative outcomes, it is useful to think of the multiracial category issue as a barometer of legislative responsiveness, at least on symbolic matters, to minority interests. Conceptualizing the multiracial category issue within this rubric allows us to link this study to the broader literature on minority representation. This body of work is fundamentally concerned with explaining the conditions under which elected officials promote or thwart the interests of minorities in the legislative arena.[23]

Although the minority representation literature guides us in the right direction, two engaging problems become immediately apparent in tying this study to that body of work. First, this literature rests implicitly on the notion that there are monolithic minority interests. Hence the interesting question: Is multiracial category legislation in the minority interest or opposed to it? As discussed earlier, the black legislators who have become involved in this issue appear to be divided on this point. That the minority representation literature does not deal well with the possibility of divergent visions for the representation of racial interests, though empirically, different visions are becoming increasingly observable. The second interesting problem involved in applying the insights of the minority representation literature, particularly to the case at hand, is that, by and large, "minority interests" have been used in this body of work to denote "black interests."

---

[22] Erickson, Wright, and McIver (1993) provide a typology of states from most conservative to most liberal. Also see Hero (1998).

[23] See, for example, Swain (1993) and Lublin (1997).

This essay raises questions about that assumption as well, in that it is difficult to view multiracial category legislation as relating exclusively to the interests (however defined) of one and only one minority group. However, albeit with some modifications, the minority representation literature takes us the furthest in understanding the outcomes in question.

My first concern, about the need to problematize "interests," is in practice mediated by the fact that, except in Michigan, no excessively vocal opponents emerged at the state level. By and large, the multiracial category issue *has* been accepted as a feel-good, cost-free measure related to, as State Senator Howard Carroll (D-IL) put it, the "quality-of-life interests of minorities."[24] As such, multiracial category legislation has evoked little controversy at the state level in general, and the largely unanimous roll-call votes support this view. In other words, the question of whether or not this sort of legislation is in the interest of minorities has provoked more contention among minority legislators than it has in the broader context of the state legislatures involved. Thus, in terms of the way in which multiracial category legislation has been viewed by state legislative bodies as a whole, we may aptly regard the issue as most legislators seem to have viewed it: as a symbolic gesture related to minority interests.

Figure 7.1 schematizes the relationships predicted by the most prevalent models employed in the minority representation literature to explain legislative responsiveness to black interests. (Recall that the minority representation literature is predominantly concerned with *black* interests.) All of these models share the view that legislative responsiveness to black interests is, in some way, related to the racial composition of the state, namely, to the percentage of black residents therein. Relating the patterns of multiracial category legislative activity at the state level to these models, we see that provisionally a modified majoritarian model holds the most explanatory promise. The hypothesis advanced by this model in its original formulation is as follows: Blacks will have little influence on the voting behavior of their representatives until they constitute a majority, at which point voting behavior will take a discrete jump toward black-favored policies.

The first modification that we should make to this model relates to the fact that we are concerned with a symbolic issue, and as such, the threshold for legislative responsiveness to minority issues is likely to be lower than

[24] Illinois State Sen. Howard Carroll, telephone interview, November 17, 1998.

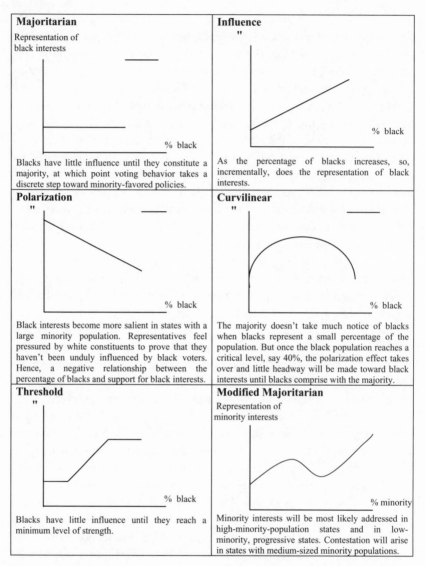

Figure 7.1 Models of minority representation. *Source*: Cameron et al. (1996), for all but modified majoritarian.

on substantive issues related to the allocation of resources. Although I am not aware of any studies directly addressing the threshold question for symbolic bills at the state level, most students of Congress agree that responsiveness to substantive black concerns rises dramatically once a district passes a threshold of around 40% black. I use 25% as the threshold for legislative responsiveness to symbolic racial issues in state legislatures.[25] Applying this first adjustment to the majoritarian model, we could explain the outcomes of interest as follows: We see multiracial category legislative activity in Georgia, Maryland, and North Carolina because these are states that reach the threshold for legislative responsiveness to black interests. We see activity in California, Minnesota, Massachusetts, and Oregon because these are generally liberal/progressive states that are more likely to pay attention to symbolic black interests than conservative states with few blacks, such as Idaho or Montana. But why do we see multiracial category legislative activity in Georgia (28.7% black) and Maryland (27.9% black) as opposed to other states with large black populations, such as Alabama (26% black) and Mississippi (36.3% black)? At the other end of the spectrum, why do we not see legislative activity in a number of other low-black-population, liberal/progressive states (e.g., Vermont, Wisconsin)? Finally, how do we explain all of the cases with medium-sized black populations (Illinois, Florida, Michigan, Texas, Ohio, and Indiana)? Most of these questions can be answered if we make a second modification to the majoritarian model by viewing multiracial category legislative activity as related to the *total minority population* of the states involved, not just the black population (Table 7.8).[26]

The overall dynamic can be explained as follows: Although we have what amounts to four different case types (large minority population; large minority population of predominantly blacks; medium-sized minority population; very small minority population), we end up with a relatively unadorned line of reasoning to explain the outcomes in question. *Multiracial category legislation is most likely to succeed in one of two types of states: those with a minority population above the national mean (25% or more) or liberal/progressive states with a relatively small (10% or less) minority population.* This is because, as adapted from the majoritarian model, when the minority population is small, minority interests are not given much attention (except in liberal/progressive states). At the other end of the spectrum, as the percentage

---

[25] Analysts disagree on the point at which substantive black interests begin to be viewed differently in Congress. I use 25% for state legislatures because minoritiés make up 25% of the U.S. population and because this is a symbolic issue.

[26] Looking at the total minority population as opposed to solely the black population renders a dramatically different picture in some cases and a negligible difference in others. Not surprisingly, in the South, most of the minority populations are blacks.

Table 7.8. *Percentage of Minority Populations in States with Multiracial Category Activity*

Above 25% Minority Population		Below 25% Minority Population	
California	**54.7% minority**	Michigan	**21.2% minority**
	6.7% Black		14.2% Black
	10.9% Asian		1.8% Asian
	32.4% Latino		3.3% Latino
	4.7% Two or More Races		1.9% Two or More Races
Texas	**48.7% minority**	Massachusetts	**18.3% minority**
	11.5% Black		5.4% Black
	2.7% Asian		3.8% Asian
	32.0% Latino		6.8% Latino
	2.5% Two or More Races		2.3% Two or More Races
Maryland	**38.2% minority**	Ohio	**16.0% minority**
	27.9% Black		11.5% Black
	4.0% Asian		1.2% Asian
	4.3% Latino		1.9% Latino
	2.0% Two or More Races		1.4% Two or More Races
Georgia	**37.5% minority**	Oregon	**15.7% minority**
	28.7% Black		1.6% Black
	2.1% Asian		3.0% Asian
	5.3% Latino		8.0% Latino
	1.4% Two or More Races		3.1% Two or More Races
Florida	**35.5% minority**	Indiana	**14.1% minority**
	14.6% Black		8.4% Black
	1.7% Asian		1.0% Asian
	16.8% Latino		3.5% Latino
	2.4% Two or More Races		1.2% Two or More Races
Illinois	**32.7% minority**	Minnesota	**11.0% minority**
	15.1% Black		3.5% Black
	3.4% Asian		2.9% Asian
	12.3% Latino		2.9% Latino
	1.9% Two or More Races		1.7% Two or More Races
North Carolina	**29.0% minority**		
	21.6% Black		
	1.4% Asian		
	4.7% Latino		
	1.3% Two or More Races		

Note: Following Census Bureau procedures, I include in the minority population those marking Two or More Races. The Native American population is negligible in all of the states under consideration.

Source: U.S. Census Bureau (2000).

of minorities in a state reaches or exceeds the national mean of 25%, minority interests are more likely to be addressed favorably.

In states where blacks comprise the majority of the minority population, the reasonable question was raised earlier: Why, for example, Georgia (37.5% minority but, of that, 28.7% black) and North Carolina (29% minority but, of that, 21.6% black) as opposed to other states with large black populations such as Alabama (26% black) or Mississippi (36.3% black)? Note, however, the southern states in which we see legislative activity: Georgia, Florida, North Carolina, and Texas. These states do not represent the classic Deep South states; rather, they are states whose economies are strongly linked to international trade and services, with rapidly growing service-based urban centers and suburban middle classes. Particularly over the past ten to fifteen years, analysts have found that these "New South" cases diverge significantly from Deep South states in terms of the voting behavior of elected officials.[27] In fact, "since 1980, 'New South' Democrats have started to behave a lot like northern Democrats" (Rhode 1991, p. 56). All of the states in which we see multiracial category legislative activity in the South are in fact new South states.

This still leaves us with the medium-sized (roughly 10–25%) minority population states: Michigan, Ohio, Massachusetts, Oregon, Indiana, and Minnesota. All things being equal, it is in this set of states that we should expect to find the most contestation surrounding the multiracial category issue. Indeed, the roll-call votes (Table 7.3) reflect this in Michigan and Ohio. Although the multiracial category bills in Massachusetts, Oregon and Minnesota never came up for a vote – thus, the only state for which my general theory conclusively does not hold is Indiana – it is interesting to speculate about these states. It seems plausible that the votes in these very liberal states could have just as easily demonstrated contestation (because of the growing minority population) or consent (because of the exceptionally liberal/progressive characteristics of these states). In general, however, extending the overall line of reasoning to other states, we might have expected states such as New York (39.6% minority population) and New Jersey (35.1% minority population) to be likely candidates for the adoption of multiracial category legislation, as well as Vermont and Wisconsin, two states with small minority populations but liberal/progressive tendencies.

[27] See, for example, Whitby and Gilliam (1991) and Nye and Bullock (1992).

Conclusions

It is no coincidence that all state-level multiracial category legislative activity came to an abrupt halt in 1997: As noted earlier, in that year and under pressure from myriad actors, the OMB changed the federal guidelines for the collection of racial data. Thus, because of MATA, it is unlikely that more states will adopt multiracial category legislation. Is this the end of the story?

It is interesting that, in the aftermath of the move to MATA, a new set of state initiatives designed to either ban the collection of racial statistics altogether or otherwise eliminate race as a factor of consideration in state institutions is gaining momentum. "Racial privacy" and/or "civil rights" initiatives have been introduced in California (2001), Florida (1999), and Washington State (1998). Although I believe that the intentions and incentives driving racial privacy initiatives differ from those behind multiracial category bills, the two are conceptually related and raise the kinds of questions that, in the future, we will see more of rather than less.

Thus, even though the state-level multiracial category issue is a low-stakes symbolic matter that resulted in negligible levels of controversy, it is worthy of exploration for a number of reasons. In analyzing legislative activity surrounding this matter at the state level, we are also asking which elected officials, representing what kinds of constituencies, are most receptive to this country's shift away from a monotypic definition of race. In the context of multiracial category bill sponsorship, the state actors most amenable to more flexible ideas of race are predominantly new-generation black elected officials and progressive white Democrats, all of whom represent affluent suburban districts. Furthermore, minority (not just black) demographics help to explain statewide legislative outcomes.

Beyond the politics of the moment, this essay also demonstrates the salience of an often overlooked relationship between constituencies, social movements, and political parties. The conventional pluralist model of U.S. politics prompts us to focus on the ways in which movements try to influence parties to achieve outcomes. But in this case, the factors necessary to sustain a pluralist line of explanation are absent: The strength and activity of the multiracial category movement are poor guides to movement success, and the multiracial category issue generally drew minimal opposition in state legislatures. Thus, the observable outcomes cannot be viewed as a matter of one party or the other achieving a victory.

[28] See www.acrc1.org/rpi.htm; www.fcri.net/FAQ.htm; www.adversity.net/i200.htm.

Clearly, the relationship between movements and parties is incomplete; what matters is the intersection of movements, parties, and constituencies. State legislators did not initiate or support multiracial category bills because they were strong-armed into doing so by a powerful movement, nor did they back such legislation as a way to outmaneuver the other party. Rather, success came because the involved legislators gauged the ways in which their responses to the multiracial category initiative would be received by their broader constituencies.

In other words, the work that movements do to frame issues is potentially valuable to legislators in gaining the support of constituencies, even if most constituents are not active in the movement. Thus, even limited social movements may mediate between larger constituencies and party politicians. Traditional notions of social movements as effective only to the degree that they mobilize supporters or exploit legislative divisions are inadequate to explain the success of multiracial category laws. Rather, the multiracial movement has raised an issue that has, in turn, been seized upon by certain state legislators to signal their constituents as to their stance on new versus traditional approaches to important issues regarding race and civil rights. The implication is that the influence of movements on legislatures is perhaps more pervasive than the respective literatures on social movements and legislative politics presume.

8

Protest Cycles and Party Politics

THE EFFECTS OF ELITE ALLIES AND ANTAGONISTS ON STUDENT PROTEST IN THE UNITED STATES, 1930–1990

Nella Van Dyke

Social movement scholars have demonstrated that political opportunities influence the emergence and dynamics of social movements (e.g., Costain 1992; Kriesi et al. 1995; McAdam 1982; Meyer 1990; Tarrow 1989). Groups are more likely to mobilize when the institutionalized political system is open to them. Doug McAdam (1996) and Sidney Tarrow (1996) describe a number of dimensions of the political opportunity system that may influence mobilization, including the stability or instability of elite alignments and the presence or absence of elite allies. Although elites are central to political opportunity theory, we do not know *which* elites may influence mobilization.

In this essay, I examine the effect of elites in different branches and levels of government on student protest mobilization from 1930 to 1990. Using Democratic Party officials in office as a proxy for left-wing allies, I examine the impact of Democrats (and Republicans) in the executive and legislative branches of the federal and state governments on student mobilization. I conduct an event history analysis of 2,496 protest events to examine the relationship between different governmental positions, parties, and protest. I suggest that elite allies in some locations may inspire increased protest activity, as suggested by political opportunity theory, but that powerful elites sometimes serve as antagonists that inspire mobilization by threatening the goals of a movement.

Political Opportunity Theory

Scholars studying a variety of social movements demonstrate that political opportunity structure influences mobilization. For example, Doug McAdam (1982) shows that African Americans mobilized to fight for their

226

civil rights in the United States partially in response to a number of changes that occurred within the institutionalized political system in the 1950s. Repression in the form of lynchings decreased steadily throughout the first half of the twentieth century, Supreme Court cases were increasingly decided in favor of African Americans, and northern Democrats began to court the black vote. As their opportunities increased, African Americans became more convinced that change was possible and began to mobilize. Other scholars have shown similar effects for other movements, including the women's movement of the 1960s (Costain 1992), the nuclear freeze movement in the United States and Europe (Kitschelt 1986; Meyer 1990; Rucht 1990), the Italian protest cycle of the 1960s (Tarrow 1989), the "new" social movements in Western Europe (Kriesi et al. 1995), and the fall of the Soviet Union (Oberschall 1996).

Synthesizing much of the recent work on political opportunities, Sidney Tarrow (1996) and Doug McAdam (1996) identify four dimensions of the political opportunity structure that may influence mobilization:

1. The relative openness or closure of the institutionalized political system
2. The stability or instability of elite alignments
3. The presence or absence of elite allies
4. The state's capacity and propensity for repression.

The general idea is that when the political system opens up to a group, or when they come to have allies in the system, they will be more likely to protest as they perceive that change may be possible. Groups mobilize to make their interests known and to influence these allies.

Numerous scholars have demonstrated the importance of elite allies to the mobilization and success of movements. Craig Jenkins and Charles Perrow (1977) compare the American farmworkers' movement in the late 1940s to the movement in the 1960s. They demonstrate that the support of liberal organizations and organized labor explains why the movement was better able to mobilize and achieve its goals in the 1960s than it had been in the earlier period. Almeida and Stearns (1998) examine the influence of allies on outcomes in a local environmental campaign in Japan. They find that increased support from external allies, including local support groups, national environmental social movements, students, the Communist Party, and the mass media all helped the movement achieve success in the early 1970s. Allies can also play a role in the decline of movement activity. Doug McAdam (1982) demonstrates that the spread of rioting to northern cities in the second half of the 1960s led to diminished support for the civil rights movement. The resulting loss of allies, with the election of Richard Nixon in 1968 and diminished support of northern liberals, was one factor influencing the movement's shift into a period of abeyance.

However, elites may not only serve as allies to a movement, they may also present a threat to movement goals. Charles Tilly (1978) argues that protesters will mobilize in response to opportunities *or* threats and will be least likely to protest when faced with little of either. Like current formulations of political opportunity theory, he suggests that groups may mobilize in response to the presence of allies, when there is evidence that elites may be receptive to their claims. However, he also argues that groups will mobilize in response to a threat, that is, when those in power threaten to deny them the realization of their interests. When there is little possibility for change, good or bad, groups have little incentive to mobilize. Although the idea that groups will mobilize when they experience an expansion of their political opportunities has seen increasing investigation over the past decade, political opportunity scholars have generally failed to recognize that groups may also mobilize in response to perceived threats.

There are some exceptions to this rule, as social movement scholars increasingly recognize the mobilizing potential of threat. Jack Goldstone and Charles Tilly (2001), for example, argue that threat is not merely the opposite of opportunity, but also an independent factor that may influence mobilization. They suggest that levels of mobilization will vary based on the levels of threat and opportunity faced by the protest group. Threats may include increasing violence against the group, the removal of rights or property, or the use of repression in response to protest actions. Hanspeter Kriesi and his colleagues (1995) argue that the political opportunity structure influences protest by altering the costs and benefits of protest, and also by changing the possibility that a movement's goals will be met. When institutional political actors are reform oriented, there may be little need for collective action since the goals of a movement will be met without it. At other times, political actors may threaten movement goals, and collective action may be necessary to prevent an erosion of valued goods.

Several lines of research demonstrate that mobilization sometimes occurs in response to threat: research on ethnic conflict and right-wing mobilization, research on repression, and research on "suddenly imposed grievances." A number of recent studies of right-wing extremism and racial violence suggest that mobilization may occur in response to threats produced by economic problems and changes in minority populations (Barret 1987; Beck 2000; Blee 1996; Kimmel and Ferber 2000; Kitschelt 1995; Koopmans 1996; McVeigh 1999; Van Dyke and Soule 2000). Studies of the interaction between protesters and the state suggest that under certain conditions, the threat produced by repression inspires protest. Several scholars demonstrate that arrests may have a curvilinear effect on protest: Some arrests may anger activists and mobilize them for additional protest (DeNardo 1985; Muller and Weede 1990), but severe levels of repression may effectively squelch mobilization. Others show that people sometimes mobilize in response to catastrophic events or suddenly imposed grievances. People mobilized rapidly in response to the Three Mile Island nuclear accident (Walsh 1981) and in response to an oil spill in Santa Barbara (Molotch 1970).

I argue that, in addition to the conditions just described, the presence of antagonists, or political actors who oppose the goals of a movement, may also create a threat that inspires protest. David Meyer's (1990, 1993) study of the nuclear freeze movement in the United States provides support for this argument. The actions and policies of Ronald Reagan during the 1980s had a profound mobilizing effect on nuclear freeze activists. Reagan's talk of "limited nuclear war" and his Star Wars initiative served to mobilize previously quiescent activists, resulting in an extended campaign including one of the largest protests in United States history. While this case study demonstrates the mobilizing effect that a threat caused by a political antagonist may have on protest activity, theoretical conceptions of political opportunity have not been revised to recognize such findings. Elite allies are included as factors influencing mobilization, but elite antagonists are not.

In this essay, I examine the influence of specific political allies in the government on the overall mobilization of protest on college campuses. I examine their impact on levels of activity on the part of all left-wing movements active on campuses between 1930 and 1990. I conceptualize this as an examination of left-wing movement activity on the part of a distinct population. However, one could also conceptualize this as a single movement, the student movement. The latter formulation strikes me as problematic, however, as students have historically been highly active on a number of different issues, including U.S. military actions, women's status, and civil rights, among others. Therefore, to conceptualize the sum total of student protests as a single movement separate from these specific issue movements

229

seems conceptually inconsistent. The study of student protest activity is worthwhile as it focuses on a population that includes representatives of virtually all left-wing movements. Student protest is also an ideal movement family to examine for a number of methodological reasons, discussed in the following data and methods section.

Political Elites: Political Parties

Elite allies or antagonists can include members of the judicial system, the legislature, the president, business, political parties, organized labor, scientists, the church, and intellectuals, among others. Although research has demonstrated the importance of allies for particular movements, few have examined the impact of particular kinds of allies or their effect on overall levels of mobilization. Numerous social movement scholars assert that social movements are not discrete entities (McAdam 1995; Meyer and Whittier 1994; Taylor 2000; Van Dyke 1998). Sidney Tarrow's concept of protest cycles (1989, 1998a) is built on the observation that movements tend to occur in clusters; some periods are characterized by heightened levels of protest. In spite of calls to study protest cycles or entire social movement sectors (Garner and Zald 1987), few social movement researchers have done so (with some notable exceptions, e.g., della Porta and Rucht 1995; Kriesi et. al. 1995).

In this essay, I examine the influence of one particular set of allies on levels of student protest activity: political parties within the legislative and executive branches of government. I consider Democrats to be allies of the left, based on numerous research studies that demonstrate that this is indeed the case. V. O. Key demonstrates that the Democrats have consistently been more liberal than the Republicans (Key 1964). Since 1896, Key argues, the Democratic Party has tended to represent the interests of lower-income groups and union members, while the Republicans have consistently represented the interests of upper-income groups and financial and corporate entities. Social scientists have demonstrated that Democrats tend to be more supportive of civil rights policies (Browning, Marshall, and Tabb 1984; Button 1989; Santoro 1995) and certain women's movement initiatives (Sorensen 1994). Left-leaning parties tend to be perceived as allies by environmental movement organizations in Europe, whether or not they actually act in the movement's interests (Dalton 1995). Similarly, the women's movement in the United States, though often pursuing bipartisan influence, has tended to align itself with the Democratic Party (Costain and Costain 1987; Young 1996). There are powerful reasons for expecting political parties to have an influence on social movement activity.

Garner and Zald (1987, p. 312) argue that

party structure is probably the single most important variable for understanding the patterning of social movements.[1] Movements can be understood as one part of a range of options that also includes political parties. Parties spin off movements, either deliberately or in the process of factionalizing. Movements appear within parties. Both are organizational forms for pursuing political ends, so it is not surprising that they are so closely intertwined.

Parties may be the targets of movements because they may be seen as allies with the ability to help movements achieve their goals. Parties may also interact with and support movements in their search for electoral support.

Debra Minkoff (1997) demonstrates that the presence of Democrats in the federal legislature influenced levels of protest in the civil rights movement and the women's movement in the United States. She found that increased Democratic Party control in the federal legislature was associated with increased levels of protest in the civil rights movement and, when accompanied by civil rights protest, higher levels of protest among feminists as well. Thus, we know that Democratic Party control in the legislature may inspire higher levels of protest activity, but further questions remain.

The Relationship between Allies and Mobilization

Although it has been shown that political allies may influence movement activity, the exact nature of this relationship remains understudied. While it does seem clear that elite allies may facilitate mobilization, we don't know whether the relationship is monotonic, where the presence of more allies means more protest, or curvilinear, where levels of mobilization may increase or decrease depending on the extent of support. Common sense might suggest the prior relationship: The more allies, the better. However, the relationship may be curvilinear, as suggested by early political opportunity theorists.

Peter Eisinger (1973) argues that protest is most likely to occur in cities in which there is a combination of "open" and "closed" structures. He suggests that protest is unlikely to occur in extremely closed or repressive systems

---

[1] Garner and Zald (1987) are referring specifically to the importance of parties in explaining cross-national differences in social movement activity. However, their point remains relevant for this study.

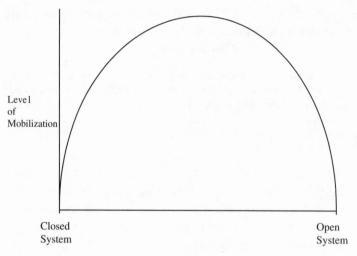

Figure 8.1 Eisinger's model of mobilization.

or in extremely open systems. Repression would discourage mobilization in the prior case, while a completely open and favorable political configuration would render protest unnecessary. His hypothesis regarding political opportunity and levels of mobilization can be represented graphically as in Figure 8.1.

The presence of divided elites is one example of a partially open, partially closed political opportunity system. Some elites may be sympathetic to the claims of a movement, while others may be antagonistic, a mixed situation compared to a system composed of primarily friendly or primarily unfriendly elites. Political opportunity scholars have shown that divided elites signal to aggrieved populations that they have some political opportunity and thereby facilitate protest activity. Doug McAdam (1982) finds that changing alignments influenced the mobilization of the civil rights movement in the early 1960s. The coalition between northern and southern Democrats fell apart and left northern Democrats searching for electoral support. They began to court the black vote, which gave more power to the civil rights movement. Similarly, Paul Almeida and Linda Stearns (1998) find that the erosion of consensus among governmental agencies and the election of environmentalists in Japan created an opportunity for a local grassroots movement to achieve some of its goals. When elites are divided and the movement has some political allies, these allies may be vulnerable to movement claims. This hypothesis is consistent with Peter Eisinger's (1973)

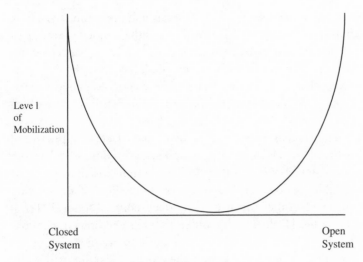

Figure 8.2 Tilly's model of mobilization.

conception of mobilization. It suggests that levels of mobilization will be higher when the political system is not completely closed to contenders or when success is not assured through a completely favorable political configuration. Groups mobilize when their chances of success are uncertain, with some possibility of success.

Charles Tilly (1978) suggests a curvilinear model of the relationship between opportunities and mobilization that is quite different from Eisinger's. He argues that protesters will mobilize in response to threats or opportunities and will be least likely to protest when faced with little of either. Groups will mobilize when those in power threaten to deny them the realization of their interests or when there is evidence that elites may be receptive to their claims. When there is little possibility for change, good or bad, groups have little incentive to mobilize. His hypothesis can be represented as in Figure 8.2.

Based on these theoretical notions, there are several possible trajectories for the dynamics of elite influence on protest. An exploration of these will help nuance political opportunity theory. First, it is unclear whether the mere presence of *some* allies is all that is necessary for mobilization or whether the level of protest increases as the number of allies increases. In addition, little research examines the possibility that elite antagonists, producing a threat, may influence levels of mobilization. And it is possible that levels of mobilization take a curvilinear form, with contenders responding either to divided elites or to threats and opportunities. These issues are all the more complicated in a country with a divided governmental structure such as the United States. Allies and divisions between elites may occur within different levels of government. Thus, the federal government may be divided, with a Democrat president and a Republican legislature, and state government may be similarly divided. It is unclear which elites matter.

Little social movement research has recognized the fact that elites within different levels and branches of government may have a differential impact on protest activity. Debra Minkoff (1997), for example, examines the influence of allied legislators, but fails to examine the effect of allies within the executive branch or the influence of state-level political actors. Political parties exist as potential allies within different levels and branches of government, and it is possible that allies in one position are more important than allies in others. I therefore examine the influence of elites within the executive *and* legislative branches of both federal *and* state government on the mobilization of student protest activity between 1930 and 1990. Because I am studying student protest, I also examine the effect of local elites: faculty and college administrators. It is possible that elites within different levels have a distinct effect on levels of protest.

Data and Methods

In order to examine the effect of elites on protest activity, I use a dataset of 2,496 protest events that occurred at nine U.S. colleges between 1930 and 1990. This dataset is well suited for examining the effect of allies on protest for several reasons. First, the nine schools are located in nine different states. Thus, I can assess the differential effects of state versus federal elites on protest activity, which would not be possible given national-level data on protest activity. Second, I have a complete record of protest activity in nine discrete locations over a sixty-year time span. This enables me to measure accurately the association between elite allies and protest activity over time. Data collected from a national newspaper source would not include such a complete count of protests in each location, and therefore the findings would be subject to stronger reporting biases.

In order to choose the colleges for the study, I randomly selected 200 schools and sent letters to their libraries inquiring whether their student newspaper was available on microfilm. The newspaper was available from only 25% of the schools. I then selected colleges ensuring diversity

Table 8.1. *Sample Colleges, Organized by Selection Criteria*

	Private	Public	N	M	H	Small	Large
Grinnell College, IA	X				X	X	
Harvard University, MA	X				X		X
Ottawa University, KS	X		X			X	
Midland Lutheran College, NE	R		X			X	
Muhlenberg College, PA	R				X	X	
St. Mary's College of CA	R			X		X	
Illinois State University		X	X				X
University of Arizona		X		X			X
University of Southern Mississippi		X	X				X

R, religious college; N, nonselective; M, moderately selective; H, highly selective.

on a number of characteristics that previous research (Van Dyke 1998) has shown to be important in influencing the location of student protest activity, including the size of the institution, how selective the school is, whether it is public or private, and if private, whether or not the college has a religious affiliation. Table 8.1 presents a description of the colleges and their characteristics.

For every issue of the student newspapers from these schools from 1930 to 1990, all articles on student protest were copied and then coded. I defined protest events as any action that collectively expressed a grievance and had a goal of causing or resisting social change, based on the work of Charles Tilly (1978) and Doug McAdam and his colleagues (1997). Thus, events had to be collective, public, and express a grievance. The events range from petitions and demonstrations to lawsuits and the passage of resolutions. Figure 8.3 shows the total number of events in the dataset over time.

Although students have historically been active on numerous issues related to the broader society, including the Civil War and abolition, for example, the issues that have most consistently occupied their attention have been those of their own circumstances: college administration. Throughout every decade included in this study, campus issues occupied a significant portion of the students' attention. Other issues have triggered higher levels of protest during certain decades, however. The two issues that mobilized the highest number of protest events were the Vietnam War and U.S. involvement with the apartheid system in South Africa. Peace issues and U.S.

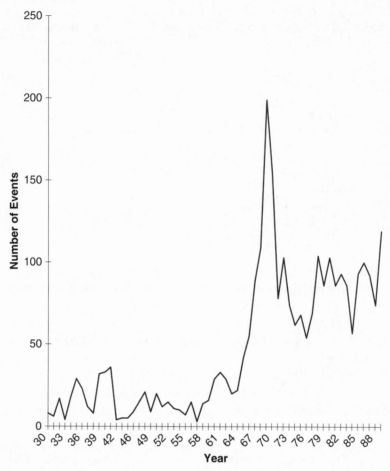

Figure 8.3 Total protest events, all colleges.

military actions, in fact, have consistently been an area of primary concern to students. These issues saw high levels of protest in every decade other than the 1950s. Interestingly, as can be seen in Figure 8.4, the number of issues generating significant levels of student protest has increased over time.

These analyses include data on all protests covering left-wing issues. A number of social movement scholars suggest that social movements are not distinct entities but are part of social movement families (McAdam 1995; Meyer and Whittier 1994; Taylor 2000; Van Dyke 1998). However,

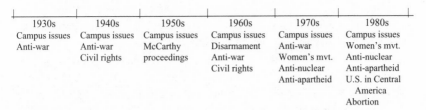

1930s	1940s	1950s	1960s	1970s	1980s
Campus issues	Campus issues	Campus issues	Campus issues	Campus issues	Campus issues
Anti-war	Anti-war	McCarthy	Disarmament	Anti-war	Women's mvt.
	Civil rights	proceedings	Anti-war	Women's mvt.	Anti-nuclear
			Civil rights	Anti-nuclear	Anti-apartheid
				Anti-apartheid	U.S. in Central America
					Abortion

Figure 8.4 Timeline of protest issues on campus.

most students of social movements study individual movements due to the difficulty of collecting data on a large number of issues. Due to the unique nature of my dataset, I am able to examine the entire left-wing movement family on the selected college campuses.

Variables

The dependent variable for the analyses presented in this essay is the duration between protest events on college campuses, or the frequency of protest events. I expect that under certain conditions, protest events will be more likely to occur and, thus, that the duration between events will be shorter.

In order to examine whether the presence of elite allies in different branches and levels has an effect on the frequency of protest events, I examine the party membership of the executive branch and the legislature. Specifically, I look at the influence of a Democrat as president or governor and the impact of the presence of Democrats in Congress and state legislatures on protest activity. I use the number of Democrats in the state and federal legislatures as a proxy for elite allies. I realize that not all Democrats support left-wing movements; however, research has demonstrated that Democrats are consistently more left-wing than Republicans and have been since 1896 (Key 1964). Therefore, I expect that the more Democrats there are in Congress, the more allies there will be for the left. These archival data are from *The Statistical Abstract of the United States* (U.S. Bureau of the Census 1959, 1963, 1968, 1974, 1980, 1986, 1991), the *Book of the States* (The Council of State Governments 1937, 1939, 1941, 1943, 1948, 1950, 1952, 1954, 1956, 1958), and the *Congressional Quarterly* (1998).[2]

---

[2] The statistical method I use, as described later, controls for the fact that Democrats in Mississippi are different from northern Democrats.

For my first analysis, I simply examine the relationship between allies and the frequency of protest. I operationalize allies in the legislatures (federal and state) as the percentage of Democrats in office and use dummy variables to indicate Democratic president and governor. In order for the elite allies hypothesis to be supported, we would expect Democrats in the executive office and a higher percentage of Democrats in the legislature to lead to higher levels of protest. In order to examine the influence of local-level allies, I look at faculty and administrative responses to previous protest events. Specifically, I look at whether or not the previous event had a favorable response from faculty or the administration.

Political opportunity theory argues that groups will be more likely to protest when elites are divided. The concept of divided elites is also relevant to an examination of whether or not people are more likely to mobilize when the government is divided, or whether they are more likely to do so when they face a threat or great opportunities. Therefore, I examine the impact of divided elites, within both the federal and state legislatures, on the likelihood of student protest activity. I operationalize divided elites as the presence of one party in the executive and the other party in the legislature. For example, the federal government would be considered divided when Republicans are the dominant party in both houses of the federal legislature but there is a Democrat in the executive office. If there is a monotonic relationship between allies and levels of protest, then Democrats in the legislature and executive should lead to high levels of protest, while Republicans in both branches should lead to low levels of protest. According to Charles Tilly's (1978) hypothesis, mobilization will be higher when Republicans dominate both houses or when Democrats dominate. According to Peter Eisinger (1973), levels of protest will be higher when the branches are divided rather than when one party dominates both.

The dataset contains a number of other variables that could potentially serve as controls for these analyses, and are of central interest to other questions not explored here. However, for simplicity in this analysis, I use fixed effects statistical models, which control for any aspect of the college that might influence the incidence of protest events over time. I do include a dummy variable that is coded 1 for the Vietnam War years due to the unusually high levels of protest during that era. There were clearly other factors that influenced protest during this period other than college characteristics and the political opportunity structure, and this variable should control for these other effects.

Statistical Method

In order to evaluate the effect of elite allies on the timing of protest events, I use event history models, which predict the frequency of events or the likelihood that an event will occur. The specific method I use is called "fixed effects partial likelihood" and is a variant of proportional hazards regression (Allison 1995). Proportional hazards regression calculates the likelihood that an event will occur. Thus, coefficients can be interpreted as influencing this likelihood, with a positive sign indicating that a variable increases the likelihood that a protest event will occur at any given moment and a negative sign indicating that it makes a protest event less likely. The model can be represented as

$$\log h_{ij}(t) = \alpha_i(t) + \beta x_{ij}(t)$$

Proportional hazards has several features that make it suitable for examining this question. Event history methods are generally appropriate because they take the timing of events into account. Thus, it is easy to examine the influence of time-varying factors, such as the composition of Congress, on the incidence of events. Proportional hazards has an advantage over other event history methods in that it does not require a specification of any particular relationship between the events and time. Because I have little theoretical reason for assuming that time, over the course of sixty years, influences the incidence of protest activity in a particular way, this method produces more accurate estimates.

I also use fixed effects methods because of the nature of my data: I have multiple events occurring within each location. Therefore, it is highly likely that unmeasured attributes of the different locations influence the frequency of protest events in that location. A fixed effects model takes into account and controls for the influence of the location or any unmeasured quality of the location. Therefore, although the models presented in this essay do not include controls for college characteristics, such as whether the school has a unique culture, these factors are implicitly controlled for. Since each college is located in a different state, the fixed effects model also controls for any unmeasured attribute of the state that might influence levels of protest.

Findings

I ran a series of event history models in order to examine the impact of elite allies at different levels and branches of government on the incidence of

Table 8.2. *Impact of Elite Allies on the Likelihood of Student Protest Activity, 1930–90 (Total Sample)*

	Model 1	Model 2	Model 3	Model 4
Local level				
Faculty support	−0.007	–	–	−0.005
	0.993			0.995
Administration support	0.031	–	–	0.014
	0.969			1.014
State level				
Democratic governor	–	−0.132*	–	−0.130*
		0.858		0.861
Percent Democrats in the	–	1.426***	–	1.181***
state legislature		4.163		3.258
Federal level				
Democratic president	–	–	−0.346***	−0.248***
			0.587	0.718
Percent Democrats in the	–	–	0.514	0.031
federal legislature			1.673	1.032
Period effect control				
Vietnam War years	0.400***	0.307***	0.387***	0.299***
	1.492	1.360	1.473	1.349
−2 log likelihood	28283.102	28213.649	28222.077	28181.289

$n = 2,496$ events.
* $p < .05$ ** $p < .01$ *** $p < .001$.
Note: First number is the value of the coefficient; second number is the odds ratio.

protest events surrounding all issues (see Table 8.2). The most striking and consistent finding is that having *allies* in the legislature at the *state level* of government makes protest *more likely*, consistent with current formulations of political opportunity theory. However, contrary to political opportunity theory, having *allies* in the *executive* branch at either level of government makes protest *less likely*. In other words, having an antagonist in the executive position may increase the likelihood of protest. This finding is consistent with the hypothesis that protesters will mobilize in response to a threat. Before I explore the implications of these findings, let me go through the different statistical models in more detail.

The first model (Model 1) includes only the local-level variables, including faculty support and support from the administration. Local-level college allies seem to have little impact on the incidence of student protest; neither the faculty nor administration support variables are significant.

The second model (Model 2) includes variables for the executive and legislature at the state level. The presence of a Democratic ally in the executive position makes protest less likely to occur. In other words, having a Republican governor makes protest *more likely* to occur. Having a Republican in office makes protest 14% more likely to occur at any given point in time. This is contrary to predictions suggested by most versions of political opportunity theory. This effect remains in the full model (see Model 4). Allies in the state legislature, on the other hand, do make protest more likely to occur. Each additional percentage of the legislature that is Democratic increases the likelihood of protest by over 3%. This effect remains in the full model, though its magnitude is slightly reduced.

The third model (Model 3) includes variables for the federal-level executive and legislature. The effects are similar to those found for the state level. Having an ally in the executive decreases the likelihood of protest occurring, while having allies in the legislature increases the likelihood of protest, though the latter result is not statistically significant. Again, the first finding is inconsistent with political opportunity theory. Having a Democrat for president makes protest 41% less likely at any given point in time, whereas having a Republican president makes protest 41% more likely. Again, the effect of allies in the legislature is nonsignificant, though in the expected direction. These effects remain in the full model (Model 4), though the effect of the executive office variable is reduced. In the full model, the presence of a Republican president increases the likelihood of protest by 28%.

The full model (Model 4) combines the three previous models. As mentioned, the effects found in the previous three models remain virtually unchanged in the full model. Allies in the state legislature increase the likelihood of protest, while antagonists in the executive branch of either level increase the likelihood of protest. I explore these findings further in the following section.

In order to examine further the relationship between allies and levels of protest, I ran additional models that examine the impact of Democratic domination of the executive and legislative branches, divided control, and Republican control over both branches. These results are presented in Table 8.3.

I ran separate models including a variable for divided elites at each level: local, state, and federal. Model 1 includes only the variable for divided local elites, faculty and administration, and a control variable for the

241

Table 8.3. *Impact of Party Control and Divisions between Elites on the Likelihood of Student Protest Activity, 1930–1990 (Total Sample)*

	Model 1	Model 2	Model 3	Model 4
Local level				
Divided faculty and	−0.016	–	–	–
administration	0.984			
State level				
Divided state government	–	−0.248***	–	−0.199***
		0.780		0.820
Republican-controlled state		−0.375***		−0.322***
government		0.687		0.724
Federal level				
Divided federal government	–	–	0.234***	0.216***
			1.264	1.241
Republican-controlled federal			0.405***	0.362***
government			1.500	1.436
Vietnam War years	0.402***	0.519***	0.443***	0.535***
	1.495	1.681	1.557	1.707
−2 log likelihood	28283.121	28249.448	28229.049	28206.434

$n = 2,496$ events.
* $p < .05$ ** $p < .01$ *** $p < .001$.
Note: First number is the value of the coefficient; second number is the odds ratio.

Vietnam War years. The divided local elites variable is a dummy coded 1 when either faculty or members of the administration indicate support for protesters but the other group fails to do so. As this model demonstrates, divided faculty and administration have no effect on the likelihood of protest activity.

Model 2 includes a variable for divided state government and a variable for Republican control of both branches. Democratic control of both branches is the omitted variable. The divided control variable is a dummy coded 1 when the executive branch is an ally but the legislature is dominated by nonallies, or vice versa. Concerning the effect of the configuration of power at the state level, protest is most likely to occur when Democrats control both the executive and the legislature, and is second most likely to occur when the government is divided. It is least likely to occur when Republicans control the executive and the legislature. When Republicans control both branches, protest is 31% less likely than when Democrats control both. Protest is 14% more likely when there is divided control than when Republicans are in control, but it is 22% less likely when control is divided than when Democrats are in control.[3] These findings are consistent with the idea that elite allies make protest more likely and that the more allies, the more likely is protest.

The findings concerning the composition of the federal government are very different, however. A third model (Model 3) examines the impact of divided federal elites on the likelihood of student protest activity. Interestingly, the results are the opposite of those in the state-level model. That is, protest is most likely when Republicans control both the executive and the legislature, and is second most likely when the federal government is divided, with Republicans in control of one branch and Democrats in control of the other. Protest is 50% more likely when Republicans are in control of both branches than when Democrats are in control. This finding suggests that contenders may mobilize in response to threat. A divided federal government, with one party in control of the executive and the other in control of the legislature, makes protest 26% more likely than when Democrats are in control of both branches. When elites are divided, protesters may perceive that there is an opportunity for greater influence, as elites look for support.

The fourth model (Model 4) combines the state and federal models. The findings remain largely unchanged, though the magnitude of the effects decreases slightly. Republican control of the federal government makes protest most likely, while Democrat control of the state government makes protest more likely.

Conclusions

These findings suggest that elite allies *and* elite antagonists may influence mobilization. As Charles Tilly (1978) suggests, protesters may mobilize in response to both threats and opportunities. Thus, Republicans in the executive branch of either the state or federal government may trigger mobilization. However, the findings also suggest that we need to pay attention to the location of elites before we can determine their effect. Elites in different levels and branches of government have a differential effect on levels of protest activity. Thus, Republicans in the legislative branch do not trigger mobilization, but allies in this location do. In addition, there are differences

---

[3] The comparison between divided elites and Republican control is not represented in Table 8.3, in which Democrats are the left-out variable. However, a separate run produced this finding, which is statistically significant.

in the effect of allies in different levels of government. Protest is most likely when Republicans control both branches of the federal government but less likely when they control both branches of state government. I hypothesize that different elites may play a dissimilar role in the mobilization of protest for two reasons: access and grievances.

Access

Actors at different levels of the political system are more or less accessible to their constituents. Legislators are more accountable to their constituents than are presidents or governors: Legislators often make visits home; you can schedule an appointment with a legislator. State legislators are even more accessible than federal legislators. Therefore, we might expect protesters to be more influenced by the presence of allies or divisions between elites within the legislative branch, and at the state and local levels, because they have more access to these actors. Contenders may assume that they can have more influence on politicians at lower levels of the system, and may be more likely to mobilize when they see an opportunity for influence at this level.

Grievances/Threat

Actors at higher levels of the political system have more power to make policies that influence broader publics. They also are more visible, and their actions impact more people than do the actions of a single legislator. Therefore, the presence of antagonists at higher levels of the system, such as a governor or president, may trigger increased levels of protest activity. These findings suggest that protesters do respond to threat and that elite antagonists as well as elite allies may be important.

The findings regarding whether the influence of allies on protest levels takes a linear or curvilinear shape are inconclusive. They are complicated by the multilevel nature of our political system. According to Peter Eisinger's (1973) formulation, we would expect levels of mobilization to be highest when elites are divided. The findings do not support this hypothesis. According to Charles Tilly's (1978) argument, we would expect levels of mobilization to be high when allies control both branches of government and when antagonists control both. However, this hypothesis was not fully supported either. At the federal level, threats increase mobilization, while at the state level allies mobilize contenders. It should be noted that these analyses

244

are not a systematic test of either hypothesis, as threat and opportunity can involve more than the composition of the state and federal legislative and executive offices. However, the theories provided hypotheses that, when applied to the relationship between political allies and mobilization, were not supported.

Students of social movements have recognized the complicated effect that government repression can have on protest activity. They also have recognized that particular individuals within the institutional political system may be antagonistic to movement goals, such as President Reagan and the nuclear freeze movement. However, many political opportunity theorists have failed to recognize the influence of these individuals. We talk about the presence or absence of elite allies but not about the possible presence or absence of elite antagonists. These findings demonstrate that we need to do so, and that more work is necessary before we will fully understand the dynamic influence that threat can have on protest activity.

Afterword

AGENDAS FOR STUDENTS
OF SOCIAL MOVEMENTS

Charles Tilly

Readers who have worked their way through *States, Parties, and Social Movements* from beginning to end have probably noticed an agreeable irony. Colleagues McAdam, Goldstone, Luders, Cunningham, Swarts, Cadena-Roa, Glenn, Desai, Williams, and Van Dyke not only study social movements, but also engage in intellectual parallels to social movements: They challenge authorities and conventional wisdom in the name of suppressed or misunderstood alternatives. Collectively, they set before students of social movements a vigorous, vital agenda for the next round of theory and research. As their outstanding contributions to this volume prove, they will surely lead the way in future implementations of that agenda.

Or, rather, those agendas. For each of our authors has selected a different aspect of social movement politics for investigation. Not all agree on such questions as how externally generated opportunities and threats produce their effects on social movement activism, or under what conditions and how social movement challenges generate new political parties. Since Jack Goldstone has opened the book with a splendid review and synthesis of the individual essays, I will resist the temptation to offer my own evaluations and adjudications in favor of spelling out the forthcoming agenda. To do so, however, will require laying out some elementary observations concerning social movements. Our authors generally take these observations for granted, but readers who are not immersed in previous discussions of the subject will no doubt benefit from seeing them out in the open.

In democratic countries, social movements have been providing political outsiders with effective means of announcing their presence and of making collective claims for almost two centuries. A cluster of features distinguishes social movement politics from the prescribed politics of democratic

246

regimes: *a sustained challenge to power holders in the name of a population living under the jurisdiction of those power holders by means of repeated public displays of that population's worthiness, unity, numbers, and commitment.* Such a definition excludes coups d'état, civil wars, insurrections, feuds, and many other forms of contentious politics. It shares some performances with industrial conflict, electoral campaigns, and interest-group politics but by no means exhausts those domains. Many an election, for example, proceeds without either sustained challenges to power holders or repeated public displays of worthiness, unity, numbers, and commitment. Such an election occurs without social movements.

At a minimum, social movements involve continuous interaction between challengers and power holders. Beginning with Goldstone himself, to be sure, authors in this volume repeatedly deny both (1) that challengers constitute a peculiar, separate class of untamed political actors and (2) that movement politics operates independently of or in utter defiance of routine politics. Their contribution, however, is not so much to eliminate the distinction between the two kinds of politics as to clarify the nature of their interaction and to show how social movements range from close integration to sharp separation from other forms of politics.

Social movement participants join in making two overlapping sorts of claims: *existence* claims and *program* claims. Existence claims assert political identities; they announce that a connected set of people have entered the political scene, possess the capacity to act together, and deserve attention as players. Program claims announce that significant categories of people support or oppose some person, organization, proposal, or public action. Sometimes social movement participants come from the constituencies they claim to represent – workers, women, neighborhood residents, military veterans, and so on. On other occasions, however, activists assemble on behalf of slaves, fetuses, war victims, animals, trees, or other absent constituencies. Social movement claim making usually engages third parties such as other power holders, repressive forces, allies, competitors, and the citizenry as a whole. Despite considerable standardization of form, social movements adapt to a startling range of actors and programs.

The social movement itself, thus understood, consists of repeated interactions among challengers, objects of their claims, relevant publics, and various third parties such as rival challengers, counterdemonstrators, bystanders, incidental victims, and police. Social movement organizers often rely on or create social movement *organizations*. The movement itself, however, consists not of organizations but of sustained interaction, of political struggle. Our authors clearly distinguish between movements and the organizations they engage.

This definition occupies a middle ground between a narrow and a broad definition of social movements. A narrow view singles out the particular bundle of structures and activities that social movement activists began to fashion in Western Europe and North America during the later eighteenth century: associations, public meetings, petition drives, demonstrations, and circulation of programmatic texts. That bundle has its own history and culture as a model for collective challenges; I have frequently followed that bundle with care in my own historical work. A broad view takes any popular, collective challenge to existing power structures as a social movement. In the broad view, the formation of new religions, the spread of subversive political doctrines, and the rise of nationalism throughout the world all qualify as social movements of sorts.

For all their odor of academic nit-picking, distinctions among broad, narrow, and middling definitions of social movements actually matter. Each of the three definitions lays a claim to causal coherence – that all popular, collective challenges have common properties, that the European-American bundle operates differently from other sorts of politics, or that the midrange phenomenon I have here identified as a social movement works in similar ways across a considerable variety of times and places. I choose the middle ground here on the bet that this book's authors are carrying on a fruitful theoretical conversation at that level. In closing, I will say how they and we can incorporate the other two levels into a common enterprise.

Although the social movement as such never acquired the legal standing of such forms of political participation as elections, referenda, parties, and petitions, social movements promoted the legalization – or at least the legal toleration – of a number of familiar forms: public meetings; demonstrations; rallies; special-interest associations; strikes; occupations of public buildings, public spaces, and workplaces. Social movements are thus partly causes, partly effects, and almost invariably concomitants of democratic freedoms to speak, assemble, associate, and complain.

Elections and social movements have important parallels and interdependencies. Both of them gauge support or opposition for authorities' actions, potential or actual. Both of them also identify blocs of like-minded people who might take further action if conditions continue to incite their disapproval. Social movements often gain impact from the presence of binding elections because movements signal the presence of connected, aggrieved populations that could either vote together or otherwise disrupt politics as usual. Successful social movement activists often enter electoral politics individually or as members of new parties, their issues gain places on party platforms, and their constituencies become forces to reckon with in future elections. As a result, social movements have generally increased in frequency, scope, and impact where and when binding contested elections based on broad suffrage have become more central to political life.

Social movements also differ from elections in several crucial ways. On the average, they demand much higher levels of energy than elections. Although candidates and party organizers may turn elections into full-time occupations, and although some people do no more for a social movement than contribute money now and then, for the most part the minimum participation in social movement activity requires greater effort and more extensive interaction with other people than does an ordinary citizen's voting. Elections focus attention primarily on candidates for office and secondarily on parties or programs, while social movements generally give primacy to programs or even to very specific demands. Elections pay off on sheer numbers; victory is virtually ensured by getting out enough supporters, regardless of their motivations and commitments. Social movement challengers always seek more complex objectives, including both specific claims and general recognition. As a consequence, numbers alone do not suffice for social movement success.

More differences between elections and social movements follow. One election generally resembles the last not only in its prescribed actions but also in its outcomes: Routines of campaigning and voting change incrementally for the most part. Participants therefore attach great importance to relatively small shifts in turnout or expressed preference. In contrast, social movement activists invest a great deal of effort in differentiating this action from the last or the next, not to mention from the actions of rivals or enemies. Finally, participants in elections sometimes make a public point of their partisan identity or support for a particular candidate but often do nothing of the sort; such displays of identity, support, and membership figure centrally in social movements.

Differences between elections and social movements result from their contrasting relations to the existing structure of power. People who already hold power set the rules of elections and usually benefit from them. Incumbents tend to win reelection, established parties to prevail despite shifts in relative strength among them, newcomers to experience difficulty even getting on ballots, advocates of new programs to have trouble injecting their issues into electoral campaigns. Social movements specialize in creating political space for newcomers, marginal populations, neglected programs, and unheard grievances. Whereas elections commonly pass with no strong public expressions of collective identity and no demonstrations of intense support for one demand or another, social movements center on coupling assertions of shared identity with statements of well-defined claims. Elections and social movements do sometimes converge, as when hotly contested races for office generate rallies, marches, and fights or when movement activists throw their support to maverick candidates. On the whole, nevertheless, elections pivot on insiders' politics, social movements on outsiders' politics.

Remember the elements that together set off social movements from other forms of politics: sustained challenge; direction of that challenge to power holders; action in the name of a distinctive population; repeated public demonstrations that the distinctive population or its advocates are worthy, unified, numerous, and committed. Each element has its own historically formed political underpinnings. Let us review each one in turn.

Sustained Challenge

In social movements, participants make collective claims not once but repeatedly, and openly rather than in disguised ways. They voice their claims as active demands, complaints, or proposals instead of as humble supplications or subtle indications of preference. Over the long sweep of political history, most regimes have suppressed any such claims when they have arisen, persecuted advocates of such claims when it was feasible, turned deaf ears when it was not, and undermined the social conditions that promote sustained, direct, popular, collective statements of claims. Generalization of social movement claim making rests on relative freedom of association, assembly, and speech – all of them historically exceptional, all of them hard-won democratic rights.

Power Holders

More often than not, social movement activists direct their claims at governmental officials. Less often, they aim at members of privileged social categories, owners of economic enterprises, operators of significant public facilities, and similar wielders of one kind of influence or another. Historically, such direct targeting of power holders has always been risky; except with the protection of a patron, the cover of anonymity, or the chaos of civil war, it has typically invited direct retaliation, cutting off of patronage, and discrimination against people connected with the claimant. Social movements capitalize on some combination of lawful rule, institutionalized protection for dissidents, vulnerability of power holders (e.g., to their own rivals), and capacity of movement supporters for protection or counteroffense. These conditions overlap historically with the conditions for sustained challenge – which means they appear more frequently in democratic regimes – but they also become more salient when a visible split has opened up within ruling classes.

Distinctive Population

Very powerful people rarely engage in social movements; they have less costly, more effective ways of pursuing their interests. Completely powerless people likewise rarely form or join social movements; they have neither the social connections nor the resources it takes. In between those extremes, social movement participants articulate a collective sense of wrong either on their own behalf or on behalf of some valued constituency. Movements vary enormously in the degree of overlap between activists and those for whom they claim to speak, from movements demanding protection of forests from clear-cutting or of fetuses from abortion to other movements aligning all of a neighborhood's squatters against the mayor who has signed their eviction notice. Rarely does a whole population for whom movement militants claim to speak actually mobilize – a fact that makes militants vulnerable to the contrary claim that they do not represent the actual will or interest of their announced constituency, to rivalries for recognition as legitimate leaders, and to the organization of countermovements within the same population. In all cases, however, movement leaders take care to emphasize wrongs or dangers endured by their constituency: deprivation of rights, threats to well-being, denial of earned recognition, or something of the sort.

Displays of WUNC

Social movements include public displays of *WUNC* – Worthiness, Unity, Numbers, and Commitment – on the part of activists, on the part of their constituency, or both. An implicit scale for movement strength applies. Worthiness, unity, numbers, and commitment each run from 0 (none) to 1 (the maximum possible in the circumstances). Strength then equals $W \times U \times N \times C$, which means that if any of the values falls to 0, so does strength.

A high value on one element (say, commitment) makes up for a low value on another (say, numbers). Thus, a few highly committed hunger strikers can have the same impact as thousands of people who merely sign a petition. Relevant codes run roughly as follows:

Worthiness: sobriety, propriety of dress, incorporation of priests and other dignitaries, endorsement by moral authorities, evidence of undeserved previous suffering

Unity: uniforms, marching or dancing in unison, chanting of slogans, singing, cheering, linking of arms, wearing or bearing of common symbols, direct affirmation of a common program or identity

Numbers: filling of public spaces, presentation of petitions, representations of multiple units (e.g., neighborhood associations), direct claims of numerical support by means of polls, membership inscriptions, and financial contributions

Commitment: persistence in costly or risky activity, declarations of readiness to persevere, resistance to attack.

With variation in the precise means used to display these characteristics (for example, the partial displacement of identifying banners by signs on sticks late in the nineteenth century), emphasis on *WUNC* has persisted from early in the social movement's history. The chief deviations from the code have occurred in pursuit of visibility and in deliberate assertions of difference, as when members of dissident factions have broken the façade of unity by resistance to marching orders or gay militants have violated conventional standards of worthiness by cross-dressing.

Because social movements sometimes succeed in their demands, because they sometimes achieve political recognition of their constituencies, because they sometimes result in acceptance of their previously repressed forms of claim making, and because struggle between challengers and authorities itself produces alterations in toleration and repression, social movements contribute to the redefinition of routine politics. As a result, unauthorized action for one generation becomes authorized action for the next; the locus of social movement innovation shifts accordingly.

In mid-eighteenth-century America, for instance, ordinary citizens had no right to meet publicly at their own initiative for political deliberation or to form politically active associations; the proliferation of such activities during the American Revolution clearly had a social movement flavor. Half a century later, however, the rights to assemble and form associations were so firmly established in the new United States that assembly and association no longer qualified in themselves as social movement activities. Later, the strike, the sit-in, and a number of other social movement innovations underwent similar transitions into legality, or at least into the zone of governmental toleration.

Social movements' sustained challenges to power holders necessarily interact with and depend upon a great deal of social life outside the public arena. Some kinds of connection deserve special attention:

- Heavy reliance of almost all movements on nonmovement networks (for example, friends, classmates, neighbors, and coworkers) for recruitment, resources, and moral support
- Formation of solidarities and mutual aid among movement activists
- Extensive behind-the-scenes recruiting, organizing, persuading, coalition forming, lobbying, and strategizing that underlie complex public events.

Movements differ enough in their approaches to these activities and in their relative stress on public versus private activity that we can distinguish roughly among three types: *professional* (the continuous, specialized, and sparse social movement conducted by experienced organizers using funds supplied by a weakly committed set of supporters); *ad hoc* (temporary, specialized, and relatively rich mobilization by members of a connected community against a specific threat); and *communitarian* (the continuous, unspecialized movement giving rise to a new community of the faithful, a community whose sustenance becomes a major preoccupation of movement supporters). The three tend to exit the social movement arena – the arena of sustained public challenge – in different directions, with professional activists moving into interest-group and electoral politics, ad hoc activists returning to their lives before the threat, and communitarian activists devoting their full time to community building. Intense involvement in any of the three, nevertheless, commonly reshapes people's social lives, giving them new ties, new priorities, and new understandings of political realities.

Careful readers of the essays can easily find partial dissents from the views I have just presented as an implicit consensus – for example, Joseph Luders's analysis of collusion between state authorities and countermovement activists, Heidi Swarts's description of quietist alternatives to public confrontation, or Jorge Cadena-Roa's detection of ties between movement activists and established political parties. No universal laws apply to all social movements everywhere. Indeed, social movement politics gains some of its

253

great strength from the adaptability of its tactical repertoire to a wide variety of claimants, issues, and locales. Yet (as the volume's essays also indicate) social movements bear family resemblances to each other. The challenge to social movement analysts is therefore the simultaneous explanation of similarity and difference.

What paths will get us there? I see four agendas, one negative and three positive: (1) abandon general movement models; (2) take seriously the history and comparative politics of particular social movement elements; (3) compare and relate movement politics to other varieties of politics; (4) search out robust causal mechanisms and processes in the course of (2) and (3). Let me sketch each of the agendas briefly.

Abandon General Movement Models

This volume's authors display ambivalence about general models of social movements. On the one hand, they find it convenient to say how their arguments and findings dispute general statements of the form "All movements_____." On the other, they hesitate between declaring that they have discovered new universals and concluding that no universals exist. Thus Kim Williams orients her informative analysis of multiracial categories as an American political issue to ostensibly general resource mobilization and political process descriptions of social movements, concluding that neither one offers much explanatory leverage. She is right. Resource mobilization, political process, and similar general portraits of social movements have served a generation of scholars usefully as questionnaires but not as replies to those questionnaires. No amount of tinkering will turn them into systematic explanations of similarity, difference, and change.

The History and Comparative Politics of Social Movement Elements

Just as the historical and comparative study of electoral systems, legislative procedures, legal codes, and bureaucratic organizations has proven essential to the explanation of change and variation in contemporary politics, social movement analysts could usefully devote their energy to tracing the demonstration, the street march, the rally, the special-interest association, the public meeting, the petition drive, and related forms of collective action as culturally specific, historically evolving, yet generalizable contributions to public politics. Perhaps the neglect of historical-comparative work on these topics by social movement analysts stems (as Jack Goldstone and collaborators suggest) from persisting assumptions of fundamental differences between social movements and institutionalized politics. I can't help thinking that it also results in part from one of the virtues of social movement analysis: its recurrent recruitment of scholars who care deeply about contemporary social movement issues, sympathize with current movements, and/or emerge from the ranks of activists. That proximity to today's movements constantly renews the energy of discussions concerning social movements, but it also inhibits direction of the energy into historical-comparative analysis.

Comparisons and Relations with Other Sorts of Politics

As Goldstone and a number of his collaborators argue, the distinctive contribution of the present volume lies in making comparisons and connections between social movements and other sorts of political processes. The program deserves further elaboration. If (as I suggested earlier) social movements and electoral politics interbreed, then their covariation deserves much more systematic analysis. The findings of Luders, Swarts, Cadena-Roa, Glenn, Desai, Williams, and Van Dyke all suggest some such interdependence but permit no simple generalization across movements and levels of government. In earlier work, Goldstone has called attention to parallels, differences, and mutations between revolutions and social movements. Now that researchers have abandoned the equations social movement = irrational = spontaneous = antipolitical, it is time to systematize the comparisons.

Robust Mechanisms and Processes

Analysts differ honestly, and perhaps even fruitfully, over the extent to which proper explanations of social processes take the form of general laws, identification of actors' orientations, location of elements within larger systems, or specification of widely occurring but smaller-scale mechanisms and processes. (Mechanism- and process-based accounts select salient features of episodes, or significant differences among episodes, and explain them by identifying within those episodes robust mechanisms of relatively general scope. Similarly, they search for recurrent concatenations of mechanisms into more complex processes.) Regardless of how great debates about explanation come out, students of social movements have much to gain from looking carefully at specific mechanisms and processes that figure

255

recurrently in mobilization, demobilization, and mutation of movements. Brokerage, activation of we–they boundaries, polarization, and cross-class coalition formation, for example, all play significant parts in a wide variety of social movements. Surely social movement analysts can learn a great deal by singling out those mechanisms and processes for systematic comparison across times, places, issues, and settings.

In pursuing the four-step agenda, a new generation of social movement analysts – superbly represented by the authors of this book's essays – will contribute to making their chosen subject a rigorous, systematic field.

References

Acosta, Miguel and Jorge A. Castañeda. 1994. *La observación internacional de las elecciones*. México: Porrúa.

All India Kisan Sabha [All India Peasants Union]. 1944–5. Organizational Reportage No. 4 of 1944–5.

Allison, Paul. 1995. *Survival Analysis Using the SAS System*. Cary, NC: SAS Inc.

Almeida, Paul and Linda Brewster Stearns. 1998. "Political Opportunities and Local Grassroots Environmental Movements: The Case of Minamata." *Social Problems* 45:37–60.

Alonso, Antonio. 1972. *El movimiento ferrocarrilero en México, 1958–1959*. México: Era.

Amenta, Edwin. 1998. *Bold Relief: Institutional Politics and the Origins of Modern American Social Policy*. Princeton, NJ: Princeton University Press.

Aminzade, Ronald. 1995. "Between Movement and Party: The Transformation of Mid-Nineteenth Century French Republicanism." In Jenkins and Klandermans, pp. 39–62.

Anderson, Bo and James D. Cockroft. 1972. "Control and Co-optation in Mexican Politics," pp. 219–44 in *Dependence and Underdevelopment: Latin America's Political Economy*, edited by J. D. Cockroft, A. G. Frank, and D. L. Johnson. New York: Anchor Books.

Andrews, Kenneth. 2001. "Social Movements and Policy Implementation: The Mississippi Civil Rights Movement and the War on Poverty, 1965 to 1971," *American Sociological Review* 66:71–95.

Antalova, Ingrid, ed. 1998. *Verenost' Proti Nasiliu 1989–1991: Svedectva a dokumenty* [Public against Violence 1989–1991: Testimony and documents]. Bratislava: Milan Simecka Foundation.

Appleman, Jeannie. 1996. *Evaluation Study of Institution-Based Organizing*. Prepared for the Discount Foundation, Rockville, MD.

Ash, Timothy Garton. 1991. "Tell Me Your Europe and I Will Tell You Where You Stand," pp. 122–5 in *Europe From Below*, edited by Mary Kaldor. London: Verso.

Ashmore, Herbert. 1957. *An Epitaph for Dixie*. New York: W. W. Norton.

Bachrach, Peter and Morton Baratz. 1962. "Two Faces of Power." *American Political Science Review* 56:947–52.

Banaszak, Lee Ann. 1998. "Use of the Initiative Process by Woman Suffrage Movements." In Costain and McFarland, pp. 99–114.

Barberán, José, Cuauhtémoc Cárdenas, Adriana López, and Jorge Zavala. 1988. *Radiografia del Fraude.* Mexico City: Neustro Tiempo.

Barkan, Steven. 1984. "Legal Control of the Southern Civil Rights Movement." *American Sociological Review* 49:552–65.

Barone, Michael. 1998. *State Legislative Elections: Voting Patterns and Demographics.* Washington, DC: Congressional Quarterly.

Barret, Stanley R. 1987. *Is God Racist? The Right Wing in Canada.* Toronto: University of Toronto Press.

Bartley, Numan V. 1969. *The Rise of Massive Resistance: Race and Politics in the South During the 1950's.* Baton Rouge: Louisiana State University Press.

Bartolini, Stefano and Peter Mair. 1990. *Identity, Competition, and Electoral Availability: The Stabilisation of European Electorates 1885–1985.* New York: Cambridge University Press.

Baumgartner, Frank R. and Bryan D. Jones. 1993. *Agendas and Instability in American Politics.* Chicago: University of Chicago Press.

Beck, E. M. 2000. "Guess Who's Coming to Town: White Supremacy, Ethnic Competition and Social Change." *Sociological Focus* 33:153–74.

Belknap, Michael. 1987. *Federal Law and Southern Order: Racial Violence and Constitutional Conflict in the Post-Brown South.* Athens: University of Georgia Press.

Bennett, Vivienne. 1992. "The Evolution of Urban Popular Movements in Mexico Between 1968 and 1988," pp. 240–59 in *The Making of Social Movements in Latin America,* edited by A. Escobar and S. E. Alvarez. Boulder, CO: Westview Press.

Berrueto, Federico. 2000. "Geografia Electoral." *Voz y Voto* 83:27–30.

Berry, Jeffrey M., Kent E. Portney, and Ken Thomson. 1993. *The Rebirth of Urban Democracy.* Washington, DC: The Brookings Institution.

Bhattacharyya, Janabrata. 1978. "An Examination of Leadership Entry in Bengal Peasant Revolts, 1937–1947." *Journal of Asian Studies* 37:611–35.

Black, Earl. 1976. *Southern Governors and Civil Rights: Racial Segregation as a Campaign Issue in the Second Reconstruction.* Cambridge, MA: Harvard University Press.

Blahoz, Josef. 1994. "Political Parties in the Czech and Slovak Federal Republics: First Steps toward the Rebirth of Democracy," pp. 229–47 in *How Political Parties Work: Perspectives from Within,* edited by Kay Lawson. Westport, CT: Praeger.

Blee, Kathleen M. 1996. "Becoming a Racist: Women in Contemporary Ku Klux Klan and Neo-Nazi Groups." *Gender and Society* 10:680–702.

Bloom, Jack S. 1987. *Class, Race, and the Civil Rights Movement.* Bloomington: Indiana University Press.

References

Boli, John and George M. Thomas. 1997. "World Culture in the World Polity: A Century of International Non-Governmental Organization." *American Sociological Review* 67:171–90.

Bose, Sugata. 1986. *Agrarian Bengal: Economy, Social Structure and Politics, 1919–49.* Cambridge: Cambridge University Press.

Bositis, David A. 2001. *Diverging Generations: The Transformation of African American Policy Views.* Washington, DC: Joint Center for Political and Economic Studies.

Bouchier, Josiane. 1988. "La Coordinadora Nacional del Movimiento Urbano Popular (CONAMUP): Una historia de odios y amores, encuentros y desencuentros entre organizaciones políticas." Licenciatura thesis, FCPyS–UNAM, México.

Brovkin, Vladimir. 1990. "Revolution from Below: Informal Political Associations in Russia 1988–89." *Soviet Studies* 42:233–58.

Browning, Rufus P., Dale Rogers Marshall, and David H. Tabb. 1984. *Protest Is Not Enough.* Berkeley: University of California Press.

Brustein, William. 1996. *The Logic of Evil: The Social Origins of the Nazi Party, 1925–1933.* New Haven, CT: Yale University Press.

Burstein, Paul. 1985. *Discrimination, Jobs, and Politics: The Struggle for Equal Employment Opportunity in the United States since the New Deal.* Chicago: University of Chicago Press.

    1998a. "Bringing the Public Back In: Should Sociologists Consider the Impact of Public Opinion on Public Policy?" *Social Forces* 77:27–62.

    1998b. "Interest Organizations, Political Parties, and the Study of Democratic Politics." In Costain and McFarland, pp. 39–56.

    1999. "Social Movements and Public Policy," pp. 3–21 in *How Social Movements Matter*, edited by Marco Giugni, Doug McAdam, and Charles Tilly. Minneapolis: University of Minnesota Press.

Burstein, Paul, Rachel L. Einwohner, and Jocelyn A. Hollander. 1995. "The Success of Political Movements: A Bargaining Perspective." In Jenkins and Klandermans, pp. 275–95.

Burt, Ronald. 1992. *Structural Holes: The Social Structure of Competition.* Cambridge, MA: Harvard University Press.

Burton, Michael and John Higley. 1987. "Elite Settlements." *American Sociological Review* 52:295–307.

Butora, Martin and Zora Butorova. 1993. "Slovakia: The Identity Challenges of the Newly Born State." *Social Research* 60:705–36.

Butorova, Zora. 1993. "A Deliberate 'Yes' to the Dissolution of the CSFR?" *Czech Sociological Review* 1:58–72.

Button, James W. 1989. *Blacks and Social Change.* Princeton, NJ: Princeton University Press.

Cadena-Roa, Jorge. 1988. "Las demandas de la sociedad civil, los partidos políticos y las respuestas del sistema," pp. 285–327 in *Primer informe sobre la democracia: México 1988*, edited by P. González Casanova and J. Cadena-Roa. México: Siglo Veintiuno-CIIH, UNAM.

1995. "New Social Movements of the Early Nineteenth Century," pp. 173–215 in *Repertoires and Cycles of Collective Action*, edited by Mark Traugott. Durham, NC: Duke University Press.

Camp, Roderic Ai. 1992. *Generals in the Palacio: The Military in Modern Mexico.* New York: Oxford University Press.

1995. *Mexican Political Biographies 1935–1975.* Tucson, AZ: The University of Arizona Press.

Campbell, David. 1986. "Organizing Grassroots Power: Transcending Alinsky-Style Leadership." Paper presented at the annual meeting of the American Political Science Association in Washington, DC, August 28–31, 1986.

Canon, David. 1999a. *Race, Redistricting, and Representation: The Unintended Consequences of Black Majority Districts.* Chicago: University of Chicago Press.

1999b. "Electoral Systems and the Representation of Minority Interests in Legislatures." *Legislative Studies Quarterly* 24:331–83.

Carnogursky, Jan. 1992. "Politics Does Not Always Have to Be Ethical: An Interview." *Uncaptive Minds* (Winter), pp. 91–2, 61–8.

Carothers, Thomas. 1996. *Assessing Democracy Assistance.* Washington, DC: Carnegie Endowment for Peace.

Carpizo, Jorge. 1978. *El presidencialismo mexicano.* México: Siglo Veintiuno Editores.

Carr, Barry. 1992. *Marxism and Communism in Twentieth Century Mexico.* Lincoln: University of Nebraska Press.

Casillas, Miguel. 1987. "Notas sobre el proceso de transición de la universidad tradicional a la moderna: Los casos de expansión institucional y la masificación." *Sociológica* 2:121–44.

Castillo, Ed. PACT leader. 1998. Interview, San Jose, CA.

Castillo, Heberto. 1986. *Desde la trinchera.* México: Océano.

Census of Travancore, 1931. Travancore: Superintendent Government Press.

Chalmers, David M. 1965. *Hooded Americanism: The History of the Ku Klux Klan.* Garden City, NY: Doubleday.

Chatterjee, Partha. 1984. *Bengal: 1920–1947.* Calcutta: K. P. Bagchi and Company.

1986. "The Colonial State and Peasant Resistance in Bengal, 1920–1947." *Past and Present* 110:169–203.

Chaudhuri, Aseem Kumar. 1980. *Socialist Movement in India: The Congress Socialist Party from 1934 to 1947.* Calcutta: Progressive Publishers.

Churchill, Ward and Jim VanderWall. 1988. *Agents of Repression: The FBI's Secret Wars Against the Black Panther Party and the American Indian Movement.* Boston: South End Press.

1990. *The COINTELPRO Papers: Documents from the FBI's Secret War Against Dissent in the United States.* Boston: South End Press.

Cigar, Norman. 1995. *Genocide in Bosnia: The Politics of Ethnic Cleansing.* College Station: Texas A&M University Press.

Clark, Ann Marie, Elizabeth J. Frieidman, and Kathryn Hochstetler. 1998. "The Sovereign Limits of Global Civil Society: A Comparison of NGO Participation in UN World Conferences on the Environment, Human Rights, and Women." *World Politics* 51:1–35.

References

Clemens, Elisabeth S. 1997. *The People's Lobby: Organizational Innovation and the Rise of Interest Group Politics in the United States, 1890–1925*. Chicago: University of Chicago Press.

Cloward, Richard A. and Frances Fox Piven. 1999. "Disruptive Dissensus: People and Power in the Industrial Age," pp. 165–93 in *Reflections on Community Organization*, edited by Jack Rothman. Itasca, IL: F. E. Peacock.

Cobb, James C. 1982. *The Selling of the South: The Southern Crusade for Industrial Development 1936–1980*. Baton Rouge: Louisiana State University Press.

Cobb, Roger W. and Charles D. Elder. 1972. *Participation in American Politics: The Dynamics of Agenda-Building*. Baltimore: Johns Hopkins University Press.

Cohen, Cathy. 1999. *The Boundaries of Blackness: AIDS and the Breakdown of Black Politics*. Chicago: University of Chicago Press.

Collier, David and Steven Levitsky. 1997. "Democracy with Adjectives: Conceptual Innovation in Comparative Research." *World Politics* 49:430–51.

Collier, Ruth Bernis. 1992. *The Contradictory Alliance: State–Labor Relations and Regime Change in Mexico*. Berkeley: University of California Press.

Concha, Miguel. 1988. "Las violaciones a los derechos humanos individuales en México, periodo 1971–1976," pp. 115–87 in *Primer informe sobre la democracia: México 1988*, edited by P. González-Casanova and J. Cadena-Roa. México: Siglo Veintiuno Editores.

Concha, Miguel, Oscar González Gary, and Lino F. Salas. 1986. *La participatión de los cristianos en el proceso popular de liberación en México*. México: Siglo Veintiuno Editores.

Congressional Quarterly. 1998. *Gubernatorial Elections, 1787–1997* Washington, DC.

Corley, Robert: 1982. "In Search of Racial Harmony: Birmingham Business Leaders and Desegregation, 1950–1963," pp. 170–90 in *Southern Businessmen and Desegregation*, edited by Elizabeth Jacoway and David Colburn. Baton Rouge: Louisiana State University Press.

Cornelius, Wayne and Ann L. Craig. 1991. *The Mexican Political System in Transition*. San Diego: University of California, San Diego, Press.

Costain, Anne N. 1992. *Inviting Women's Rebellion*. Baltimore: The Johns Hopkins University Press.

   1998. "Women Lobby Congress." In Costain and McFarland, pp. 171–84.

Costain, Anne N. and W. Douglas Costain. 1987. "Strategy and Tactics of the Women's Movement in the United States: The Role of Political Parties," pp. 196–214 in *The Women's Movements of the United States and Western Europe*, edited by Mary Fainsod Katzenstein and Carol McClurg Mueller. Philadelphia: Temple University Press.

Costain, Anne N. and Andrew S. McFarland, eds. 1998. *Social Movements and American Political Institutions*. Lanham, MD: Rowman & Littlefield.

Costain, W. Douglas and James P. Lester. 1998. "The Environmental Movement and Congress." In Costain and McFarland, pp. 185–98.

Council of State Governments. 1937–1959. *The Book of the States*, Vols. 3–12. Chicago.

Craig, Ann L. and Wayne Cornelius. 1995. "Houses Divided: Parties and Political Reform in Mexico," pp. 249–97 in *Building Democratic Institutions: Party Systems in Latin America*, edited by S. Mainwaring and T. R. Scully. Stanford, CA: Stanford University Press.

Cress, Daniel M. and David A. Snow. 2000. "The Outcomes of Homeless Mobilization: The Influence of Organization, Disruption, Political Mediation, and Framing." *American Journal of Sociology* 105:1063–1104.

Cunningham, David. 2000. "Organized Repression and Movement Collapse in a Modern Democratic State." Ph.D. dissertation, University of North Carolina at Chapel Hill.

Dalton, Russell J. 1995. "Strategies of Partisan Influence: West European Environmental Groups." In Jenkins and Klandermans, pp. 296–323.

Dalton, Russell and Manfred Kuechler, eds. 1990. *Challenging the Political Order*. New York: Oxford University Press.

Dasgupta, Biplab. 1984. "Sharecropping in West Bengal: From Independence to Operation Barga." *Economic and Political Weekly* 19:A85–A96.

Davenport, Christian. 2000. *Paths to State Repression: Human Rights Violations and Contentious Politics*. Lanham, MD: Rowman & Littlefield.

Davis, James Kirkpatrick. 1997. *Assault on the Left: The FBI and the Sixties Antiwar Movement*. Westport, CT: Praeger.

de Candole, James. 1991. "Czechoslovakia: Too Velvet a Revolution?" *European Security Study #11*, Institute for European Defense and Strategic Studies.

de la Rosa, Martín. 1985. "Iglesia y sociedad en el México de hoy," pp. 268–92 in *Religión y politica en México*, edited by M. d. l. Rosa and C. A. Reilly. México: Siglo Veintiuno Editores.

della Porta, Donatella and Herbert Reiter, eds. 1998. *Policing Protest: The Control of Mass Demonstrations in Western Democracies*. Minneapolis: University of Minnesota Press.

della Porta, Donatella and Dieter Rucht. 1995. "Left Libertarian Movements in Context: A Comparison of Italy and West Germany 1965–1990." In Jenkins and Klandermans, pp. 229–72.

Dellinger, Dave. 1975. *More Power Than We Know: The People's Movement Toward Democracy*. New York: Anchor Press/Doubleday.

Democratic Research Service. 1957. Indian Communist Party Documents, 1930–1956. Bombay: Democratic Research Service.

DeNardo, James. 1985. *Power in Numbers: The Political Strategy of Protest and Rebellion*. Princeton, NJ: Princeton University Press.

Dhanagare, D. N. 1983. *Peasant Movements in India, 1920–1950*. Oxford: Oxford University Press.

Diamond, Larry and Juan J. Linz. 1989. "Introduction: Politics, Society, and Democracy in Latin America," pp. 1–58 in *Democracy in Developing Countries: Latin America*, vol. 4, edited by L. Diamond, J. J. Linz, and S. M. Lipset. Boulder, CO: Lynne Rienner.

Draper, Theodore. 1993. "The End of Czechoslovakia." *The New York Review of Books*, January, 28, pp. 20–6.

References

Dreze, Jean and Amartya Sen. 1995. *India: Economic Development and Social Opportunity.* Oxford: Oxford University Press.

Edles, Laura Desfor. 1995. "Rethinking Democratic Transition: A Culturalist Critique and the Spanish Case." *Theory and Society* 24:355–84.

Edmonston, Barry and Charles Schultze, eds. 1995. *Modernizing the U.S. Census.* Washington, DC: National Academy Press.

Eichhorn, Robert L. 1954. "Patterns of Segregation, Discrimination and Interracial Conflict: Analysis of a Nationwide Survey of Intergroup Practices." Ph.D. dissertation, Cornell University.

Eisinger, Peter K. 1973. "The Conditions of Protest Behavior in American Cities." *American Political Science Review* 67:11–28.

Ekiert, Grzegorz. 1991. "Democratization Processes in East Central Europe: A Theoretical Reconsideration." *British Journal of Political Science* 21:285–313.

———. 1992. "Peculiarities of Postcommunist Politics: The Case of Poland." *Studies in Comparative Communism* 25:341–62.

Elazar, Daniel J. 1984. *American Federalism: A View from the States,* 3d ed. New York: Harper & Row.

Elster, Jon, Claus Offe, Ulrich K. Preuss. 1998. *Institutional Design in Post-Communist Societies: Rebuilding the Ship at Sea.* Cambridge: Cambridge University Press.

Erikson, Robert S., Gerald C. Wright, and John P. McIver. 1993. *Statehouse Democracy: Public Opinion and Policy in the American States.* Cambridge: Cambridge University Press.

Estrada, Alba Teresa. 1986. "El Movimiento anticaballerista: Guerrero 1960. Crónica de un conflicto." Licenciatura thesis, FCPyS (Sociología), UNAM, México.

———. 1994. *Guerrero: Sociedad, economía, política y cultura.* México: CIIH-UNAM.

Evans, Geoffrey and Stephen Whitefield. 1993. "Identifying the Bases of Party Competition in Eastern Europe." *British Journal of Political Science* 23: 521–48.

Fairclough, Adam. 1995. *Race and Democracy: The Civil Rights Struggle in Louisiana, 1915–1972.* Athens: University of Georgia Press.

Fernandez, Carlos. 1992. "La Raza and the Melting Pot: A Comparative Look at Multiethnicity." In *Racially Mixed People in America,* edited by Maria Root. Newbury Park, CA: Sage.

Fitzpatrick, Jody L. and Rodney E. Hero. 1988. "Political Culture and Political Characteristics of the American States: A Consideration of Some Old and New Questions." *Western Political Quarterly* 41:145–53.

Francisco, Ronald A. 1995. "The Relationship between Coercion and Protest: An Empirical Evaluation in Three Coercive States." *Journal of Conflict Resolution* 39:263–82.

Franda, Marcus. 1971. "Radical Politics in West Bengal," pp. 183–222 in *Radical Politics in South Asia,* edited by Paul R. Brass and Franda Marcus. Cambridge, MA: MIT Press.

Franke, Richard and Barbara Chasin. 1989. *Kerala: Radical Reform as Development in an Indian State.* San Francisco: Institute for Food and Development Policy.

Frey, William. 2001. *Melting Pot Suburbs: A Census 2000 Study of Suburban Diversity.* The Brookings Institution, Census 2000 Series, June.

Frey, William and William O'Hare. 1992. "Becoming Suburban, and Black." *American Demographics* 30–8.

1993. "Vivan Los Suburbios!" *American Demographics* 30–7.

Fric, Pavol. 1992. "Who Loves Ya Meciar?" *East European Reporter* July–August:79.

Fukuyama, Francis. 1992. *The End of History and the Last Man.* New York: Free Press.

Gamson, William A. 1990. *The Strategy of Social Protest,* 2nd ed. Belmont, CA: Wadsworth.

Gamson, William, Bruce Fireman, and Steve Rytina. 1982. *Encounters with Unjust Authority.* Homewood, IL: Dorsey.

Gamson, William and David Meyer. 1996. "The Framing of Political Opportunity." In McAdam, McCarthy, and Zald, pp. 275–90.

Garland, James H. 1993. "Congregation-Based Organizations: A Church Model for the 90's." *America* November 13.

Garner, Roberta Ash and Mayer N. Zald. 1987. "The Political Economy of Social Movement Sectors," pp. 293–317 in *Social Movements in an Organizational Society,* edited by Mayer N. Zald and John D. McCarthy. New Brunswick, NJ: Transaction Publishers.

Gibson, James L. 1989. "The Policy Consequences of Political Intolerance: Political Repression During the Vietnam War Era." *Journal of Politics* 1:13–35.

Glassberg, Andrew D. 1991. "St. Louis: Racial Transition and Economic Development, pp. 86–96 in *Big City Politics in Transition,* edited by H. V. Savitch and John Clayton Thomas. *Urban Affairs Annual Reviews,* vol. 38. Newbury Park: Sage.

Goffman, Erving. 1974. *Frame Analysis: An Essay on the Organization of Experience.* New York: Harper Colophon.

Goldstone, Jack A. 1980. "The Weakness of Organization." *American Journal of Sociology* 85:1917–42.

1991. *Revolution and Rebellion in the Early Modern World.* Berkeley: University of California Press.

Goldstone, Jack A. and Charles Tilly. 2001. "Threat (and Opportunity): Popular Action and State Response in the Dynamics of Contentious Action," pp. 179–94 in *Silence and Voice in Contentious Politics,* by Ronald Aminzade, Jack Goldstone, Doug McAdam, Elizabeth N. Perry, William Sewell, Jr., Sidney Tarrow, and Charles Tilly. Cambridge: Cambridge University Press.

González Casanova, Pablo 1970. *Democracy in Mexico.* New York: Oxford University Press.

ed. 1990. *Segundo informe sobre la democracia: México, el 6 de Julio de 1988.* México: Siglo Veintiuno Editores.

Goodwin, Jeff. 2001. *No Way Out: States and Revolutionary Movements, 1945–1991.* Cambridge: Cambridge University Press.

Gopalan, A. K. 1959. *Kerala: Past and Present.* London: Lawrence and Wishart.

1974. *In the Cause of the People: Reminiscences.* Madras: Orient Longman.

References

Gordon, Leonard. 1974. *Bengal: The Nationalist Movement 1876–1940*. New York: Columbia University Press.

Granovetter, Mark. 1973. "The Strength of Weak Ties." *American Journal of Sociology* 78:1360–80.

1978. "Threshold Models of Collective Behavior." *American Journal of Sociology* 83:1420–43.

Gray, Virginia and Herbert Jacob. 1996. *Politics in the American States: A Comparative Analysis*. Washington, DC: Congressional Quarterly Press.

Green, John C., James L. Guth, and Clyde Wilcox. 1998. "Less Than Conquerors: The Christian Right in State Republican Parties." In Costain and McFarland, pp. 117–35.

Grofman, Bernard, Robert Griffin, and Amihai Glazer. 1988. *La democracia en la calle: Crónica del movimiento estudiantil mexicano*. México: Siglo Veintiuno Editores.

1992. "The Effect of Black Population on Electing Democrats and Liberals to the House of Representatives." *Legislative Studies Quarterly* 17:365–79.

Gupta, Dipak K., Harinder Singh, and Tom Sprague. 1993. "Government Coercion of Dissidents: Deterrence or Provocation?" *Journal of Conflict Resolution* 73:301–39.

Gurr, Ted Robert. 1970. *Why Men Rebel*. Princeton, NJ: Princeton University Press.

1986. "The Political Origins of State Violence and Terror: A Theoretical Analysis," pp. 45–71 in *Government Violence and Repression: An Agenda for Research*, edited by Michael Stohl and George A. Lopez. Westport, CT: Greenwood Press.

1989. "Political Terrorism: Historical Antecedents and Contemporary Trends." pp. 201–30 in *Violence in America: Volume II, Protest, Rebellion, Reform*, edited by Ted Robert Gurr. Newbury Park, CA: Sage.

Haas, Peter M. 1992. "Introduction: Epistemic Communities and International Policy Coordination." *International Organization* 46:1–35.

Harding, Susan. 1987. "Reconstructing Order through Action: Jim Crow and the Southern Civil Rights Movement," pp. 378–402 in *Statemaking and Social Movements: Essays in History and Theory*, edited by Charles Bright and Susan Harding. Ann Arbor: University of Michigan Press.

2001. *Cultural Dilemmas of Progressive Politics: Styles of Engagement among Grassroots Activists*. Chicago: University of Chicago Press.

Harvey, Neil. 1990. *The New Agrarian Movement in Mexico, 1976–1990*. London: University of London Press.

Hayden, Tom. 1988. *Reunion: A Memoir*. New York: Random House.

Heberle, Rudolph. 1951. *Social Movements*. New York: Appleton-Century-Crofts.

Heidenheimer, Arnold, Hugh Heclo, and Carolyn Teich Adams. 1990. *Comparative Public Policy: The Politics of Social Choice in America, Europe, and Japan*, 3rd ed. New York: St. Martin's Press.

Hero, Rodney. 1998. *Faces of Inequality: Social Diversity in American Politics*. Oxford: Oxford University Press.

Hibbs, Douglas. 1973. *Mass Political Violence*. New York: Wiley.

Higley, John and Richard Gunther, eds. 1992. *Elites and Democratic Consolidation in Latin America and Southern Europe*. Cambridge: Cambridge University Press.

Hirales, Gustavo. 1982. "La guerra secreta, 1970–1978." *Nexos* 54:34–42.

Hirst, Paul. 1991. "The State, Civil Society and the Collapse of Soviet Communism." *Economy and Society* 20:217–42.

Hollinger, David. 1995. *Postethnic America*. New York: Basic Books.

Horn, Miriam. 1990. "Campaign Carnival: A Velvet Election?" *The New Republic* 203:11–13.

Huntington, Samuel. 1973. "Transnational Organizations in World Politics." *World Politics* 25:333–68.

Imig, Douglas R. 1998. "American Social Movements and Presidential Administrations." In Costain and McFarland, pp. 159–170.

Innes, Abby. 1997. "The Breakup of Czechoslovakia: The Impact of Party Development on the Separation of the State." *East European Politics and Societies* 11:393–435.

Jacoway, Elizabeth and David Colburn, eds. 1982. *Southern Businessmen and Desegregation*. Baton Rouge: Louisiana State University Press.

Jaramillo, Rubén and Froylán C. Manjarréz. 1967. *Autobiografía y asesinato*. México: Nuestro Tiempo.

Jeffrey, Robin, ed. 1978. *People, Princes and Paramount Power*. Oxford: Oxford University Press.

1984. " 'Destroy Capitalism!' Growing Solidarity of Alleppey's Coir Workers, 1930–1940." *Economic and Political Weekly* 19:1159–65.

1985. *The Politics of Insurgency*. New York: Columbia University Press.

Jenkins, J. Craig and Bert Klandermans, eds. 1995. *The Politics of Social Protest*. Minneapolis: University of Minnesota Press.

Jenkins, J. Craig and Charles Perrow. 1977. "Insurgency of the Powerless: Farm Worker Movements 1946–1972." *American Sociological Review* 42:249–68.

Johnson, Paul B. Family Papers. n.d., University of Southern Mississippi (Hattiesburg), Series II, Sub-Series 9, Sovereignty Commission.

Jose, A. V. 1984. "Poverty and Inequality – The Case of Kerala," pp. 107–36, in *Poverty in South Asia*, edited by Azizur Rahman Khan and Eddy Lee. Bangkok: International Labour Organization.

Kannan, K. P. 1988. *Of Rural Proletarian Struggles: Mobilization and Organization of Rural Workers in South-West India*. Delhi: Oxford University Press.

Karapin, Roger. 1994. "Community Organizations and Low-Income Citizen Participation in the U.S.: Strategies, Organization, and Power since the 1960s." Paper presented at the annual meeting of the American Political Science Association, September 1–4.

Katzenstein, Mary Fainsod. 1998. "Stepsisters: Feminist Movement Activism in Different Institutional Spaces." In Meyer and Tarrow (1998b), pp. 195–216.

Keck, Margaret and Kathryn Sikkink. 1998. *Activists Beyond Borders: Advocacy Networks in International Politics*. Ithaca, NY: Cornell University Press.

Keesing's Research Reports. 1970. *Race Relations in the USA, 1954–1968*. New York: Charles Scribner's Sons.

References

Keller, William W. 1989. *The Liberals and J. Edgar Hoover: Rise and Fall of a Domestic Intelligence State*. Princeton, NJ: Princeton University Press.

Keohane, Robert O. and Joseph S. Nye. 1972. *Transnational Relations and World Politics*. Cambridge, MA: Harvard University Press.

Key, V. O. 1964. *Politics, Parties, and Pressure Groups*, 5th ed. New York: Thomas Y. Crowell.

Kim, Hyo Joung and Peter S. Bearman. 1997. "The Structure and Dynamics of Movement Participation." *American Sociological Review* 62: 70–93.

Kimmel, Michael and Abby Ferber. 2000. "'White Men Are This Nation': Right Wing Militias and the Restoration of Rural American Masculinity." *Rural Sociology* 654:582–604.

Kingdon, John W. 1984. *Agendas, Alternatives, and Public Policies*. Boston: Little, Brown.

Kitschelt, Herbert P. 1986. "Political Opportunity Structures and Political Protest: Anti-Nuclear Movements in Four Democracies." *British Journal of Political Science* 16:57–95.

    1995. *The Radical Right in Western Europe: A Comparative Analysis*. Ann Arbor: University of Michigan Press.

    1996. "Formation of Party Cleavages in Post-Communist Democracies." *Party Politics* 1:447–72.

Klandermans, Bert and Dirk Oegema. 1987. "Potentials, Networks, Motivations and Barriers: Steps Toward Participation in Social Movements." *American Sociological Review* 52:519–31.

Klandermans, Bert, Marlene Roefs, and Johan Olivier. 1998. "A Movement Takes Office." In Meyer and Tarrow (1998b), pp. 173–94.

Klaus, Vaclav. 1992. *Dismantling Socialism: A Preliminary Report (A Road to a Market Economy II)*. Prague: Top Agency.

    1997. *Renaissance: The Rebirth of Liberty in the Heart of Europe*. Washington, DC: The Cato Institute.

Knight, Alan. 1992. "Mexico's Elite Settlement: Conjuncture and Consequences," pp. 113–45 in *Elites and Democratic Consolidation in Latin America and Southern Europe*, edited by John Higley and Richard Gunther. New York: Cambridge University Press.

Knopf, Jeffrey W. 1989. "From Elite Activism to Democratic Consolidation: The Rise of Reform Communism in West Bengal," pp. 367–415 in *Dominance and State Power in Modern India*, vol. 2, edited by Francine Frankel and M. S. A. Rao. Oxford: Oxford University Press.

    1993. "Beyond Two-Level Games: Domestic–International Interaction in the Intermediate-Range Nuclear Forces Negotiations." *International Organization* 47:599–628.

Koopmans, Ruud. 1995. *Democracy from Below: New Social Movements and the Political System in West Germany*. Boulder, CO: Westview Press.

    1996. "Explaining the Rise of Racist and Extreme Right Violence in Western Europe: Grievances or Opportunities?" *European Journal of Political Research* 30:185–216.

1997. "Dynamics of Repression and Mobilization: The German Extreme Right in the 1990's." *Mobilization* 2:149–65.

Koordinacni Centrum OF Praha [Coordination Center of Civic Forum, Prague]. 1990. Mimeo draft of membership principles. Private collection of Ivan Havel.

Krejčí, Oskar. 1995. *History of Elections in Bohemia and Moravia*. Boulder, CO: East European Monographs; New York, distributed by Columbia University Press.

Kriesi, Hanspeter. 1995. "The Political Opportunity Structure of New Social Movements: Its Impact on Their Mobilization." In Jenkins and Klandermans, pp. 167–98.

Kriesi, Hanspeter, Ruud Koopmans, Jan W. Duyvendak, and Marco G. Guigni. 1995. *New Social Movements in Western Europe: A Comparative Analysis*. Minneapolis: University of Minnesota Press.

Kubik, Jan. 1992. "The Infirmity of Social Democracy in Postcommunist Poland: A Cultural History of the Socialist Discourse, 1970–1991." Program on Central and Eastern Europe Working Paper Series, #20, Harvard University, Cambridge, MA.

1998. "Institutionalization of Protest during Democratic Consolidation in Central Europe." In Meyer and Tarrow (1998b) pp. 131–52.

Kumar B. G. 1982. *Government Intervention and Levels of Living in Kerala, India*. Unpublished D. Phil. dissertation, Oxford University.

Kunhi Krishnan, V. 1993. *Tenancy Legislation in Malabar 1880–1970*. New Delhi: Northern Book Centre.

Kurzman, Charles. 1996. "Structural Opportunities and Perceived Opportunities in Social Movement Theory: Evidence from the Iranian Revolution of 1979." *American Sociological Review* 61:153–70.

Landry, David M. and Joseph B. Parker. 1976. *Mississippi Government and Politics in Transition*. Dubuque, IA: Kendall/Hunt.

Lau, Rubén. 1991. "Historia política del CDP," pp. 11–67 in *Movimientos populares en Chihuahua*, edited by R. Lau and V. Quintana. México: Universidad Autonoma de Ciudad Juarez.

Laushey, David. 1975. *Bengal Terrorism and the Marxist Left: Aspects of Regional Nationalism in India, 1905–1942*. Calcutta: Firma K. L. Mukhopadhyay.

Leff, Carol. 1997. *The Czech and Slovak Republics: Nation versus State*. Boulder, CO: Westview Press.

Lewis, Paul G. 1998. "Party Funding in Post-Communist East-Central Europe," pp. 137–79 in *Funding Democratization*, edited by Peter Burnell and Alan Ware. Manchester and New York: Manchester University Press.

Lichbach, Mark. 1987. "Deterrence or Escalation?: The Puzzle of Aggregate Studies of Repression and Dissent." *Journal of Conflict Resolution* 31:266–97.

Lichbach, Mark and Ted Robert Gurr. 1987. "The Conflict Process: A Formal Model," *Journal of Conflict Resolution* 25:3–29.

Lindenberg, Siegwart. 1989. "Social Production Functions, Deficits, and Social Revolutions: Pre-revolutionary France and Russia." *Rationality and Society* 1: 50–76.

References

Linz, Juan. 1975. "Totalitarian and Authoritarian Regimes," pp. 175–411 in *Handbook of Political Science*, vol. III, edited by Fred Greenstein and Nelson Polsby. Reading, MA: Addison-Wesley.

Lipset, Seymour Martin and Stein Rokkan. 1967. "Cleavage Structures, Party Systems and Voter Alignments," pp. 1–64 in *Party Systems and Voter Alignments: Cross-National Perspectives*, edited by S. M. Lipset and S. Rokkan. New York: Free Press.

Lo, Clarence Y. H. 1982. "Countermovements and Conservative Movements in the Contemporary U.S." *Annual Review of Sociology* 8:107–34.

———. 1990. *Small Property versus Big Government: Social Origins of the Property Tax Revolt*. Berkeley: University of California Press.

Loaeza, Soledad. 1999. *El Partido Acción Nacional: La larga marcha, 1939–1994*. México: FCE.

Logan, William [1887]. 1951. *Malabar*, vol. 2. Madras, India: Superintendent Government Press.

Lowi, Theodore. 1964. "American Business and Public Policy: The Politics of Foreign Trade" [review]. *World Politics* 16:677–715.

Loyo, Aurora. 1979. *El movimiento magisterial de 1958 en México*. México: Era.

Loyola, Rafael and Samuel Léon. 1992. "El Partido Revolucionario Institucional: los intentos del cambio," pp. 53–80 in *El nuevo Estado mexicano*, vol. 2, edited by J. Alonso, A. Aziz, and J. Tamayo. México: Nueva Imagen.

LSA (Lousiana State Archives). 1965. Letter from Jack N. Rogers to Mr. Anderson (April 29, 1965), Box #1, JLCUA (Joint Legislative Committee on Un-American Activities); Folder: Ku Klux Klan.

Lublin, David. 1997. *The Paradox of Representation: Racial Gerrymandering and Minority Interests in Congress*. Princeton, NJ: Princeton University Press.

Luders, Joseph E. 2000. "The Politics of Exclusion." Ph.D. dissertation, New School for Social Research.

Lukes, S. 1974. *Power: A Radical View*. London: Macmillan.

Maciel, Carlos. 1990. *El Movimiento de Liberación Nacional: Vicisitudes y aspiraciones*. México: Universidad Autónoma de Sinaloa.

Macín, Raúl. 1985. "Los protestantes y las luchas populares en México," pp. 313–27 in *Religión y política en México*, edited by M. d. l. Rosa and C. A. Reilly. México: Siglo Veintiuno Editores.

Maguire, Diarmuid. 1995. "Opposition Movements and Opposition Parties: Equal Partners of Dependent Relations in the Struggle for Power and Reform?" In Jenkins and Klandermans, pp. 199–228.

Mallick, Ross. 1993. *Development Policy of a Communist Government*. Cambridge: Cambridge University Press.

Markoff, John. 1996. *Waves of Democracy: Social Movements and Political Change*. London and Thousand Oaks, CA: Sage/Pine Forge Press.

Marván, Ignacio. 1990. "La dificultad del cambio," pp. 255–90 in *El partido en el poder. Seis ensayos*, edited by IEPES. México: El Día.

Marwell, Gerald and Pamela Oliver. 1993. *The Critical Mass in Collective Action*. Cambridge: Cambridge University Press.

Marx, Gary T. 1982. "External Efforts to Damage or Facilitate Social Movements: Development, Participation, and Dynamics," pp. 181–200 in *Social Movements*, edited by J. Wood and M. Jackson. Belmont, CA: Wadsworth Publishers.

Mathews, Jessica T. 1997. "Power Shift." *Foreign Affairs*, January–February, pp. 50–66.

McAdam, Doug. 1982. *Political Process and the Development of Black Insurgency: 1930–1970*. Chicago: University of Chicago Press.

1995. "Initiator and Derivative Movements: Diffusion Processes in Protest Cycles," pp. 217–39 in *Repertoires and Cycles of Collective Action*, edited by Mark Traugott. Durham, NC: Duke University Press.

1996. "Conceptual Origins, Current Problems, Future Directions," In McAdam, McCarthy, and Zald, pp. 23–40.

McAdam, Doug, John D. McCarthy, Susan Olzak, and Sarah A. Soule. 1997. "NSF Grant Proposal: The Dynamics of Collective Protest." Unpublished manuscript.

McAdam, Doug, John D. McCarthy, and Mayer N. Zald. 1988. "Social Movements," pp. 695–737 in *Handbook of Sociology*, edited by Neil Smelser. Beverly Hills, CA: Sage.

eds. 1996. *Comparative Perspectives on Social Movements: Political Opportunities, Mobilizing Structures and Cultural Framings*. New York: Cambridge University Press.

McAdam, Doug, Sidney Tarrow, and Charles Tilly. 2001. *Dynamics of Contention*. Cambridge: Cambridge University Press.

McCarthy, John D., Jackie Smith, and Mayer N. Zald. 1996. "Accessing Public, Media, Electoral, and Governmental Agendas." In McAdam, McCarthy, and Zald, eds., pp. 291–311.

McCarthy, John D. and Mayer N. Zald. 1977. "Resource Mobilization and Social Movements: A Partial Theory." *American Journal of Sociology* 82:212–41.

McManus, Susan and Lawrence Morehouse. 1997. "Redistricting in the Multiracial Twenty-First Century: Changing Demographic and Socioeconomic Conditions Pose Important New Challenges," in *Race and Representation*, edited by Georgia Persons. New Brunswick, NJ: Transaction Publishers.

McMillan, George. 1960. *Racial Violence and Law Enforcement*. Atlanta: Southern Regional Council.

1962. "The South's Pattern of Violence Has Changed." *Washington Post*, October 7, pp. E1, E7.

McMillen, Neil R. 1971. *The Citizens' Council: Resistance to the Second Reconstruction*. Urbana: University of Illinois Press.

1973. "Development of Civil Rights 1956–1970," pp. 154–76, in *A History of Mississippi*, vol. 2, edited by Richard Aubrey McLemore. Jackman, MS: University and College Press of Mississippi.

McVeigh, Rory. 1999. "Structural Incentives for Conservative Mobilization: Power Devaluation and the Rise of the Ku Klux Klan, 1915–1925." *Social Forces* 774:1461–96.

Melucci, Alberto. 1989. *Nomads of the Present*. London: Hutchinson Radius.

References

Menon, Dilip. 1994. *Caste, Nationalism and Communism in South India*. Cambridge: Cambridge University Press.

Meyer, David S. 1990. *A Winter of Discontent: The Nuclear Freeze and American Politics*. New York: Praeger.

1993. "Institutionalizing Dissent: The United States Structure of Political Opportunity and the End of the Nuclear Freeze Movement." *Sociological Forum* 82:157–79.

Meyer, David S. and Suzanne Staggenborg. 1996. "Movements, Countermovements, and the Structure of Political Opportunity." *American Journal of Sociology* 101:1628–60.

Meyer, David and Sidney Tarrow. 1998a. "A Movement Society: Contentious Politics for a New Century." In Meyer and Tarrow (1998b), pp. 1–28.

eds. 1998b. *The Social Movement Society: Contentious Politics for a New Century*. Lanham, MD: Rowman & Little field.

Meyer, David S. and Nancy Whittier. 1994. "Social Movement Spillover." *Social Problems* 422:277–98.

Meyer, John W., John Boli, George M. Thomas, and Francisco O. Ramirez. 1997. "World Society and the Nation-State." *American Journal of Sociology* 103: 144–81.

Meyer, Lorenzo. 1977a. "El estado Mexicano contemporáneo," pp. 5–36 in *Lecturas de política mexicana*, edited by C. d. E. Internacionales. México: El Colegio de México.

1977b. "Historical Roots of the Authoritarian State in Mexico," pp. 3–22 in *Autoritarianism in Mexico*, edited by J. L. Reyna and R. S. Weinert. Philadelphia: Institute for the Study of Human Issues.

Michels, Robert. 1958. *Political Parties: A Sociological Study of the Oligarchical Tendencies of Modern Democracy*. Glencoe, IL: Free Press.

1962. *Political Parties: A Sociological Study of the Oligarchical Tendencies of Modern Democracies*. New York: Free Press.

Minkoff, Debra C. 1997. "The Sequencing of Social Movements." *American Sociological Review* 625:779–99.

Misztal, Bronislaw and J. Craig Jenkins. 1995. "Starting from Scratch Is Not Always the Same: The Politics of Protest and the Post-Communist Transitions in Poland and Hungary." In Jenkins and Klandermans, pp. 324–40.

Mlynar, Vladimir. 1992. "Jak bohate jsou nase strany? [How rich are our parties?]" *Respekt* No. 48, November 11:4.

Molinar, Juan. 1990. *El tiempo de la legitimidad*. México: Cal y Arena.

Mollenkopf, John H. 1983. *The Contested City*. Princeton, NJ: Princeton University Press.

Molotch, Harvey. 1970. "Oil in Santa Barbara and Power in America." *Sociological Inquiry* 40:131–44.

Montes de Oca, Rosa Elena. 1977. "The State and the Peasants," pp. 47–63 in *Autoritarianism in México*, edited by J. L. Reyna and R. S. Weinert. Philadelphia: Institute for the Study of Human Issues.

Moore, Barrington. 1966. *Social Origins of Dictatorship and Democracy.* Boston: Beacon Press.

Moravcsik, Andrew. 1993. "Introduction: Integrating International and Domestic Explanations of World Politics," pp. 3–42 in *Double-Edged Diplomacy: International Bargaining and Domestic Politics,* edited by Peter B. Evans, Harold K. Jacobson, and Robert D. Putnam. Berkeley: University of California Press.

Morris, Aldon D. 1984. *The Origins of the Civil Rights Movement.* New York: Free Press.

Mottl, Tahi L. 1980. "The Analysis of Countermovements." *Social Problems* 27:620–35.

Muller, Edward N. 1985. "Income Inequality, Regime Repressiveness, and Political Violence." *American Sociological Review* 50:47–61.

Muller, Edward N. and Erich Weede. 1990. "Cross-National Variation in Political Violence: A Rational Action Approach." *Journal of Conflict Resolution* 34: 624–51.

Muse, Benjamin. 1964. *Ten Years of Prelude: The Story of Integration since the Supreme Court's Decision.* New York: Viking Press.

Namboodiripad, E. M. S. 1976. *How I Became a Communist.* Trivandrum: Chinta Publishers.

National Archives of India, New Delhi. Home Political Files, 1930 to 1947.

National Democratic Institute for International Affairs. 1996. "What Is the National Democratic Institute for International Affairs?" *Mission statement.* Washington, DC.

National Research Council Committee on National Statistics. 1996. *Spotlight on Heterogeneity: The Federal Standards for Racial and Ethnic Classification.* Washington, DC: National Academy Press.

NCDAH (North Carolina Division of Archives and History). 1958a. Papers of Governor Hodges, Box 313, File: Segregation, Ku Klux Klan and Governor Hodges Papers, General Correspondence, Box 227, File: Segregation, General.

1958b. Statement by Governor Hodges (30 January 1958). Hodges Papers, Box 313, Folder: Segregation: Ku Klux Klan.

1960. News Release (10 March 1960). Governor Hollings Papers, Box 1, Folder 36.

1963a. Report on Goldsboro 23, September 1963. Sanford Papers, Box 112, Folder: Segregation W. II.

1963b. Report of State Highway Patrol (12 September 1963). Sanford Papers, Box 348, Folder: Segregation, W II.

Neidhardt, Friedhelm. 1989. "Gewalt und Gegengewalt. Steigt die Bereitschaft zu Gewaltaktionen mit zunehmender staatlicher Kontrolle und Repression?" pp. 233–43 in *Jugend-StaatGewalt. Politische Sozialisation von Jugendlichen, Jugendpolitik und politische Bildung,* edited by W. Heitmeyer, K. Möller, and H. Sünker. Weinheim: Juventa.

Nelson, Barbara J. 1984. *Making an Issue of Child Abuse: Political Agenda Setting for Social Problems.* Chicago: University of Chicago Press.

References

New York Times. 1957. "Klan Pickets in South Dispersed." September 2, p. 26.

1958. "Klan Charged in Dynamite Plot." February 22, p. 32.

1961a. "Biracial Unit Tells of Beating in South." May 11, p. 25.

1961b. "Negroes Get Service: Eat at Formerly Segregated Counter in Columbia, S.C." May 31, p. 23.

1961c. "Police Guard 32 on Freedom Ride." June 15, p. 38.

1963. "Tear Gas in Carolina." September 12, p. 30.

1964. "2 Held for Trying to Burn North Carolina Church." July 15, p. 16.

1965. "Clean Bill of Health." August 1, p. 57.

Nicholls, William. 1960. *Southern Tradition and Regional Progress*. Chapel Hill: University of North Carolina Press.

Núñez, Oscar. 1990. *Innovaciones democrático-culturales del movimiento urbano-popular*. México: UAM.

Nye, Mary Alice and Charles S. Bullock III. 1992. "Civil Rights Support: A Comparison of Southern and Border State Representatives." *Legislative Studies Quarterly* 17:81–94.

Oberschall, Anthony. 1993. *Social Movements*. New York: Transaction Books.

1994. "Rational Choice in Collective Protests." *Rationality and Society* 6:79–100.

1996. "Opportunities and Framing in the Eastern European Revolts of 1989." In McAdam, McCarthy, and Zald, pp. 93–121.

O'Donnell, Guillermo and Philippe Schmitter. 1986. *Transitions from Authoritarian Rule: Tentative Conclusions about Uncertain Democracies*. Baltimore: Johns Hopkins University Press.

1993. "Vivan Los Suburbios!" *American Demographics* 30–7.

Oliver, Pamela. 1989. "Bringing the Crowd Back In. The Non-Organizational Elements of Social Movements," pp. 1–30 in *Research in Social Movements, Conflict and Change*, Vol. 11., edited by L. Kriesberg. Greenwich, CT: JAI Press.

Oliver, Pamela, Gerald Maxwell, and Ruy Teixeira. 1985. "A Theory of the Critical Mass I. Interdependence, Group Heterogeneity, and the Production of Collective Action." *American Journal of Sociology* 91:522–56.

Olson, David M. 1993. "Dissolution of the State: Political Parties and the 1992 Election in Czechoslovakia." *Communist and Post-Communist Studies* 26:301–14.

Olzak, Susan. 1989. "Analysis of Events in the Study of Collective Action." *Annual Review of Sociology* 15:119–41.

Opp, Karl-Dieter and Wolfgang Roehl. 1990. "Repression, Micromobilization, and Political Protest." *Social Forces* 2:521–47.

Orozco, Victor. 1976. "Las luchas populares en Chihuahua." *Cuadernos Políticos* 9:49–66.

Ortíz, Orlando. 1972. *Genaro Vázquez*. México: Diógenes.

Ost, David. 1991. "Shaping a New Politics in Poland." Program on Central and Eastern Europe Working Papers Series #8, Harvard University, Cambridge, MA.

Overstreet, Gene. D. and M. Windmiller. 1959. *Communism in India*. Berkeley: University of California Press.

Paige, Jeffrey. 1975. *Agrarian Revolution*. New York: Free Press.

Panebianco, Angelo. 1988. *Political Parties: Organization and Power*. Cambridge: Cambridge University Press.

Panikkar, K. N. 1989. *Against Lord and State: Religion and Peasant Uprisings in Malabar, 1836–1921*. Delhi: Oxford University Press.

Peck, James. 1962. *Freedom Ride*. New York: Simon & Schuster.

Pellicer, Olga. 1968. "La revolución Cubana en México." *Foro Internacional* 8:360–83.

Pereira, Bresser, Luiz Carlos, Jose Maria Maravall, and Adam Przeworski. 1993. *Economic Reforms in New Democracies: A Social-Democratic Approach*. Cambridge: Cambridge University Press.

Peterson, Paul E. 1981. *City Limits*. Chicago: University of Chicago Press.

ed. 1995. *Classifying by Race*. Princeton, NJ: Princeton University Press.

Pinto-Duschinsky, Michael. 1991. "Foreign Political Aid: The German Political Foundations and Their U.S. Counterparts." *International Affairs* 67:33–63.

1997. "Consolidating the Third Wave Democracies," pp. 295–324 in *Consolidating Third Wave Democracies*, edited by Larry Diamond, Marc F. Plattner, Yun-han Chu, and Hung-mao Tien. Baltimore: Johns Hopkins University Press.

Pozas Horcasitas, Ricardo. 1997. "La observación electoral: Una modalidad de la militancia ciudadana." *Revista Mexicana de Sociología* 59:23–40.

Presidencia de la República. 1987. *Las razones y las obras: Gobierno de Miguel de la Madrid*, vol. 4. México: FCE.

1994. *Crónica del Gobierno de Carlos Salinas de Gortari*. Sexto año. México: FCE.

Pridham, Geoffrey. 1995. "Parties and Their Strategies in the Transition," pp. 1–28 in *Party Formation in East-Central Europe: Post-communist Politics in Czechoslovakia, Hungary, Poland, and Bulgaria*, edited by Gordon Wightman. Brookfield, VT: Edward Elgar.

1996. "Transnational Party Links and Transition to Democracy: Eastern Europe in Comparative Perspective," pp. 187–219 in *Party Structure and Organization in East Central Europe*, edited by Paul G. Lewis. Cheltenham, U.K.: Edward Elgar.

Przeworski, Adam. 1985. *Capitalism and Social Democracy*. Princeton, NJ: Princeton University Press.

1990. "The Games of Transition." Center for Social Theory and Comparative History Colloquium, UCLA.

1991. *Democracy and the Market*. Cambridge: Cambridge University Press.

Purcell, Susan Kaufman. 1977. "The Future of the Mexican System," pp. 173–91 in *Autoritarianism in Mexico*, edited by J. L. Reyna and R. S. Weinert. Philadelphia: Institute for the Study of Human Issues.

Putnam, Robert. 1993. "Diplomacy and Domestic Politics: The Logic of Two-Level Games," pp. 431–68 in *Double-Edged Diplomacy: International Bargaining and Domestic Politics*, edited by Peter B. Evans, Harold K. Jacobson, and Robert D. Putnam. Berkeley: University of California Press.

1996. "The Strange Disappearance of Civic America." *American Prospect* 24: 34–48.

References

2000. *Bowling Alone: The Collapse and Revival of American Community.* New York: Simon & Schuster.

Quigley, Kevin F. F. 1997. *For Democracy's Sake: Foundations and Democracy Assistance in Central Europe.* Washington, DC: Woodrow Wilson Center Press.

Ramsden, William E. and John C. Montgomery. 1990. *Biblical Integrity and People Power: A New Look at Church-Based Community Organizing in the 1990s.* Chicago: Institute on the Church in Urban-Industrial Society.

Ranga, N. G. 1939. "Jenmi System Doomed in Malabar," *Congress Socialist* vol. 4, no. 4.

Rascón, Marco and Patricia Ruíz. 1986. "Chihuahua: La disputa por la dependencia." *Cuadernos Políticos* 47:25–39.

Rasler, Karen. 1996. "Concessions, Repression, and Political Protest in the Iranian Revolution." *American Sociological Review* 61:132–52.

Rasul, M. A. 1969. *History of the All India Kisan Sabha.* Calcutta: National Book Agency.

Ravelo, Renato. 1978. *Los Jaramillistas.* México: Nuestro Tiempo.

Reitzes, Donald D. and David C. Reitzes. 1987. *The Alinsky Legacy: Alive and Kicking.* Greenwich, CT: JAI Press.

Reyna, José Luis. 1977. "Redifining the Authoritarian Regime," pp. 155–71 in *Autoritarianism in México,* edited by J. L. Reyna and R. S. Weinert. Philadelphia: Institute for the Study of Human Issues.

Rhode, David W. 1991. *Parties and Leaders in the Post-reform House.* Chicago: University of Chicago Press.

Robinson, William I. 1966. "Globalization, the World System, and 'Democracy Promotion' in U.S. Foreign Policy." *Theory and Society* 25:615–55.

Robles, Rosario and Julio Moguel. 1990. "Los nuevos movimientos rurales, por la tierra y por la apropiación del ciclo productivo." pp. 377–450 in *Historia de la cuestón agraria: Los tiempos de la crisis 1970–1982* (segunda parte), vol. 9, edited by J. Moguel. México: Siglo Veintiuno-CEHAM.

Rogozinski, Jacques. 1993. *La privatización de empresas paraestatales.* México: FCE.

Rondfeldt, David. 1984. *The Modern Mexican Military: A Reassessment.* La Jolla: University of California Press.

Root, Maria P.P. 1996. *The Multiracial Experience.* London: Sage.

Rose, Richard. 1984. *Do Parties Really Matter?* 2nd ed. London: Macmillan.

Rosenbaum, H. Jon and Peter C. Sederberg. 1974. "Vigilantism: An Analysis of Establishment Violence." *Comparative Politics* 6:541–70.

Rothschild, Joseph. 1974. *East Central Europe between the Two World Wars.* Seattle: University of Washington Press.

Roy, Subodh, ed. 1976. *Communism in India: Unpublished Documents, 1935–1945.* Calcutta: National Book Agency.

Rucht, Dieter. 1990. "Campaigns, Skirmishes and Battles: Anti-Nuclear Movements in the USA, France and West Germany." *Industrial Crisis Quarterly* 4:193–222.

——— 1998. "The Structure and Culture of Collective Protest in Germany since 1950." In Meyer and Tarrow (1998b), pp. 29–57.

Rueschemeyer, Dietrich, John Stephens, and Evelyn Huber Stephens. 1992. *Capitalist Development and Democracy*. Chicago: University of Chicago Press.

Rusch, Thomas A. 1973. *The Role of the Congress Socialist Party in the Indian National Congress, 1931–1942*. Unpublished Ph.D. dissertation, University of Chicago.

Rusk, David. 1995. *Cities without Suburbs*. Washington, DC: Woodrow Wilson Center Press.

Russell, Cheryl. 1996. *The Official Guide to Racial and Ethnic Diversity*. Ithaca, NY: New Strategist.

Sale, Kirkpatrick. 1973. *SDS*. New York: Vintage Books.

Sanders, Elizabeth. 1999. *Roots of Reform: Farmers, Workers, and the American State 1877–1917*. Chicago: University of Chicago Press.

Santoro, Wayne A. 1995. "Black Politics and Employment Policies." *Social Science Quarterly* 76:794–806.

Sanyal, Hitesranjan. 1979. "Congress Movements in the Villages of East Midnapore, 1921–1931," pp. 169–78 in *Asie du sud: Traditions et changements*, edited by Marc Gaborieau and Alice Thorner. Paris: CRNS.

Sarkar, Sumit. 1983. *Modern India: 1885–1947*. New Delhi: Macmillan India Ltd.

Sarkar, Tanika. 1987. *Bengal: 1928–1934: The Politics of Protest*. Oxford: Oxford University Press.

SCDAH (South Carolina Department of Archives and History). 1963. Letter from William Lowndes to Governor Russell (March 26, 1963), Governor Russell Papers, Folder: College Presidents.

n.d. [a]. "Overall Plan for Law Enforcement at Clemson College," Governor Russell Papers, Folder: Clemson Case to Council of College Presidents.

n.d. [b]. Oral History, Governor Robert McNair Papers (n.d.), 29.

Schattschneider, E. E. 1960. *The Semisovereign People: A Realist's View of Democracy*. New York: Holt, Rinehart and Winston.

Schmitter, Philippe C. 1992. "The Consolidation of Democracy and Representation of Social Groups. *American Behavioral Scientist* 35:422–49.

1996. "The Influence of the International Context upon the Choice of National Institutions and Policies in Neo-Democracies," pp. 26–54 in *The International Dimension of Democratization: Europe and the Americas*, edited by Laurence Whitehead. Oxford: Oxford University Press.

Scott, James. 1976. *The Moral Economy of the Peasant*. New Haven, CT: Yale University Press.

Seidman, Gay. 2001. "Guerrillas in Their Midst: Armed Struggle in the South African Anti-Apartheid Movement." *Mobilization* 6:111–27.

Sen, Sunil. 1972. *Agrarian Struggle in Bengal, 1946–47*. New Delhi: People's Publishing House.

SERS (Southern Education Reporting Service). 1964. *Statistical Summary of School Segregation-Desegregation in the Southern and Border States*. Nashville, TN: SERS

Sikkink, Kathryn. 1993. "Human Rights, Principled Issue–Networks, and Sovereignty in Latin America." *International Organization* 74:411–41.

Skocpol, Theda. 1996. "Unravelling from Above," pp. 292–301 in *Ticking Time Bombs*, edited by Robert Kuttner. New York: New Press.

References

Skocpol, Theda and Morris P. Fiorina. 1999. *Civic Engagement in American Democracy*. Washington, DC, and New York: The Brookings Institution and the Russell Sage Foundation.

Snow, David A., E. Burke Rochford, Jr., Steven K. Worden, and Robert D. Benford. 1986. "Frame Alignment Processes, Micromobilization, and Movement Participation." *American Sociological Review* 51:464–81.

Sorensen, Elaine. 1994. *Comparable Worth*. Princeton, NJ: Princeton University Press.

Spencer, Rainer. 1999. *Spurious Issues: Race and Multiracial Identity Politics in the United States*. Boulder, CO: Westview Press.

Staniszkis, Jadwiga, 1991. *The Dynamics of the Breakthrough in Eastern Europe: The Polish Experience*. Berkeley: University of California Press.

Stevens, Evelyn P. 1970. "Legality and Extra-Legality in Mexico." *Journal of Inter-American Studies and World Affairs* 12:62–75.

1974. *Protest and Response in Mexico*. Cambridge, MA: MIT Press.

Stohl, Michael and George A. Lopez, eds. 1986. *Government Violence and Repression: An Agenda for Research*. Westport, CT: Greenwood Press.

Suárez, Luis. 1976. *Lucio Cabañas, guerrillero sin esperanza*. México: Roca.

Sullivan, William C. with Bill Brown. 1979. *The Bureau: My Thirty Years in Hoover's FBI*. New York: W. W. Norton.

Swain, Carol. 1993. *Black Faces, Black Interests: The Representation of African-Americans in Congress*. Cambridge, MA: Harvard University Press.

Swarts, Heidi. 2001. "Boxed In: The U.S. Multiracial Movement." Ph.D. dissertation, Cornell University.

Synnott, Marcia. 1980. South Carolina Library, *Modern Political Collections, Oral History Project*, July 8.

Tarrow, Sidney. 1989. *Democracy and Disorder: Protest and Politics in Italy, 1965–1975*. Oxford: Oxford University Press.

1996. "States and Opportunities." In McAdam, McCarthy, and Zald, pp. 41–61.

1998a. *Power in Movement: Social Movements and Contentious Politics*. Cambridge: Cambridge University Press.

1998b. "'The Very Excess of Democracy': State-Building and Contentious Politics in America." In Costain and McFarland, pp. 20–38.

In press. "Contentious Politics in Western Europe and the United States." In *Governing Europe: Essays in Honor of Vincent Wright*, edited by Jack Hayward and Anand Menon. Oxford: Oxford University Press.

Taylor, Verta. 2000. "Mobilizing for Change in a Social Movement Society." *Contemporary Sociology* 29:219–30.

Tesoro, Jose Manuel. 1999. "Who's in Charge of East Timor?" *Asiaweek*, April 30.

Tharakan, P. K. Michael. 1984. "Intra-Regional Differences in Agrarian Systems and Internal Migration of Farmers from Travancore to Malabar, 1930–1950." Working Paper No. 194. Trivandrum, India: Center for Development Studies.

The John Lewis Mumford Center for Comparative Urban and Regional Research. 2001 (July 9). "The New Ethnic Enclaves in America's Suburbs."

http://mumford1.dyndns.org/cen2000/suburban/SuburbanReport/page1.
html

The State, (Columbia, SC), June 8, 1961.

Tilly, Charles. 1978. *From Mobilization to Revolution*. Reading, MA: Addison-Wesley.

1984. "Social Movements and National Politics," pp. 297–317 in *Statemaking and Social Movements*, edited by Charles Bright and Susan Harding. Ann Arbor: University of Michigan Press.

1995. *Popular Contention in Great Britain 1758–1834*. Cambridge, MA: Harvard University Press.

1998. "Democratization." New York: Columbia University and Center for Advanced Study in the Behavioral Sciences.

Tilly, Charles and Lesley Wood. In press. "Contentious Connections in Great Britain." In *Relational Approaches to Collective Action*, edited by Mario Diani and Doug McAdam. Oxford: Oxford University Press.

Tolnay, Stewart E. and E. M. Beck. 1992. *A Festival of Violence: An Analysis of Southern Lynchings, 1882–1930*. Chicago: University of Chicago Press.

U.S. Bureau of the Census. 1959–86. *Statistical Abstract of the United States*, 80th (1959), 84th (1963), 89th (1968), 95th (1974), 101st (1980), 106th (1986), and 111th (1991) eds. Washington, DC: U.S. Government Printing Office.

1990. Census of Population and Housing of the United States. Summary Tape File 1 (STF-1), Tables P-006 and P-008. Washington, DC: U.S. Government Printing Office.

1960, 1970, 1980. *Subject Reports on Marital Status*. Washington, DC: U.S. Bureau of the Census.

1991, 1992. *Current Population Reports*, Series P-20, nos. 461 and 468. Washington, DC: U.S. Bureau of the Census.

1994. *County and City Data Books*. Washington, DC: Office of Management and Budget.

1998a. "Marital Status and Living Arrangements." *Current Population Reports*, Series P-20, No. 514, March. Washington, DC: U.S. Bureau of the Census.

1998b. "Composition of State Legislatures by Political Party Affiliation: 1990 to 1996." *Statistical Abstract of the United States*, 118th ed. Washington, DC: U.S. Government Printing Office.

2000. Census of Population and Housing of the United States. Summary File 1 (SF-1), Tables P7 and P8. Washington, DC: U.S. Government Printing Office.

2001a. "Composition of State Legislatures by Political Party Affiliation: 1994 to 2000." *Statistical Abstract of the United States*, 121st edition. Washington, DC: U.S. Government Printing Office.

2001b. *Percent of Population by Race and Hispanic or Latino Origin, for the United States, Regions, Divisions, and States, and for Puerto Rico: 2000*. Washington, DC: U.S. Bureau of the Census.

U.S. House of Representatives. 1967. Committee on Un-American Activities, *The Present-Day Ku Klux Klan Movement*. Washington, DC: U.S. Government Printing Office.

References

1974. Hearing before the Civil Rights and Constitutional Rights Subcommittee of the Committee on the Judiciary, 3rd Congress, Second Session on FBI Counterintelligence Programs.

United States v. Guest. 383 vs 745 (1966).

United States v. Price. 383 vs 787 (1966).

United States White House Central Files. 1964. Memorandum for the President, Johnson Presidential Library, White House Central Files, Box 26, File January 1–July 16, 1964.

Valencia, Guadalupe. 1994. "Guanajuato," pp. 64–83 in *La República Mexicana. Modernización y democracia de Aguascalientes a Zacatecas*, vol. II, edited by P. González Casanova and J. Cadena-Roa. México: La Jornada-CIIH-UNAM.

1998. *Guanajuato: Sociedad, economía, política y cultura*. México: CEIICH-UNAM.

Valenzuela, J. S. 1989. "Labor Movements in Transition to Democracy." *Comparative Politics* 2:445–72.

Vander Zanden, James W. 1965. *Race Relations in Transition: The Segregation Crisis in the South*. New York: Random House.

Van Dyke, Nella. 1998. "Hotbeds of Activism: Locations of Student Protest." *Social Problems* 452:205–20.

Van Dyke, Nella and Sarah A. Soule. 2000. "Explaining Variation in Levels of Patriot and Militia Organization." Paper presented at the annual meeting of the American Sociological Association, August 12–16.

Varghese, T. C. 1970. *Agrarian Change and Economic Consequences*. Bombay: Allied Publishers Private Ltd.

Verba, Sidney, Kay Lehman Schlozman, and Henry E. Brady. 1996. *Voice and Equality*. Cambridge, MA: Harvard University Press.

Voss, Kim. 1993. *The Making of American Exceptionalism: The Knights of Labor and Class Formation in the Nineteenth Century*. Ithaca, NY: Cornell University Press.

Walsh, Edward J. 1981. "Resource Mobilization and Citizen Protest in Communities Around Three Mile Island." *Social Problems* 29:1–21.

Walton, Carl. 1995. "The Congressional Black Caucus and Its Liberal Ideology: A Search for Explanation." Paper presented at the annual meeting of the American Political Science Association, Chicago.

Walton, John. 1984. *Reluctant Rebels*. New York: Columbia University Press.

Wapner, Paul. 1995. "Politics beyond the State: Environmental Activism and World Civil Politics." *World Politics* 47:311–40.

Weede, Erich. 1987. "Some New Evidence on Correlates of Political Violence: Income Inequality, Regime Repressiveness, and Economic Development." *European Sociological Review* 3:97–108.

Welsh, Helga. 1996. "Dealing with the Communist Past: Central and East European Experiences after 1990." *Europe-Asia Studies* 48:413–28.

Wheaton, Bernard and Zdenek Kavan. 1992. *The Velvet Revolution: Czechoslovakia*. Boulder, CO: Westview.

Whipple, Tim, ed. 1991. *After the Velvet Revolution: Vaclav Havel and the New Leaders of Czechoslovakia Speak Out*. New York: Freedom House Press.

Whitby, Kenny J. and Franklin D. Gilliam, Jr. 1991. "A Longitudinal Analysis of Competing Explanations for the Transformation of Southern Congressional Politics." *Journal of Politics* 53:504–18.

White, Robert W. 1989. "From Peaceful Protest to Guerrilla War: Micromobilization of the Provisional Irish Republican Army." *American Journal of Sociology* 94:1277–302.

1999. "Comparing State Repression of Pro-State Vigilantes and Anti-State Insurgents: Northern Ireland, 1972–75." *Mobilization* 4:189–202.

Wightman, Gordon. 1991. "Czechoslovakia," pp. 53–69 in *New Political Parties in Eastern Europe and the Soviet Union*, edited by Bogdan Szajkowski. Harlow, U.K.: Longman Press.

Williams, Kim. 2001. "Boxed In: The U.S. Multiracial Movement." Ph.D. dissertation, Cornell University.

Wolchik, Sharon. 1995. "The Politics of Transformation and the Break-up of Czechoslovakia," pp. 225–44 in *The End of Czechoslovakia*, edited by Jiri Musil. Budapest: Central European University Press.

Wolf, Eric. 1969. *Peasant Wars of the Twentieth Century*. New York: Harper & Row.

1987. *The Moplah Rebellion and Its Genesis*. New Delhi: People's Publishing House.

World Bank. 1998. *Reducing Poverty in India: Options for More Effective Public Services, 1988–91*. Economic Report. No. 17881. Washington, DC: World Bank.

Wyn, Craig Wade. 1987. *The Fiery Cross: The Ku Klux Klan in America*. New York: Simon & Schuster.

Young, Lisa. 1996. "Women's Movements and Political Parties." *Party Politics* 22:229–50.

Zack, Naomi, ed. 1985. *American Mixed Race: The Culture of Microdiversity*. London: Rowman & Littlefield.

Zak, Vaclav. 1995. "The Velvet Divorce – Institutional Foundations," pp. 245–68 in *The End of Czechoslovakia*, edited by Jiri Musil. Budapest: Central European University Press.

Zald, Mayer and Bert Useem. 1987. "Movement and Countermovement Interaction: Mobilization, Tactics, and State Involvement," pp. 247–72 in *Social Movements in an Organizational Society*, edited by Mayer N. Zald and John D. McCarthy. New Brunswick, NJ: Transaction.

Index

Index

Index